Revive Us Again

Revive Us Again

Biblical Principles for Revival Today

Walter C. Kaiser Jr.

CHRISTIAN FOCUS

This edition published in 2001, reprinted in 2003 by
Christian Focus Publications, Geanies House, Fearn,
Ross-shire, IV20 1TW, Scotland

www.christianfocus.com

Cover design by Alister MacInnes

Printed and bound by
Mackays of Chatham

Previously published in 1999 by
Broadman & Holman Publishers, Nashville, Tennessee
Page Design and Typesetting: TF Designs, MT. Juliet, Tennessee

*Dedicated to
the memory of great revivalists
of previous Great Awakenings
and
especially to
the memory of
Colman M. Mockler,
a most effective leader in
the business community and
in the Christian community,
in whose honor the chair I presently hold is named
and to his wife, Joanna, who carries on
so effectively
the work Colman began*

Contents

Foreword

The heart cry for true revival rises up to God from many parts of the world in our time. Nowhere is the need more evident than in those places where reformation and revival were once the norm, North America and Western Europe. While thousands pray for revival throughout the world, in western nations few understand it, either its nature or its true effects. Yet western nations are presently experiencing a moral bankruptcy rarely, if ever, seen in our history. Spiritual life in the churches is the only answer to the free fall of our society.

What is needed is spiritual awakening. We need prayer for revival, but we also need fresh God-given passion. Passion, if it is truly from God, is born and nurtured in an atmosphere of truth. Truth is birthed and fanned into a flame by the clear understanding of the Bible and its message of covenant and grace. Ultimately the Word of God, used directly by the Spirit of God, is the only proven means for bringing about the reformational revival needed in our time.

Walter Kaiser, a world-renowned Old Testament scholar, provides in this extremely helpful book an accurate and faithful understanding of biblical revival. He uncovers the spiritual principles inherent in revivals recorded in Holy Scripture by surveying sixteen specific revival accounts in the Old Testament, including those under both Moses and John the Baptist. What makes his treatment so genuinely helpful is that he always stays so close to the text of the Bible.

By staying close to the text of the Word of God Walter Kaiser gives us a clear analysis of both the need for true revival and exactly what it is we pray for when we ask God "to rend the heavens and come down" (Isaiah 64:1). Besides giving us a good working definition of true revival Kaiser sets forth a clear apologetic for why we should not give up the Word or the biblical truth contained in it. By looking at these biblical accounts Kaiser also identifies the blessings and dangers of biblical revival.

One of the continual tensions faced by those who speak of, and pray for, true revival is the question of human means and divine sovereignty. Kaiser embraces divine sovereignty without compromise but he never runs away from human responsibility in the process. For this reason his work is biblically based and personally convicting. Kaiser forces the serious reader to do much more than agree with mere definitions and historical accounts. He provides the actual fuel needed to actively pursue God for the gift of true revival. A helpful study guide makes this book even more useful for groups in churches and prayer fellowships.

I am grateful to commend this excellent book to a much wider audience in both North America and Europe. I pray that it will spark a movement of serious thought and earnest prayer. "Who knows, he [the Lord] may turn and have pity and leave behind a blessing" (Joel 2:14).

John H Armstrong, President
Reformation & Revival Ministries

Preface

*A*bout ninety years ago, a college student in Wales named Evan Roberts, age twenty-six, obtained permission to leave college to return to his home village of Loughor to preach his first sermon. Seventeen people showed up to listen to his four points: confess any known sin to God and put away any wrong done to others, put away any doubtful habit, obey the Holy Spirit promptly, and confess faith in Christ openly.

No one could have predicted the nationwide impact that event would have. J. Edwin Orr related that "within three months a hundred thousand converts had been added to the churches of Wales. Five years later a book debunking the revival was published and the main point made by the scholarly author was that of the 100,000 added to the churches, only 80,000 remained after five years."[1] This same revival jumped the ocean and spread to America's shores and was the last major nationwide revival we have seen since 1905.

It would seem that events and forces have moved in the meantime to make us more than ready for the special work of God in revival once again. It is hoped that this volume may be used by the Spirit of God to make one more small contribution toward that end.

Originally, reviews of ten of these sixteen revivals were printed under the title *Quest for Renewal: Personal Revival in the Old Testament.*[2] That original volume went through two printings, but there were a number of foreign translations as well: they include two separate Korean translations and one Arabic translation in Egypt.

To these original chapters we have added the study of Psalm 85 and five New Testament revivals along with the epilogue. Another unique feature are the eighteen study guides that appear in the back of this book. It is hoped that they will be used as the basis for collegiate and neighborhood Bible studies as well as groups of Christians actively seeking and praying for revival. These eighteen chapters could well serve as the basis for many preaching and teaching and small group Bible study series—a veritable 125-day spiritual journey for the people of God.

There is no doubt that the need is desperate and the concern of the believing community has begun to mount nationwide for a special work of God. Such a great awakening will come at the pleasure of God, but he does wait for us to seek his face and to pray for such a rejuvenation of heart, soul, and mind. May our Lord be gracious to us and surprise us by raining righteousness from heaven once again.

It is a joy to acknowledge the compilation of the indices by my graduate assistant, Jim Cheshire, who is a second generation student of mine, being born while his dad was studying with me during his seminary days. A special note of thanks also goes to Broadman & Holman Publishers for undertaking this second volume we have worked on together. Thanks are especially due to John Landers for his help in guiding this work through the press.

May God be praised through this work.

Introduction

*W*hen in the course of human events there lies such a heavy sense of injustice and despair over the proliferation of evil and the failure of any forces for good or righteousness to carry the sentiment of the day, there remains only one answer: revival. This has been the experience of men and women throughout history, as the biblical record testifies.

If I (and a host of other observers of Western culture) am not wrong, the time is again ripe for that outcry to heaven from mortals who sense that things have gotten out of hand, that the forces of sin, evil, and destruction are beyond our ability to contain. For example, in just twenty-five years, this country has quadrupled Hitler's record for destruction of human life with our sinful flaunting of disregard for the unborn.

Hitler slaughtered 6 million Jews, and we have put to death more than 30 million babies. The question of the hour is this: if God judged Germany for her evil, then why has he not judged the United States?

Not that this is our only sin; it is merely one of many offenses that comes quickly to mind in a day when evil seems not to know any boundaries. Our sins are growing out of all manageable proportions, including child abuse, pornography, homosexuality, failure to require capital punishment, and widespread corruption in the halls of justice and government.

However, when evil and wickedness seem to grow like weeds on the landscape, God has often graciously given his people, as the first signal of revival fires, a deep yearning for relief that knows no other language than the cry for deliverance. (Five times in the history of the Judges things got so bad that finally misery found a voice to cry out to God.) It is only then that the human predicament presents God's first opportunity to be heard clearly and fairly. In my judgment, we in the United States and Canada have arrived at just such a time, and therefore it is time for revival in North America. Indeed, it would seem that it is high time once again for a worldwide revival.

What Is Revival?

What then is revival? Probably this is one of the church's most abused terms. Some see it as a synonym for mass evangelism or a special week of meetings in the local church aimed at winning the lost to Christ. Others regard the term with suspicion and automatically associate it with bizarre happenings in church meetings held under heavy orgies of emotion. Tales of emotional extravagances abound, such as barking like dogs, the "jerks," and theatrical feats of showmanship on the part of both the subjects of revival and the revivalists themselves.

But neither of these understandings can claim biblical support for what is distinctive or normative about revivals. Indeed, one of the most amazing facts about the whole subject is that in spite of a rather extensive literature of several thousand volumes on the topic, I have been able to find only five volumes (two of which are quite slender) that treat the subject of *revivals in the Bible*. These volumes, in the order of their publication, are:

Baker, Ernest. *The Revivals of the Bible*. Capetown, South Africa: Miller, 1906.

Smith, Wilbur M. *The Glorious Revival under King Hezekiah*. Grand Rapids: Zondervan, 1937. Rev. ed., 1954.

Newell, Philip R. *Revival on God's Terms*. Chicago: Moody, 1959.

Autrey, C. E. *Revivals of the Old Testament*. Grand Rapids: Zondervan, 1960.

Olford, Stephen F. *Heart-Cry for Revival: Expository Sermons on Revival*. Westwood, N.J.: Revell, 1962.

As long ago as 1937, Wilbur M. Smith observed that "the Christian Church still awaits a scholarly examination of [the] sixteen Biblical revivals, set in their historical perspective, with a very careful study of the various ways in which the Spirit of God moved upon a nation, or a city; in other words, a work comparable to that done in relation to post–Biblical revivals by James Burns in his epochal *Revivals: Their Laws and Leaders*, issued in London in 1909."[1]

Although the present work may not be everything that Smith was looking for, certainly there is much to be learned from examining the great revivals of the Bible. Inasmuch as revival remains the prerogative and special work of God, it would appear that the first requisite for any significant planning, praying, or writing in this area would be the study of revivals in the Bible.

Biblical Definition—2 Chronicles

What then is the Bible's definition of revival? Almost everyone will agree that the greatest text on the subject is 2 Chronicles 7:14, "If my people, who are called by my name, will humble themselves and pray and seek my face and turn from their wicked ways, then will I hear from heaven and will forgive their sin and will heal their land." The text does not use the term *revive* or *revival*, as does Psalm 85:6: "Will you not revive us again, that your people may rejoice in you?" However, there can be little doubt that 2 Chronicles 7:14 supplies most of the components of a definition. It identifies the subjects of revival (not just Israel, but all who are owned by God and have God's name on them), the four *conditions*[2] for revival (the same ones featured in the four key revivals that are reported by 2 Chronicles, providing its structure, as I will argue), and the three results that form the special work that makes revivals unique, distinctive among all the works of the Lord.

Moreover, the context of 2 Chronicles 7:14 identifies the circumstances where revival might apply. King Solomon had just completed his magnificent prayer of dedication for the recently completed temple. Solomon's prayer included the request that God would forgive the nation's sin whenever God was forced to introduce drought, famine, and pestilence (2 Chron. 6:26–31). It was in reply to this request that the Lord responded in 7:12–16, in words that provide both the basis and formula for all true revivals.

No doubt a significant number of God's people will object that 2 Chronicles 7:14 has no reference to them because it was addressed to Israel; it is strictly not their mail. But though the desire for a consistent hermeneutic, which underlies this objection, is admirable, the conclusion is wide of the mark on several counts. First of all, the phrase "If my people" is immediately explained by the little exegetical, or appositional, clause "who are called by my name," a clause so distinctive to both Testaments that its meaning could never be confused or mistaken. What God or man named, he owned and protected, whether that included cities (2 Sam. 12:28; Jer. 25:29; Dan. 9:19), the temple (1 Kings 8:43; Jer. 7:10–11, 14, 30; 32:34; 34:15), or men and women (Isa. 4:1; Jer. 14:9; 15:16). Thus, when Israel walked by faith, Moses promised that "all peoples of the earth shall see that you are called by the name of the LORD" (Deut. 28:10 NKJV). In the same way, James noted how God had "visited the Gentiles to take out of them a people for His name" (Acts 15:14 NKJV). Most convincing of all is the appearance of the phrase in Joel 2:32. "Everyone who calls on the name of the LORD will be saved." The fact that Peter used this expression on the day of Pentecost to inaugurate the age of the Spirit, the times of the new covenant, and the church is not altogether accidental. Therefore, although this promise was originally given to Israel, it is also most assuredly intended for us.

Another reason for applying this promise to present-day believers is that it involves the same hermeneutical principle as the one used in applying the new covenant to the church. The new covenant in its original setting was clearly addressed to the house of Israel and the house of Judah (Jer. 31:31), apparently setting aside (according to some) all claims of the church to this same promise. But the fact remains that some in the Christian body are ministers of the new covenant (2 Cor. 3:6), and all believers do drink the blood of the new covenant in the Lord's Supper (Matt. 26:28; 1 Cor. 11:25). It is true, of course, that the climactic fulfillment of the new covenant will not happen until the Deliverer comes from Zion and banishes ungodliness from Jacob in that day of the restoration of Israel to her Lord and her land (Rom. 11:25–27). Thus, without (incorrectly, in my judgment) simply equating the nation Israel with the church, it is possible to see that what appeared to be an exclusive word to Israel likewise included the believers of the New Testament era. The "people of God" are one, even though we can distinguish several aspects, such as believing Israel and believers in the church.

Finally, the assurance given in Romans 15:4 and 1 Corinthians 10:11 should keep us from insulating the contemporary Christian from 2 Chronicles 7:14. Paul teaches, "For everything that was written in the past was written to teach us, so that through . . . the Scriptures we might have hope," and, "These things happened to them as examples and were written down as warnings for us, on whom the fulfillment of the ages has come."

The centrality of 2 Chronicles 7:14 for the study of revivals in the Bible can be witnessed by the fact that it provides the outline for 2 Chronicles and sets the agenda for the material selected from the lives of five key Davidic kings of Judah. Each of the four conditions for revival is taken up separately as the single most important term for the reigns and lives of these five Judean monarchs. The resulting pattern forms an *inclusio*, with the first and last king sharing the same term. It may be plotted as follows:

Imperative	2 Chronicles	King under Whom the Revival Came
"Humble yourselves"	11–12	Rehoboam
"Seek my face"	14–16	Asa
"Pray"	17–20	Jehoshaphat
"Turn from your wicked way"	29–32	Hezekiah
"Humble yourselves"	34–35	Josiah

Fifteen of the thirty-six chapters in the book, or almost one-half of the material, are given over to the reigns and revivals of these five kings, for they honored God during their reigns by leading their people in revival. It is not an extravagant claim, then, to see the theme of revival as one of the central organizing motifs of 2 Chronicles—it is a programmatic theme for the whole of 2 Chronicles. In fact, another recent commentator on the book has also observed:

> It is quite extraordinary that none of the commentators has seen the vital significance [2 Chron. 7:14] for the Chronicler's theology. . . . Four avenues of repentance are mentioned which will lead God to forgive and restore, and these are taken up at various points in the remainder of the narrative and illustrated. . . . That this is deliberate is shown by the fact that wherever these terms occur in the earlier narrative they are often quite neutral theologically and do not mark similar miraculous turning-points.[3]

Other Definitions

By now it is clear that a revival can be defined primarily (or at least in its initial impact) in terms of something happening first of all exclusively to the believer. For Stephen Olford, revival is "the sovereign act of God, in which He restores His own backsliding people to repentance, faith and obedience."[4] Likewise, Charles Finney wrote, "It presupposes that the Church is sunk down in a backslidden state, and revival consists in the return of the Church from her backslidings and in the conversion of sinners."[5] Even though Finney included the conversion of sinners as part of his definition, it is clear from his book that he viewed this as an effect and not as part of the initial work of revival. "The fact is," warned Finney, "*Christians* are more to blame for not being revived than sinners are for not being converted."[6] C. E. Autrey agreed: "Revival is a reanimating of those who already possess life. . . . It revives spiritual life which is in a state of declension."[7] In short, in the words of the Old Testament prophet Hosea, revival consists of "breaking up fallow ground" that once had been tilled and was mellow and suitable for growing an abundant harvest but now is hardened and overgrown with weeds and all sorts of spontaneous vegetation, none of which pleases or is useful to the farmer (Hos. 10:12). Perhaps the most succinct definition of revival has come from J. Edwin Orr, who has written extensively on the subject in our generation. With an eye to Acts 3:19, he affirmed the best definition of revival is the phrase "times of refreshing from the presence of the Lord."

Why Revival Is Needed

The assumption is that revival is needed to remedy deficiencies that would not be present had real Christianity been practiced and readily observed by a watching world. Whenever such authenticity is scarce, it becomes necessary to plead, "O Lord, revive Your work in the midst of the years!" (Hab. 3:2 NKJV). Accordingly, revival presupposes a serious decline in the church's appetite for spiritual things and in her championing the cause of morality and justice in human affairs.

Furthermore, revival presupposes that believers either do not know the standards set forth in Scripture or do not care to press them as the basis for deciding what is true, just, righteous, beautiful, and pleasing to God. And when Christ's followers have ceased to function as salt and light (Matt. 5:13–16), society and the church are left without any principle or purpose when judged by the norms given in the Word of God and consequently without any check on ungodliness. Wickedness grows like weeds, and no voices are raised in protest or warning about the certainty and awesomeness of the frightening judgment of God that is to come. Thus, the consistent lack of obedience to the will of God among Christians is the problem underlying the need for revival.

Even more embarrassing, however, are the telltale signs of decadence within the church itself. This is amply illustrated in our own day. It is bad enough that the world exhibits sins that only a few years ago the most godless man would have turned away from in revulsion; now the same list of sins is shared by the church of the living God. Surely revival is needed when believers fall into such vices and scandalous sins as incest, abortion, divorce, homosexuality, and cheating on employers and on the government. Revival is also needed when worldliness so captures our hearts that we are as entrapped by our insatiable desires for leisure time, extended vacations (away from the house of God), and every kind of entertainment similar to that of the ancient Israelites who were likewise led into the idolatry of the Canaanite culture of their day. Of course there is a legitimate theology of leisure and culture in Scripture (e.g., the joy of life as traced in Ecclesiastes; see my small commentary on that book[8]), but when any form of leisure or entertainment competes for the believer's time and loyalties, equaling or exceeding the time and joy that he gives and receives from spiritual things, then he has crossed the line and entered headlong into idolatry.

Another signal that something is wrong in the church comes when a spirit of controversy arises over minor issues or even in the way in which major issues are handled. The presence of a divisive spirit in the church—jealousies, dissensions, and whisperings about fellow believers, other denominations, churches, institutions, mission agencies, and the like—indicates a desperate need for revival. The Christian life cannot flourish apart from an environment of love and brotherly concern, no matter how grievous the error or the difference among believers may be. This, too, has a current application.

But if deviations like these are not only known among our churches and Christian institutions but also widely reported and tolerated, we should not be surprised by our relative ineffectiveness or the fact that the world does not take us very seriously. Is it any wonder that the wicked continue to triumph in the marketplace and in government in opposition to the spread of the gospel? Our sins have had the net effect of reducing to a new level of impotency the efforts of pastors, evangelists, and missionaries in the spread of the gospel. Can water rise higher than its source? Can the Christianity reproduced on the worldwide fields fail to reflect the level of spiritual experience or the fervency of supportive prayer found in the sending church in North America? When the wicked become bold, insolent, reckless, and arrogant in establishing new lows for morality and godlessness, righteousness has suffered a staggering blow because of the laxity of professing Christians. Such a time will be filled with terrorists, murderers, extortionists, crooks, thieves, whoremongers, and haters of God.

The Christian's Responsibility in Revival

There is, however, an all-too-convenient explanation for latter-day spiritual decline that has been used frequently, but mistakenly, by sincere evangelicals: the imminency of the Lord's return. But this truth of Scripture is too wonderful a teaching to be strapped with the burden that some Christians would like to foist on it: that is, it is good that things are getting worse, for that is a sign that the Lord is coming very soon. Things indeed will grow worse among the wicked as we approach the time of the end. But this fact was never meant to be used as an excuse (as some seem to use it) for their own lack of purity or, worse still, as a means for giving up any and all responsibility to call for repentance and revival. Faithfulness will always be the first prerequisite of the watching, waiting, and praying believer looking for the Lord's return. Surely we can derive no satisfaction from the fact that the world is going "to the dogs," as if this would speed things along. In fact, the only way we can hasten the day of the coming of Christ, according to 2 Peter 3:11–12, is by living holy and godly lives.

Therefore, today's believers must begin by following God's program for revival as set forth in 2 Chronicles 7:14, or our land will lie fallow and overgrown. On the other hand, if we are willing to repent of our sin, then the floodgates of heaven will open, and both we and our culture will be the surprised recipients of the blessing of God.

The cost is significant, however. Every area of neglect and omission must be explored by each individual: the failure to love God with all of one's heart and soul, or to show concern for the eternal damnation of the lost outside of Christ; the neglect of earnest prayer, of the diligent study of Scripture, and of the health of our own souls, or the souls of our brethren in the household of faith; the omission of duties to family and society. In addition, we need to probe our scarred consciences for sins of commission. The list is too long to attempt a complete analysis here, but surely it begins with sins of the heart, such as envy, pride, ill will, jealousies, and hatreds, before it goes on to involve deeds of the flesh, such as lying, stealing, immorality, cheating, and all of their ilk.

How can the preaching of the gospel at home or abroad have any major effect, or how can Christians act as salt and light in society, when our hearts are frozen and in a fallow state? All our efforts for spiritual service will be handicapped and seriously curtailed in their real impact when judged by the standards of the resurrection power of Christ if we do not soon experience a genuine Holy Spirit-attended revival.

Characteristics of the Great Old Testament Revivals

What then are the features of revival as described in the Scriptures and especially in the ten great Old Testament revivals on which this book of the Bible focuses? Wilbur Smith lists nine characteristics of the great revivals.[9]

First, most revivals were preceded by a time of deep spiritual decline and despair. For example, there was the Egyptian bondage, which led to the golden calf debacle, or the time prior to the revival under King Hezekiah, which involved the revolting practice of offering children as burnt offerings on the altar of Molech. No different was the situation in Elijah's time, with the maddening spectacle of a whole nation wavering in its allegiance between the Baal and the Lord on Mount Carmel, unable to decide finally whether to worship exclusively Baal or Yahweh. All were times of deep spiritual decline, and they match our own in many ways.

Second, each of these revivals began in the heart of one of God's servants, who then became the instrument in God's hands to stir up the sleeping consciences of God's people. The list of revival leaders includes the patriarch Jacob; prophets like Moses, Samuel, Elijah, Haggai, Zechariah; kings like Rehoboam, Asa, Jehoshaphat, Hezekiah, Josiah; leaders like Nehemiah and Zerubbabel, the deacon Philip, John the Baptist, and the apostles Peter and Paul. The truth of God, which these leaders brought to the people, was the great motivating force for revival, not the mere charisma of their own persons or the dynamic of some managerial ability otherwise unknown or untapped until that time.

This leads nicely into the third characteristic. Every revival in the Old Testament rested solidly on a new and powerful proclamation of the Word of God. The most obvious evidence of this characteristic can be seen in the revival under Josiah, when the Book of the Law was found and read with great response in the presence of the king. In the revival that took place under Jehoshaphat, the Levites "taught throughout Judah, taking with them the Book of the Law of the LORD" (2 Chron. 17:9). No less central was the Word of God in the revival under Ezra and Nehemiah, for Ezra read from it from daybreak until noon (Neh. 8:3) for seven days (Neh. 8:18), "making it clear and giving the meaning" (Neh. 8:8). But even in those instances where the revival was not immediately preceded by a proclamation or reading of the Word of God, such as with Jacob or Elijah on Mount Carmel, the power and ministry of that mighty word is not very far out of the picture. All lasting revivals have their genesis in the restoration of the Word of God to its rightful place of prominence. As Wilbur Smith warned:

> A revival which does not rest solidly upon the Word of God will ultimately either fade out, because there is no fountain of divine truth continually refreshing it, or it will run into dangerous and sensational emotionalism, which, after it has passed, will make those who have been the subjects of such an experience dry and indifferent to the things of God, at times more easily accessible than ever to the inroads of Satan himself. There is something about the Word of God that men recognize as divine: when it is preached men know that they are hearing the Word of God, and nothing less will ever arouse a nation sunk in selfishness, self-satisfaction, and godlessness.[10]

The fourth characteristic is that each revival was marked by a return to the genuine worship of Yahweh. Whether it was Jacob smashing the idols of his family, Elijah exposing the impotency of Baal, or Haggai calling for authenticity in the worship and service of the Lord, they all presented the same case for authenticity. Wholehearted, genuine worship of the living God became the chief delight and one of the foremost desires of each person who was truly restored to spiritual vitality. Hence the great corrective needed for most current complaints about worship lies primarily not in the area of form, setting, or even substance, but in the area of a new reviving work of the incomparably great God.

Closely attached to this is the fifth sign of revival: a destruction of every idol that blocked the rightful acknowledgment of Yahweh as the only true and living God. This is true of every revival except the last two, which occurred after the exile, when no idols were left in Judah. It is easy, of course, to dismiss this characteristic in the modern era with a sense of relief: "At least that is one sin we do not possess or need to worry about!" But that conclusion would be incorrect, for we are involved in idolatry, even if we do not possess icons or plaster and metallic images. Whenever we allow any concept, program, committee, goal, commitment, person, or pleasure to take a place equal to or greater than that which rightfully should be occupied by the Lord alone, we are into idolatry just as much as any ancient or contemporary worshiper of icons and images was or is. God will not share his glory or honor with another, whether that be a sports team, the television, a job, family, success in the church, or any other aspiration that we make equal to or greater than our love for God alone.

In the sixth place, there was a deep sense of sin and an overpowering desire to separate themselves from it and from all its sponsoring causes. Such divinely induced anxiety and agonizing conviction of sin needs no prompting or psychological maneuvering. The work is uniquely that of the Holy Spirit. The failures of the past, even those that have been forgotten, suddenly become so real and so painfully present that no amount of comfort or personal rationalization will assuage the terrible pressure of individual guilt and heartbreak. Accordingly, so spontaneous and thorough should be the conviction and simultaneous hatred of sin that there will be no need to plead with men and women to make any decisions.

Seventh, in every revival in the Old Testament there was likewise a return to the offering of blood sacrifices. Given such a heavy sense of sin, there must be as great a remedy, and that can only be met by the one and only sufficient sacrifice of the Paschal Lamb of God. Every sacrifice in the Old Testament pointed forward to the final sacrifice that Christ would offer. Thus in Hezekiah's time there was mention of the sin offering (2 Chron. 29:21–25) and the first reference to atonement since Israel came into the land (2 Chron. 29:24). Only on this basis could the people be revived; all other schemes were bogus deals. While we do not offer the sacrifices of Israel's day, we most certainly must affirm what those sacrifices pointed to: the sole sufficiency of the blood of Christ (i.e., an offering up of his very life) to care adequately for the burden of our sins.

The eighth feature plainly set forth in the Old Testament revivals was the experience of a new sense of unbounded joy and exuberant gladness. Nowhere is this seen more clearly than in that postexilic scene with Nehemiah and Ezra. Instead of permitting the people to weep and grieve continually over their sins, Nehemiah and Ezra counseled them to stop mourning, for that day of revival was sacred to the Lord. It should be a day for celebrating, feasting, and sending gifts, for "the joy of the LORD is your strength" (Neh. 8:9–10).

The ninth and final characteristic is that each revival was followed by a time of great productivity and prosperity. This is not the health, wealth, happiness, and success message that some are offering today. Rather it is the observation that the fortunes of the soil are intimately tied up with men and women and their spiritual success or failure. We find the rationale and explanation for this feature of revivals in the biblical record as early as the garden of Eden. When Adam sinned, the ground was cursed on his account. And so it will remain until all creation is redeemed at the future coming of the Lord (Rom. 8:20–22). But if the final redemption cannot presently be offered because creation is still subjected to vanity, there can be substantial healing in the realm of nature.

This observable measure of healing for the fields and crops of the fields is always associated with the repentance of humanity and the revival of the spiritual fortunes of believers. Thus Haggai asked whether anyone had noticed that when the spiritual temperature of the community declined, so did the productivity of their fields, the enjoyment of their food and drink, and the purchasing power of their earnings (Hag. 1:5–6). Similarly, in response to the preaching of Joel's call for repentance, Yahweh answered not only with a promise of the future outpouring of the Holy Spirit (Joel 2:28–32) but also with immediate relief from the locust plague and the drought (Joel 2:19–27). The fields, Joel explained, would groan under the heavy load of the bumper crop of grain and grapes. The pastures would become green, the trees would bear their fruit in abundance, and the autumn and spring rains would come as before. The barns and storage bins would overflow because the yield would be so unexpectedly high.

We should not be surprised, therefore, to find that 2 Chronicles 7:14 promises that God will heal our land (i.e., any nation that takes serious this promise of God) if we turn to him to be revived. Must we always fail to see that the deliverance offered in Scripture is not isolated from the material world? It is not enough to view the effect of revival as only on a person's soul. Revival affects the whole of life, including agriculture, the economy, international relations, peace, and the security of a people (even in its large urban areas). To be sure, revival is no panacea or magical cure-all. To see it as such would be to reject the reality of the presence of sin in the created order until the Messiah's return. But neither should we hesitate to speak of the substantial restoration that is available now. It is to our shame that we have not utilized our spiritual power more openly and effectively; but then, how can we if we are currently in need of being revived? Before we can either experience these blessings or be the means of blessing to a watching world, we must experience God's reviving of us and our people.

Why Study the Biblical Revivals?

Before turning to examine sixteen of the Bible's revivals in detail, a final question needs to be considered. Some may still be asking why it is necessary to study the revivals of the Bible. There are at least five good reasons for exposing ourselves to an in-depth study of biblical revivals—yes, even the revivals of the Old Testament.

The first reason is motivational: a study of the biblical revivals ought to create a desire in the believer for revival today. Seeing God graciously grant his power and presence to those who so obviously had earned anything but God's mercy and grace is a strong source of encouragement to us. In this sense, the study of revival is contagious. Every legitimate inducement, especially from the Word of God, is a further encouragement for us to sense our own condition before God.

The second reason is more methodological. It answers the question, How should we go about the quest for revival? What methods will God use? For example, in some of the revivals of the past, God used a national crisis (as at Mizpah under Samuel) or a three-year drought and an outdoor meeting on Mount Carmel (under Elijah) as the occasion for times of refreshing from the Lord. Moreover, when individuals or the believing community could not be reached by the faithful preaching or teaching of the Word of God, God made that Word scarce. Eventually, those who had become deaf to the message of the Word were forced to listen to another, harsher, word from God: the harsh realities of a culture without the purifying presence and gracious provision of the hand of God. Then it was, and still is, that people's extremities become God's opportunities. If we have not observed this yet from experience, then the Word of God is still available to teach us.

A study of biblical revivals will acquaint us, in the third place, with the types of people God uses in revivals. In themselves they were nothing spectacular. They possessed the same desires, fears, and successes that many of us experience. Therefore, we should be careful about making plaster saints out of them. But we do develop a great respect for the God these men adored and trusted implicitly. We learn how they went to the school of prayer, as Elijah did for three years, before they were used of God in one great day of ministry to turn a whole nation to God. We learn that what they were externally they first were in their hearts, for "as he thinks in his heart, so is he" (Prov. 23:7 NKJV).

We are instructed, fourthly, on how we should prepare for revival. The emphasis in 2 Chronicles 7:14 on the four conditions for revival are amply illustrated, taught, and urged in every one of the sixteen great biblical revivals. It must be acknowledged that much ink has been spilled over the question of the proper source and means for expecting a revival. However, most of this debate could have been settled long ago by a full and patient listening to Scripture. This battle over whether revival is solely and always the work of God, or whether it also recognizes certain means that are requisite to promote a revival, has sorely tried the church in the past and will no doubt be used by the enemy of our souls and of revivals on every future occasion. Few will deny that God is sovereign in this whole work of revival, but many will doubt whether men and women have any necessary part. Yet most, if not all, will agree that people are not just robots, without any fault or responsibility in this affair. And surely confession and repentance, even though they are aided by the special work of God, are nonetheless also the responsibility of individuals.

The debate in this area reminds me very much of the debate that has been raging over the doctrine of sanctification. As a student I sat through many sermons by speakers who asked the audience the rhetorical question, Do you know what is wrong with Christians? Why is it that we are so far behind our beliefs in practicing a vital, sanctified life? The first time I heard this question I was all ears, for I had no idea what the desired response was. It turned out to be this: it is because we are not willing to *let go and let God be God*. The proof for this statement was found in such texts as Ephesians 2:10, "For we are God's workmanship," and Philippians 2:13, "For it is God who works in you both to will and to do His good pleasure" (NKJV).

Well, that settled that question. At least it settled it until the next day, when another chapel speaker arrived and rhetorically asked the identical question. Had it not been a dignified and most conservative setting, I might have blurted out yesterday's answer, but fortunately for my reputation and the reserved decorum of the setting, I was spared what would have been embarrassment and a great deal of theological discomfort. As it turned out, the answer had changed 180 degrees overnight. Now the problem was not the "emptiness of busyness," as a substitute for the sovereign working of God; no, the problem now was that too many Christians were lazily sitting around expecting God to do everything when the Scripture said, we are "created . . . to do good works" (Eph. 2:10), and that we should "work out [our] salvation with fear and trembling" (Phil. 2:12).

It took a number of months and years of this kind of switch hitting before I began to realize something (typical case of a slow learner). Both sides were appealing to almost the same contexts or verses. However, each was quoting only that portion of the text that held high the point in the argument they wished to make. My conclusion was staring me in the face: Scripture taught both positions, and one without the other was in danger of becoming lop-sided.

Thus I conclude that there can be no revival without the Lord's initiating it and carrying it out. But I also conclude that no one can hide behind the doctrine of God as the explanation for why we have not had a revival in our day or the reason that the last great revival in America occurred in 1905–6. There are essential factors for revival, such as repentance, prayer, the preaching of the Word of God, humbling ourselves under the mighty hand of God, and earnestly seeking his face. The study of the sixteen greatest revivals of the Bible should handily demonstrate both the balance and the dual nature of this truth without clumsily involving us in a despicable works-salvation or even in any whisper of a suggestion that we or anyone else has merited, earned, attracted, or otherwise been responsible for the favor of God.

The fifth and final reason for studying revival involves the area of preparation. Once we know how the Lord has acted in the past, we should be better prepared to accept the special working of God when it arrives. It also will warn us that no two revivals are alike, for the Lord God uniquely suits each divine visitation to the needs of the hour. Every one of our preconceptions and built-in limitations concerning what God can or cannot do or what he is likely or not likely to do in exact detail must be jettisoned if we are to learn anything from the distinctiveness of each of these biblical revivals.[11] Let us now turn to each of these sixteen teaching passages where the Word demonstrates the truth of 2 Chronicles 7:14 and the power of a revived people of God.

1   It Is Time to Ask God to Revive Us Once Again

Revival under the Sons of Korah
Psalm 85:1–13

---

*P*salm 85, in several church traditions, is usually read on Christmas Day because of its bright pictures of peace, reconciliation, and fruitfulness of land—in the last verses. It is an amazingly beautiful prayer, probably set to music, as the psalm title informs us, with the focal point coming in verse 4, "Restore [or "revive"] us again, O God our Savior."

But just as significant is the fact that it was composed by "the sons of Korah." Now the name of Korah is connected with infamy in Numbers 16. There Korah, along with certain persons from the tribe of Reuben—Dathan, Abiram, and On— became insolent when they declared that it was time for a change in leadership. Moses and Aaron had to go! They argued that all the congregation was "holy," so why should Aaron and Moses set themselves up as leaders over the Lord's assembly? (Num. 16:3).

Moses and Aaron were instructed by God to tell the congregation of Israel to move away from the tents of Korah, Dathan, and Abiram (Num. 16:23, 26). Suddenly the earth opened up, and they went down to their graves alive (Num. 16:33).

One would think that all the natural descendants of Korah would forever be cut off from the mercy and grace of God, but the title to this psalm indicates that the exact opposite is true. The same Mosaic law that taught that God would punish the sins of "fathers to the third and fourth generation of those who hate me" (Exod. 20:4) also taught that "fathers shall not be put to death for their children, nor children put to death for their fathers; each is to die for his [or her] own sin" (Deut. 24:16). Thus the marvelous grace of God did not hold against the lineal descendants of Korah the faults that overtook their forefather, but instead raised them to even greater heights by allowing them to be the authors of Scripture, including Psalms 42–49; 84–85; and 87–88. In 2 Chronicles 20:19 the Korahites stood along with the Levities and the Kohathites to praise the Lord.

How appropriate, then, that the family that had experienced so generously of the grace of God should be used by God to call their generation and ours back to that same God of grace! They did this in Psalm 85, with four strophes that laid out before the Lord four requests:

1. Grant us your restoration as in times past (85:1–3).
2. Grant us your joy and love in our times (85:4–7).
3. Grant us your peace and presence in our land (85:8–9).
4. Grant us your harmony among your people (85:10–13).

Here is the prayer for revival that should teach us how we ought to pray as we earnestly storm the gates of heaven and cry out to God that he might revive his church, our nations, and our sin-laden culture once again.

Grant Us Your Restoration as in Times Past (85:1–3)

Is it not true that past revivals have been responsible for bringing to all who live on earth the benefits and blessings we now enjoy? And that is indeed the basis on which the psalm begins: God has been favorable to the people of Israel in the past. In fact, that is the very essence of our definition of revival. A revival is a time when believers witness an extraordinary work of God enlivening, strengthening, and elevating the spiritual life and vitality already possessed, but which life is now in a state of decline and is feeble, mediocre, and dull in its outworkings. Revivals come as "times of refreshing from the Lord" (Acts 3:19) or, in the case of Israel, it was a time when God restored the fortunes of Israel.

For modern evidences of such extraordinary movements of God among his saints, one need only look to South Korea's history in the last forty years, or to what has gone on in Eastern Europe, the former Soviet Union, and the People's Republic of China in even more recent days. In each case, a cleansed church has led to fantastic enlargement of the believing family of God. For example, with less than a million believers in China prior to 1950, the Spirit of God has added, mainly since 1979, another 70 to 90 million believers in that nation that contains one-fourth of the earth's population!

And who can forget the 10 to 15 million believers in South Korea in a nation of just over 40 million citizens? Most of that growth in South Korea has come since the Korean War in the 1950s. Yes, God has "showed favor to [many lands]" (v. 1). But let Korea or any other nation forget what God has done, and the results are tragic: markets tumble, economies catapult, and prestige vanishes, until the believing community remembers where its strength and glory came from.

It is little wonder, then, that the six verbs of verses 1–3 review the way that God had worked so majestically in the past. While it is true that the context of this psalm may have been some recent national catastrophe, verse 4 was not a request that God should complete a work then in progress; instead, it was a prayer that God would once again, in that present time, do the same new work for those who currently were completely deserving of the wrath of God as others had experienced God's grace in the past.

Three important components of Israel's past history formed the basis for the request for revival: (1) confession of sin, (2) forgiveness of sin, and (3) the removal of God's wrath. The fact that God "showed favor" and that he "restored" (or literally "turned") the "fortunes of Jacob" in verse 1 implied that the people had begun their quest for renewal and revival by confessing their sin. In turn, God "forgave" their "iniquity," and he "covered all their sins" (v. 2). The people's quest for results, blessing, prestige, influence, and power had to address the issue of blockage caused by sin first. Without forgiveness, none of the sought-after results would be present, or at least, they would not be long-lasting. The sin question must always be dealt with first, or the quest for renewal and reviving of life among God's people will be dead in the water, even before it starts.

When sins are confessed and forgiven, God's restoration also involves the removal of his wrath against us sinners and our nations. That is what verse 3 affirmed: God "set aside" his wrath, and he "turned" or "called back" his fierce anger. The allusion in verse 3 is probably to Exodus 32:12; 34:7, 14; and Numbers 25:4, where the offended holiness of God is like a consuming fire that can only be set aside when an atonement for sin has made possible a reconciliation for all who will ask for forgiveness. But thanks be to God: he has restored us to his favor, and his anger no longer burns against us, when we confess our sin and he forgives us and removes the impending threat of his wrath that hung over our heads.

Grant Us Your Joy and Love in Our Times (85:4–7)

Spiritual growth cannot exist where there is unconfessed sin. Neither is the joy of singing possible where fellowship has been broken. Have you ever visited a new congregation and been struck by the absence of any heartfelt joy and vitality in the songs of the congregation? I have. In my experience, it has been possible to almost determine the spiritual sensitivities of that group, based on the way in which that congregation sang. Where the singing had been lackluster and almost begrudgingly offered as a requirement to God, the ability of that group of saints to receive the word of God with joy and to allow that word to judge them was almost defeated in its effectiveness before it began. Why? Because they needed to get rid of their festering sins and to ask the Holy Spirit of God to revive them again.

Only when God's people are restored to his favor and new life has again begun to flow through that body of believers is it possible to experience the joy believers were meant to have in our Lord. That is why the sons of Korah pleaded, "Restore [or "turn"] us again . . . and put away your displeasure toward us" (v. 4).

Notice that revival is the work of God: *You* restore us and *you* revive us (vv. 4, 6), they prayed. Revival comes from God; it cannot be imitated or self-induced. Revival is the gift of God's "love" (v. 7). The Hebrew word used for "love" in this verse is the word *hesed*, one of the most beautiful, but difficult, words to translate in all the Old Testament.[1] It is not as if we did not know what *hesed* meant; instead, it is that it contains too rich a meaning for any one English word to approximate. It includes the ideas that God is gracious, loving, and faithfully loyal in all that he has promised to do—and more. Thus, the same love that chastens us will now revive us by bringing us back to the forgiving Savior. That is why we judge the heart of this psalm and prayer to God for all ages, times, cultures, and nations to be in verse 6: "Will you not revive us again?" How else will we be able to rejoice in our Lord if we are not first revived?

The request in verse 7 to grant us "salvation" is not a request to bring us into the family of God for the first time. It is a request that we be delivered from the just consequences of our sin. For too long the body has suffered powerlessness, unhappiness, affliction, dispersion, and a cultural captivity that has made the church the laughingstock of the heathen.

Some of the sins that we need to be delivered from should be mentioned to start our hearts and minds thinking of the seriousness of the summons that is being issued here in this passage. First, we would mention the sin of nonattendance at the house of God. Hebrews 10:25 warns, "Let us not give up meeting together, as some are in the habit of doing." Not only have the baby boomers dropped out of attending church, but now many above fifty years of age have felt that worship styles have catered too much to the tastes of the yuppies (in a distorted effort to win them back to the church). As a consequence, many churches have departed from incorporating the pastoral prayer, the public reading of Scripture, and the forthright exposition and proclamation of Scripture. While this is an accurate assessment of the habits of all too many churches, it still does not relieve us of our obligation to attend the house of God and to pray for the kind of spiritual hunger in all God's people that will see past trendy styles and strive for a real meeting with God in worship.

We could also mention the sin of unreliability in Christian service. Too many have invested all of their best efforts into their professions and jobs with whatever time is left being reserved for one's own leisure time. However, 1 Corinthians 4:2 likewise warns, "Now it is required that those who have been given a trust must prove faithful." Where the fires of revival burned dimly, if at all, there it is that scores of positions for service in God's vineyard and his house go begging for faithful and dedicated workers.

In the third place, the sin of unholiness in everyday affairs could be mentioned. First Thessalonians 4:7 boldly affirms, "For God did not call us to be impure, but to live a holy life." Hence, all that offends the holiness of God is one more reason why we ought to cry out to God in repentance for his reviving power in our lives again.

All sin is actually a transgression of the law of God, as John taught in 1 John 3:4. Thus all who sin break God's law and need to be reconciled to him. But if it is claimed that this is too much to ask of those who have already been forgiven and are part of the family of God, then let it be remembered that the apostle John's letter to the seven churches of Asia Minor (i.e., present-day Turkey) advised five of the seven churches to "repent." To the church at Ephesus he declared, "Repent and do the things you did at first. If you do not repent, I will come to you and remove your lampstand [church] from its place" (Rev. 2:5). No less severe were John's words to the church at Pergamum: "Repent therefore! Otherwise, I will soon come to you and will fight against [you] with the sword of my mouth" (Rev. 2:16). The church at Thyatira had an even more damning indictment: "I have given her time to repent of her immorality, but she is unwilling. So I will cast her on a bed of suffering, and I will make those who commit adultery with her suffer intensely, unless they repent of her ways" (Rev. 2:21–22). To the church at Sardis he wrote: "Remember, therefore, what you have received and heard; obey it, and repent" (Rev. 3:3). Finally, the church of Laodicea was advised, "So be earnest, and repent. Here . . . I stand at the door and knock. If anyone hears my voice and opens the door, I will come in and eat with him, and he with me" (Rev. 3:19b–20).

Who can deny the fact that failure to recall and to act on what we have been taught from the Word of God will likewise earn the wrath of God, unless we, too, repent and return to obeying the whole counsel of God? All too frequently in this day of pluralism and minimalistic doctrine, ethical practice, and abbreviated morality, the full demands of Scripture are sacrificed in the name of every other good in Christendom, except respect for what he has taught us in his Word. We are told that we must think of the larger picture, of the need for unity among the brethren, of the need to bring as many as possible under one banner for a more effective voice in a culture that counts noses as easily as it counts beans in deciding what is the correct position in a democracy on the same basis. But will this wash with the Savior? Can we avoid the overwhelming necessity to repent and to cry out, "Do it again, Lord. Please revive us again."

In any case, God's anger, in comparison with his grace, mercy, and love, lasts but for a moment (Ps. 30:5), while his favor lasts a lifetime (Exod. 34:6). And when God's saints are restored to his favor, they are enabled to rejoice once more.

Is it not clear that oftentimes there comes a call even for the *church of God* to repent and to return to believing, acting, and living like she did when she first came to know the Lord? When we refuse to forsake our wicked practices, such as immorality, God will cast his very own people and his beloved church into a bed of intense suffering until she cries out in repentance.

The interesting point is that rejoicing is not an optional feature of the Christian life. It is an essential part of being the people of God. Thus, people who have little inner joy are probably in desperate need of his reviving work. This point is proven by the psalmist in other parts of that book: "Those who love your name may rejoice in you" (Ps. 5:11b); "May those who love your salvation always say, 'The LORD be exalted!'" (Ps. 40:16b).

Grant Us Your Peace and Presence in Our Land (85:8–9)

The promise of God is simply the reaffirmation of the word given in Leviticus 26:3–13. This promise comes in our psalm almost as if a voice interrupted the silence while an answer was awaited to the requests that had been made in verses 1–7. Just as the prophet Habakkuk had to wait to hear what God would say in his bewilderment, so the psalmist waits until he hears "what God the LORD will say" (v. 8a).

And the result of his waiting is that God "promises peace." Peace is not only protection from one's enemies and fertility of the land (as Lev. 26 makes abundantly clear), but God's *shalom* is a veritable summary of everything that he will do for his people materially, physically, socially, spiritually, and psychologically. This is not to give credence to the message of the health, wealth, and prosperity people, for that message is totally individualistic, secular, and me-centered. Instead, it affirms what has been true of every revival we have seen in the past. Wherever the voice of God has been recognized in all its fullness, there God's people have experienced the peace from God that passes all understanding. And that peace has both an inner and outer aspect that cannot be compared to any cheap tit-for-tat serving of God in order to get rich, or to a name-it-and-claim-it program of do-it-yourself egocentrism.

The people of God are called by three names in these two verses: "his people," "his saints," and "those who fear him." What a privilege to belong to God and to be chosen to be his special possession (Exod. 19:5–6). And who would ever think of the present body of Christ, at least in most of its forms, as "saints"? But that is what we are called in both the Old and New Testaments. Imagine the people at the messed-up church of Corinth being called "saints" (1 Cor. 1:2 NKJV), but so they were! And think about all the texts in Proverbs, Psalms, Ecclesiastes, and Job where we are enjoined to "fear the LORD." "The fear of the LORD is the beginning of wisdom" argued the psalmist in 111:10a.

Besides promising his peace, verse 9b observes that under these revived conditions the "glory" of God may now dwell in the land. The glory of God stood for nothing short of his very own *presence*. Indeed, the personal presence of God would come to dwell in the land or nation where the people of God had called out for a revival from above. What better exchange could we have today for all the wickedness and rampant evil than to have God's personal presence abiding with us where once the streets and cities had been all but given over to lawlessness? Is this not more than enough reason for us to call for a new work of God in our churches?

O that we would "not return to folly" (v. 8c). Such a reversal of directions would be tantamount to acting like pigs that want to get back into the mud after being cleaned up or to acting like dogs that return to their vomit after having experienced what really good eating was like (2 Pet. 2:22).

Grant Us Your Harmony among Your People (85:10–13)

In everyday affairs, strict adherence to the claims of truth sometimes prevents the display of love and kindness. But when God showers his grace on a revived people, grace and truth (Hebrew *hesed* and *'emet*) not only come together, but they embrace and kiss each other (v. 10)!

This may be looked at from two different aspects. From the terrestrial side ("springs forth from the earth," v. 11a) comes "truth" (or, as the NIV has it, "faithfulness"); but from heaven ("looks down") comes "righteousness."

In our personal lives, truth is combined with a gracious and merciful spirit when we believe and act on the assertion that "the kingdom of God is not a matter of eating and drinking, but of righteousness, peace and joy in the Holy Spirit" (Rom. 14:17). Meanwhile, our collective life manifested the reviving work of God when, as in the past, slavery was abolished, child labor laws were ended, work hours were shortened, missionary societies were formed, the YMCA was begun in many cities of the world, slums were cleared, the Sunday school movement began, homes for unwed mothers were provided, abortion was condemned, law and order was restored to the major urban centers, and many similar reforms were enacted by revived consciences of restored believers moving out into the marketplaces of the world and our society at large.

Even more amazing, the way back to the green theology of ecology was not by means of a concentration on the imbalance we have created in nature *per se*, but to tackle the problem of the heart of humanity first as a means to getting more than a fashionable response to a current eddy of thought that would no doubt only last for a period of time as long as it got recognition from the media.

Verses 12–13 promise that when God revives his people, even the land will experience a substantial healing, thereby modeling what the full restitution of the whole creation will be when our Lord returns a second time to this earth (Rom. 8:20–22). Leviticus 26:4 had predicted that "the ground will yield its crops" when God's people obey him. Generally the most prosperous times in English and American history were directly connected as aftermaths of revivals from God.

Proverbs 14:34 is still true: "Righteousness exalts a nation, but sin is a disgrace to any people." It is also exceedingly true that "Where there is no revelation [i.e., preaching of the Word of God to God's people or to any nation], the people cast off restraint"

(Prov. 29:18). What better explanation is there for the brazen effrontery of lawlessness and wickedness in our day than this verse supplies? When the pulpit fails to declare the whole counsel of God and turns, instead, to pop psychology, self-realization talks, and identity types of searches in sermonettes, be sure that the populace, both inside the church and outside it, will see all hell break loose just as Moses witnessed after a mere forty-day hiatus of his presence and preaching while he was on Mount Sinai receiving the Ten Commandments. Proverbs 29: 18 borrowed the very same word used in Exodus 32:25 when it observed that the people "were running wild" (or "had broken loose") in sacred prostitution to the golden calf. What will happen after months and years of such poor pablum and poppycock substitutes for the Word of God? Has not our culture, both church and secular, torn down the fences and gone wild? And whom shall we blame for this state of affairs? Or better still, to whom shall we go in repentance and hunger for revival given such a desperate state of affairs, no matter how they have come about?

Righteousness (i.e., the "rightness" of God) will go before the revived as a vanguard for all their steps and plans, exactly as Isaiah 58:8b had promised in a similar manner. And those who cry out so frequently for guidance and for someone or something to lay out the path they should take are relieved to know that when we are revived God lays down a path for us to walk in (v. 13b). What a blessing revival is both to the land and to its inhabitants!

Conclusion

Without the reviving power and presence of God, there can be no spiritual life or vitality. If we are to have life—real life—we must ask the source of that life.

As I write this chapter, the temperature outside is slipping to 20 degrees below zero with windchill readings of minus 50 degrees! In this kind of weather, many will experience frostbite very quickly if exposed to the elements for too long. The first sign of a frozen limb is pain—and so is the first sign of our need for revival. If we deny that we need anything, we are actually in the very jaws of death, warned John (Rev. 3:17).

The second sign of life is a voice that cries out because of the pain. Here is where the ministry of prayer begins as we entreat our heavenly Father to come to our rescue. Never have we experienced a revival that has not begun with a humbling of ourselves in recognition of our abysmal state and a heavy burden that we must beg God to help us with. Without prayer, revivals do not even begin.

A third sign of life comes when we seek help from a physician. This is equivalent to our "seeking the face of God." God is under no duress of obligation to answer us, but we know that he is most merciful and gracious.

The final sign of life for those stricken with frostbite comes when the gangrene and dead part of the limb is removed. This is true in the spiritual realm; sin must be faced. The sphere of confession, goes the very wise counsel of olden days, must be as wide as the sphere of acquaintance of the sin, whether in the community of believers or outside the church.

Then, and only then, will we have met the conditions for revival in our day. Then it will be possible to plead just as many have in the past: "Do it again, Lord; revive your people so that we may rejoice in you."

2   It Is Time to Get Rid of Our Idols

Revival under Jacob
Genesis 35:1–15

Were it not for the shocking events of life, some of us would never consider our need for revival to be very serious at all. But often, just when we have settled into the routine of our ways and thought that we were no worse off than the average believer, the Lord mercifully shocks us from the staleness of our relationship with him. How much easier it would have been to have listened to the Word of God in the first place. But God's love is so intense and so deeply desirous of our good that when we become deaf to his Word or fail to respond to it, he mercifully knows how to get our attention through the events of life. Of course he would rather have us respond to his Word without this special prompting. But when all else fails and after a long period of patience, then God speaks to us as individuals and as a nation through the problems and tragedies of life.

This is not to say that God is the author of evil. He is holy, pure, and without any sin whatsoever. He is no more the author of evil today than he was when Satan appeared before him in the book of Job to request permission to bring tragedy into Job's life. Of course the purpose of those calamities was different from the ones presently being considered. In Job's case the purpose was to answer the challenge that people serve God only because he blesses them. However, in either case it is clear that evil is only permitted by God. He is the author of the author of evil in that God created Satan before he sinned. Therefore, although God can and does allow evil or tragedy to come into our lives, he is not its author.

One of the reasons God would allow such a horrible thing to happen to us is to alarm us of the seriousness of the plight of our spiritual health and progress. We do not live by bread alone but by every word that proceeds from the mouth of God. It was in just such a circumstance that the patriarch Jacob found himself in Genesis 35. The whole problem started over his daughter, Dinah, one of his children by his wife Leah.

Jacob had just moved back into the land of Canaan from Paddan Aram (Gen. 33:18) when Shechem, the son of Hamor, ruler of that area, saw Dinah, took her, and raped her (Gen. 34:2). This tragedy set off a string of events that would permanently alter the lives of all who were touched by them. Nevertheless, God was still in control, allowing his will to be worked out in spite of the violence and reprehensible evil involved.

Hamor came to Jacob to negotiate a marriage for his son, settle the bride-price, and to establish friendly relations, only to learn that there was trouble. Dinah's brothers in particular were outraged at what had happened to their sister: "a thing that should not be done" (Gen. 34:7). Hamor offered favorable terms, involving the reciprocal offer of intermarriage between their families, but he had no understanding of the impossibilities this presented for a people who were not to be unequally yoked to unbelievers. But then, what real difference was there between these unbelieving Shechemites and Jacob's family? In practice their lives seemed to be alike.

Jacob had promised God some thirty years earlier, when he was fleeing the wrath of his deceived brother, Esau, that if God would be with him, watch over him, and return him safely to Canaan, then Yahweh would be his God, and he would serve him. But like so many of us in these so-called foxhole experiences, Jacob had forgotten his vow. Yet God had returned him safely to his land and had blessed him and had caused his life to overflow with the bounty of God's goodness (Gen. 28:20–22). How, we ask in amazement, could Jacob have been so ungrateful? Surely he had nothing when he cried out for help. And was thirty years not enough time to remember the vow made to God, or even to remember Yahweh himself? Perhaps Jacob considered himself a self-made man; after all, had it not been by his own hard work, wits, and sheer willpower and drive that he had become what he was? This argument ("I earned it by myself") sounds curiously similar to the attitude of the average middle class or newly rich American today.

But now Jacob had family trouble, and that was different. To make matters worse, Jacob's self-made sons decided to take things into their own hands and reap vengeance on the heads of Hamor's clan. First there was deceit: the sons pretended that all would be well if the men of Hamor would be circumcised; then Dinah could be given in marriage (Gen. 34:13–16). Is it not true that once evil is let loose, sometimes there is no stopping it, except through a genuine change in the lives of all who are affected? But in this situation Jacob still did not see the hand of God or the necessity for calling his sons or these heathen to repentance. In fact, he had even forgotten his own vow to God.

The situation deteriorated further. The men of Hamor's city yielded to the demand to be circumcised, totally unaware of what evil lay lurking in the hearts of Jacob's sons. On the third day after this operation, while they were still in pain, every male in the Canaanite city, including Hamor and his son Shechem, was murdered by two of Jacob's sons, Simeon and Levi (Gen. 34:25–26). None of this had the approval or consent of Yahweh.

Only then did it begin to dawn on Jacob how serious a situation he had worked himself into. For when the looting and the stealing of all livestock and goods were over, Jacob rebuked his two sons, Simeon and Levi, who had reaped this havoc on the offenders: "You have [made] me a stench to . . . the people living in this land. We are few in number, and if they join forces against me and attack me, I and my household will be destroyed" (Gen. 34:30). Their only defense was to retort, "Should he have treated our sister like a prostitute?" (34:31).

It took an atrocity like this to push Jacob to finally take the action he should have taken long before; it was time he and his family took this word to heart: "Get rid of the foreign gods you have with you" (Gen. 35:2). I believe this text is the focal point of Genesis 35, providing the basis for a threefold challenge. Thus I have used it in the title of the present chapter. Chapter 35 gives three reasons why Jacob, his sons, and *we* ought to get rid of our idols:

1. Only cleansed men and women can meet God (vv. 1–4).
2. Only God can protect us when we are in danger (vv. 5–8).
3. Only God can change our personalities and bless us (vv. 9–15).

Only Cleansed Men and Women Can Meet God (35:1–4)

In the midst of Jacob's bitter reflections and agonizing perplexities, the Lord urged Jacob to move his family approximately thirty miles south of Shechem to Bethel. This was the very spot where Jacob had sought God in a moment of deep despair some thirty years before. Here he had experienced the heavenly vision of a ladder, and here he had made his vow. In other words, God ordered him back to ground zero. It is too bad that it had taken a crisis to drive Jacob to this point, but it was better for him to have the crisis and to respond than to miss the blessing of God.

How important it is to fulfill the vows we have made. Jacob's deliberate delay had cost him the grief experienced with his daughter, Dinah. The same lesson would later be repeated with Moses, who sinfully delayed in circumcising his son, due apparently to a family argument over the rite with his Midianite wife, Zipporah (Exod. 4:24–26).

What a stern warning this is to us as well. So frequently we have no idea that there is a subtle and pernicious drift away from divine things in our lives or in our families until it is almost too late. Then events shock us to our spiritual senses and force us to take drastic and speedy spiritual measures for the saving of ourselves and our households.

It is interesting to note, as the commentator George Bush points out, that God did not order Jacob to "build an altar to me as you promised and disappointingly have not done lo these thirty years."[1] Instead, Genesis 35:1 simply says, "Go up to Bethel and settle there, and build an altar there to God, who appeared to you when you were fleeing from your brother Esau." The remonstrance is ever so gentle, not an in-your-face reminder of all the trouble Jacob had brought on himself because of his stubbornness. There are so many evidences like this of grace in the Old Testament that we can never forget that the nature of God has always been the same, and it ever will be.

The time had come to get back to God quickly. The savagery and cruelty of his sons had convinced Jacob of that. Even though there was a cost for Jacob's hesitancy to make God Lord in his life as he had promised, there still was time to put away the root of these problems. Surely there is a lesson here for us to learn.

There can be little doubt that the source of decay in this family could be traced back to the presence of foreign gods in their midst. Sometimes it seems so easy just to let some things be, but these little sins can become like foxes that burrow away in our lives until their appetite knows no limit and they have devoured us.

In the introduction of this book, a strong connecting link was observed between idolatry in another day and the contemporary challenges that come in the form of every rival of God in heart, mind, and life. Therein lies the real genius and penchant for idolatry, both ancient and modern. Nothing can have first place along with the Lord: not my job, my hobby, my goals, my organizations, my leisure time, my recreation, my marriage, my family, or even my church. If such are placed first or even share first place with my commitment to the Lord, then I have slipped into idolatry. In this case, we may as well name them Baal, Anat, Asherah, Molech, and all other rival gods.

Jacob's word, and hence God's word to us, is straightforward: "Get rid of them." Furthermore, God urges us to purify ourselves and to put off our old clothes and put on new (v. 2). This is similar to the New Testament call for us to put off the old man and to put on the new man in Christ as we purify ourselves from every form of evil (Col. 3:9–10).

We may wonder whether Jacob himself partook in any of the practices associated with these icons or if he was aware up to this point of his children's practice. Or perhaps it was simply a matter of his being unwilling to risk the resentment of those who were dear to him by ordering the removal of these gods. Indeed, the question must be asked: where had the gods come from? Perhaps from Rachel, Jacob's favorite wife, who had stolen the gods, or the seraphim, of her father, Laban (Gen. 31:19). Scholars believe that whoever possessed them was also owner of all the family property; thus they functioned, if we may judge from archaeological references in tablets from that approximate epoch, as inheritance wills to inherit the property. But did they also tempt their owners to worship them as well? Or did the entrance of this evil come from the Mesopotamian servants, who had become syncretistic in their faith, professing to worship Yahweh while holding on to remnants of their old pagan ways? One other possibility occurs to us. Could these also have been the gods stolen from the sacking and looting of Shechem? (The Targum Jonathan refers to them as "the gods which you received from the house of the idols of Shechem.") The correct answer is that we simply do not know. But the result was the same regardless of their origins. Get rid of them; that is God's command to all his people. Remove every competing loyalty from your hearts and your sight!

In addition to this command, the Lord challenges us to personal holiness. The command to "purify [our]selves" was again expanded by the Targum Jonathan as "Cleanse yourselves from the pollutions of the slain to whom you have come nigh." But this hardly meets the total demands of the text; Jacob's family was filled with more impurities than the mere contact with corpses. Surely the changing of their clothes merely symbolized the putting off of the old and the putting on of that which was new.

Holiness of life is never satisfied solely with one aspect of a person to the exclusion of all others. This theology can be illustrated with Moses' experience at the burning bush. When he was told to take off his sandals, he must have felt comfortable in those shoes. Why should he have to take them off? But Yahweh patiently explained that because God was present and because the ground Moses was standing on was holy, he needed to obey.

The lesson is clear: holiness is wholeness. In fact, the English root for both words is one and the same. Therefore, it will do no good to prepare to meet God only in our hearts or, conversely, with mere outward vestments, without real inward preparation. For the believer, holiness is not an optional spiritual luxury, nor is it an unessential feature, if we expect to see revival in our time.

After adequate and holistic preparation was made, the house of Jacob could approach the altar of God (v. 3). This was the place of forgiveness for ruptured relationships. On no other grounds or bases could full restoration to the favor, fellowship, and reviving energy of the living God be possible.

Suddenly Jacob recalled his old promise and the fact that God had "answered [him] in the day of [his] distress and [had] been with [him] wherever [he] had gone" (v. 3). If we ask why this command to build the altar had not come sooner, the response will be the same as the reason God lets us go on so long with matters degenerating to such a terrible state of affairs that only a crisis is left to awaken us from our lethargy. Harold Stigers accurately commented:

> So it is that God leaves His people to their ways so that they and others, seeing such results, may understand why believers should not live for themselves and earthly things to the exclusion of the will of God. Yet when they repent, as did Jacob,

> God is gracious to forgive. But the scars remain;
> the scars for Jacob were the lives led by his sons.[2]

Just as 2 Chronicles 7:14 would later promise, so here God promised that he would hear from heaven and answer. Moreover the expression "in the day of distress" in connection with prayer must have been on the mind of the psalmist when he wrote in Psalm 20:1, "May the Lord answer you when you are in distress; may the name of the God of Jacob protect you. May he send you help from the sanctuary." And that had indeed been the experience of Jacob, for Yahweh had been with him; he had watched over Jacob wherever he had gone, he had brought him back to his own land, and he had not abandoned him even when Jacob did not appear to have merited such gracious treatment (Gen. 28:15).

When God promises to answer, he intends to say more than merely acknowledging the petition with either an affirmative or a negative answer. Rather it means that he will effectually work on the petitioner's behalf. That is what happened when he answered Elijah by fire (1 Kings 18:24), and so it will be for our earnest petitions as well.

The surrender and dedication of Jacob's family was completed by the surrendering of their gods and earrings (which apparently served as charms, amulets, or talismans). Thus all superstitious reverences were abandoned and buried under the oak at Shechem, which, incidentally, may be the same oak near which Joshua later set up a stone of witness (Josh. 24:25–26).

But we are surprised to see such ready cooperation after so many years of neglect. Why? George Bush answered when he observed, "The incident teaches us that where our spirit is right, we have great access to the hearts of others. Duties [which are normally] difficult in prospect are rendered easy and successful the moment we have . . . faith to carry them into execution."[3]

Only God Can Protect Us When We Are in Danger (35:5–8)

When God places his repentant people under his protection, they are safer than they would be if they were protected by a whole arsenal of national weapons. His people no longer need to be overly concerned about what their enemies might be planning. Neither do they need to keep up the pretense that good-for-nothing idols can save them. (This would amount to little more than using a rabbit's foot.)

After Jacob's household had purged itself of all idolatry and returned to a full acknowledgment of the only true and living God, an astounding dread fell on their would-be detractors because of a divinely induced terror sent from God (v. 5). Once again the grace of God exceeded all the steps of faith taken by these men toward God. The Lord placed such high restraints on those who normally were vindictive that no one pursued Jacob and his family. And not only was this restraint felt by those who were directly affected, but the neighboring towns, whose populations were by far much larger than Jacob's small entourage, also decided against any pursuit of Jacob. If only we as North Americans could learn (indeed, if all the nations of the world could only learn) that our best defense does not lie primarily in our material national hardware for war or the state of our military preparedness, but in a renewed visitation of the Spirit of God in response to our decision to rid ourselves of all our idols, we would all be much better for that understanding and response.

Moving to Bethel signified more than moving to a place of safety; it was also a place of reconciliation at the altar of God. This altar, built by Jacob, was the fifth altar built by the patriarchs, for Abraham had built altars near Bethel (Gen. 12:8) and Hebron (Gen. 13:18), Isaac had built one in Beersheba (Gen. 26:25), and Jacob had also built one in Shechem (Gen. 33:20). Previously Bethel had been named Luz, meaning "almond tree," but that name, which Jacob had given to it thirty years earlier, had not yet taken hold. From now on it would be known as Bethel, meaning "the house of God," because it was here that Jacob had met with God in the past, and here it was that sacrifices would be offered on the altar of God (v. 7).

In renaming Luz *El Bethel*, Jacob unmistakably connected God's name with this site. In Hebrew, the word *El*, the shortened form of

Elohim, or "God," is distinctly separated by the Hebrew disjunctive, a separating accent mark used in the post-Christian system devised by the Hebrew scribes known as the Masoretes. The name *El*, then, is not part of the title, for in that case the place would be called (in translation) by the clumsy name "God, house of God." Some scholars think, though it is difficult to say for sure, that *El* or *Elohim* by itself signifies that God is the strong one, the miracle-working God who had been protecting and blessing Jacob during those twenty years in the land of Paddan Aram. But what we can say for certain is that Jacob, if he ever was involved in the polytheism of his sons, was certainly done with it by this point. Verse 7 places the article in front of the proper name for God (a fairly uncommon phenomenon), thus making it clear that he is the one true living God.[4]

Two wonderful hallmarks of revival now appear in the text: the revelation of God and the place of sacrifice. Where would we be without a word from God and a means of reconciliation and atonement? It was the Lord himself who took the initiative in communicating with man (even as he did when Jacob was thrown on his own resources and felt himself a stranger from the promises of God). And it was the Lord who invited Jacob to set up an altar. This place of death would be a picture of life to all who would claim the promise of God until Christ would come and personally do what no animal or human rite ever could do or promise to do. Only the word of acceptance by God combined with the authorized picture of what God would one day accomplish was the guarantee that stood behind this place of slaughter, as the word *altar* literally signified. The altar and the Word of God—these were God's means of reviving his people. And in that security, all danger was negligible, for greater was the Lord they now served than all the threats, weapons, machinations, and armies of men.

Only God Can Change Our Personalities and Bless Us (35:9-15)

When God graciously grants a revival to come, a number of changes take place in our lives. Not only do we experience freedom from the fear of our enemies, as Jacob witnessed in the preceding section, but we also experience a reorientation of our personalities. Thus it happened that Jacob received a new name.

Biblical names are more than just the vocable by which individuals are addressed. In ancient Israel they were also used to indicate the character and personality of a person. So it was that up to this point Jacob carried a name meaning "supplanter," or "he who grasps the heel" (Gen. 25:26). For that is how Jacob came into this world: he came out of the womb clutching the heel of his brother, Esau, who had preceded him. And that is the way Jacob made his own way through life (at least that is what he thought). But it was God who constantly pursued him, even when Jacob acted as if he were the only one responsible for what he had and what he had become.

On two occasions God met Jacob and so overpowered him by his love that Jacob would forever remain changed. In Jacob's early years, when God first appeared to him in the dream of the ladder to heaven prior to his leaving Canaan, the Lord was already calling him into a new and fuller relationship with God (Gen. 28:13). But at Peniel, Jacob spent a long night wrestling with the angel of the Lord, who is identified in Hosea 12:3 as none other than God himself: "In the womb he grasped his brother's heel; as a man he struggled with God." At Peniel, Jacob's name was changed to Israel, which means "he struggles with God." The Lord explained, "Your name will no longer be Jacob, but Israel, because you have struggled with God and with men and have overcome" (Gen. 32:28). Jacob named that place Peniel because, as he said, "I saw God face to face" (Gen. 32:30).

The second occasion was after the Dinah incident in Genesis 35. Once again God said, "'Your name is Jacob, but you will no longer be called Jacob; your name will be Israel.' So he named him Israel" (Gen. 35:10). Apparently the trauma of the first episode—an event that happened to Jacob while he was on his way home from Paddan Aram after many years of being filled with fears about what his brother Esau, whom he had cheated, might do to him—had not served its full purpose. Jacob was still Jacob in heart and spirit. Yet tragedy had accomplished what a lifetime of wrestling with God could not. Not even a whole night of confrontation with God face to face had stirred his slumbering soul. After the Shechemite massacre, however, Jacob's sleepy soul was aroused. Henceforth he would become a prevailer with God in prayer (Gen. 35:9). The long divine pursuit of Jacob had climaxed.

How much will it take before some people respond? How patient must God be? How long must he wait before we catch on and are revived and changed thoroughly? One thing is certain. When we put away our idols and purify ourselves under the mighty hand of God, the Lord changes our names, that is, our personalities, our characters, our natures, and our dispositions.

But there is more. When we put away our idols, the blessings of God, which lay dormant and only in word form, come to us in full measure. Revival does not necessarily mean that these blessings are totally new. Often they are blessings we have already experienced. But now they come with a freshness, force, and power not known during the days of our lackluster, dull, and equivocating walk with God.

In 35:11 the Lord announces himself as *El Shaddai*, a name used rather infrequently in the Old Testament (forty-eight times), mostly by the patriarchs and Job, who probably lived in the same era. The oldest interpretation of the name goes back to pre-Christian times when the Greek translation of the Old Testament, the Septuagint, rendered it as *pantokrator*, "all-powerful." Likewise, the Latin Vulgate translated the name as *omnipotens*. The rabbis analyzed the name as being a compound composed of the relative *she*, "who," and the Hebrew word *day*, "enough"; hence, "the one who is [self]sufficient" (Babylonian Talmud, *Hagigah* 12a). Recent scholarship has not progressed much beyond these pre-Christian and early Christian interpretations. The ending *-ay* certainly makes it an adjectival suffix; hence, "[something] of the . . . ," but we are no further in identifying the actual root. Therefore it is best to understand it as a testimony to the effectiveness, sufficiency, and power of God.[5] God appeared as *El Shaddai* to the patriarchs seven times: to Abraham (Gen. 17:1), to Isaac (Gen. 28:3), and to Jacob

(Gen. 35:11; 43:14; 48:3). The context for every one of these instances was the promise-plan of God, which in itself should tell us something about the name: He is the all-powerful one and the God of all-sufficiency to carry out his promise-plan.

This promise-plan of God stretches from one end of the Bible to the other. At its heart is the gospel: "All nations will be blessed through you" (Gen. 12:3; Gal. 3:8). But it takes its inception from the very ordinances of creation itself. The ancient promise that God would make his own fruitful and that he would multiply them is likewise repeated in Genesis 35:11.

The statement exceeded anything personal and individual and went on to include a nation that would come from Jacob—in fact, a whole community of nations. More accurately, they were to be a *qahal*, a "congregation" of nations. Was this the tip of the iceberg, a harbinger of the whole future missionary movement that was to come—the fact that God was here and now empowering and commissioning Israel to be his witnesses to the nations? In my opinion, yes.

The centerpiece of this promise doctrine was the fact that a king would come from the line of kings that were to flow out of the loins of Abraham and Jacob. From that patriarchal line, and eventually from the Judean kings, the Messiah would be heralded. The man of promise would come from Jacob's own body (35:11)—wonder of wonders and mystery of mysteries.

The sphere in which one aspect of this promise-doctrine, or promise-plan, would unfold would be the promised land. Accordingly, God would not only bring his blessing and salvation to the inner lives of these revived men and women; he would also demonstrate that he was the Lord of all history and the Lord of all real estate by assigning a tithe of the lands of the earth to Israel so that they could be the instruments of his good news to the nations. This promise is very much part and parcel of his overall promise-plan. It was just as perpetual and eternal as were the so-called spiritual parts. It would serve as an everlasting sign to the nations that the Lord had the legal claim to all territories of the world. Thus he claimed a small portion in perpetuity as a symbol of this right (35:12).

After revealing all these blessings, which were a repetition of the ancient words he gave to Abraham and Isaac, especially when the Lord had appeared to them as *El Shaddai*, God "went up from above him" (literal rendering of 35:13). This implies a visible manifestation by God to Jacob just as he had experienced years before at Bethel and more recently at Peniel. It is also similar to the experience of Abraham in Genesis 17:22, where God likewise "went up from him."

In commemoration of this outstanding episode, Jacob memorialized it by setting up a "standing stone" (35:14), for it is always good to remember those times when we have met God in a new and wonderful way. He also went on to consecrate the spot where God had performed a reviving work of grace in his life by anointing the standing stone with oil and by pouring out a libation (see Exod. 29:40; 30:9; Deut. 32:38). Once again Jacob named the spot "Bethel" (v. 15) as he had in Genesis 28:19 after his vision of the ladder to heaven.

Conclusion

Revival came to the house of Jacob because he was willing to get rid of the idols in his life. There is our challenge as well. Are we tied to the past, with its toys and ambitions that steal our hearts from loving God with everything in us? Do we have the courage to hear God's word in our day? Will we act with all due speed in the church to cleanse our lives of all this filthiness? Or will our families, churches, institutions, and nations continue to suffer because of the moral minority or failure to come to grips with the most pressing spiritual need of the hour?

Our appeal to all believers everywhere is this: let us turn from our competing loyalties to the living God, renounce all forms of wickedness, especially those involving idolatry, and act quickly before the love of God is forced to drive us to even greater calamities than we are currently facing in our lives and our society. Then we shall find the same great blessing that Jacob found for himself and his house.

3   It Is Time to Confess Our Sin

Revival under Moses
Exodus 32:1–34:7

*N*othing so separates us from the Lord as sin. It is this thief that robs us of the benefits of our standing in the Savior. It is this blockage that renders us impotent before the present system of evil and wickedness. Alas, due to the corrosive and corrupting power of sin, the believer with all his mighty potential, the salt and light for which this world hungers, is unable to function as intended. These two tragedies, the tragedy of our separation from God and the tragedy of our uselessness, are reasons enough to call for an immediate confession of sin and a prayer for God to begin his reviving work in every one of us.

Nowhere in Scripture is this need evidenced more dramatically than in the situation found in Exodus 32:1–34:7. There are few places in the Bible where such a wonderful expression of God's compassion and full forgiveness can be found simultaneously with his hatred of sin.

Moses had been called to the top of Mount Sinai to receive the law of God. But when his absence seemed to stretch out longer than the Israelites thought it should, the people panicked. All sorts of wild scenarios began to form in their minds, where the peace of God should have resided. They imagined that Moses had been struck by lightning or killed by some other violent or natural means. So they began to take matters into their own hands. This is not so uncommon as we at first might think! We need only consider our own impatience with the work of God to find similar analogies!

Their first thought was to replace God with other "gods who [would] go before [them]" (Exod. 32:1). No one remembered that Jacob and his sons had been through this routine many years before. They pummeled poor Aaron, (Moses' brother) who had been left in charge of things, with questions and urged him to cast a new, visible god that would replace the one worshiped by their absent leader, Moses. The sheer treachery of the request is enough to make us, at this safe distance in time and space, cry out in outrage on behalf of the offended Lord. But nonetheless treacherous are our stupid sins. There should and must be the same outcry of grief over them. For, like Israel's sin, they have severely offended a holy God, separated us from his favor, and rendered us impotent in the great cause of justice and righteousness here on earth.

Unfortunately, Aaron does not seem to have protested too much. Further, it would appear that he did not even attempt to dissuade them. His advice came quickly: "Take off the gold earrings . . . and bring them to me" (32:2). These he used to cast an idol in the shape of a calf. This was the same Aaron who was consecrated as high priest to Yahweh. He fashioned the monster with a tool and then, strangely, announced a festival to the Lord, Yahweh (v. 5). Once again we are back into the heavy drag of syncretism, that system that attempts to serve God and mammon. But how is this possible? How can we serve two masters? Will we not, as Jesus taught, love the one and hate the other?

There is another sin present here. The rabble-rousers showed disregard for their leadership when they whined, "As for this fellow Moses . . . we don't know what has happened to him" (32:1). Surely their tone showed anything but appreciation and regard; it was disdainful and cynical. How quickly the erring heart forgets all the mercies and gifts of God that have been given to his people through delegated leaders. This, then, becomes a further sign that we are ripe candidates for revival. When we easily reject the leadership that God bestows, it may signal that our hearts, more than the abilities of the leaders given to us, are in serious need of repair. Their situation was similar to the bumper sticker I saw the other day which read "QUESTION ALL AUTHORITY." I assume that meant all authority except the authority that had urged this action! Thus, we trade symptoms for causes and fail to face ourselves, all the while trying to relocate the blame and assign it to some remote category, such as the personalities and abilities of our leaders.

On completion of his monstrous act of blasphemy, Aaron had the nerve to declare, "These are your gods, O Israel, who brought you up out of Egypt" (v. 4). He also added an altar for offerings to this bull calf (an all too easily identifiable icon left over from their days of witnessing the idolatry in Egypt; cf. Apis, the bull-god of Egypt).

By now everything was out of hand. Out came the drinks, and away went the garments, and Israel was totally out of control. Sin always begets more sin in its wake, and it spreads like the rot. When the English text reads they "rose up to play" (32:6 RSV), it means the people began to indulge in sexual prostitution. (The same verb is used to describe Isaac "fondling" his wife in the marital act; cf. Gen. 26:8.) Therefore, the compounding of sin was a major problem. Israel risked losing all the promises of God by openly flaunting their rejection of God. What would the Lord do to them for this outrage?

The answer is not long in coming. So serious was their offense that God threatened to destroy the whole nation, except Moses. To him God would grant all the promises that had been pledged to the patriarchs (Exod. 33:1). At the very least God would withdraw his presence from the nation and refuse to be with the Israelites any longer (33:3).

This sets up the marvelous teaching of the grace of God in forgiveness. No where else does such stark contrast appear between the utter failure of human sinfulness and the absolutely limitless power of Yahweh to cleanse. The only limitation on the application of this free grace and forgiveness is to be found in Israel's (and our) stubbornness. Yet how senseless and irresponsible is refusal, given the high degree of vulnerability in sinful situations. Accordingly, we should be warned against the unnecessary risks involved in not confessing our sin. According to Exodus 32:1–34:7 and the life of Israel, we face at least four risks when we do not confess our sin:

1. We risk facing the anger and wrath of God for our sin (32:7–14).
2. We risk facing the loss of atonement for our sin (32:30–35).
3. We risk facing the loss of the presence of God for our sin (33:1–17).
4. We risk facing the loss of the goodness of God for our sin (33:18–34:7).

As 2 Chronicles 7:14 reminds us, repentance, turning from our wicked way, is an extremely important component of meeting the prerequisites for a genuine revival. Sin leads us to a defeated position. If we continue in it without major changes involving a heartfelt confession of sin, we open ourselves up to untold mischief. The risks are almost incalculable. The Lord's plea is that we might profit from the warning of Israel's example, flee as quickly as possible to the merciful side of our Lord, and claim his restoring grace. May the rehearsal of each of these risks do more than merely move us cognitively. May they stir us to mourn over our sin and to ask our Lord to change us inside out.

We Risk Facing the Anger and Wrath of God for Our Sin (32:7–14)

There is no sense in trying to hide our sin or to pretend that it is not there or that it is not as bad as it first seemed. Sin will not just disappear by itself. Even if we bury it deep in our subconsciousness, it will still need to be dealt with. The reason is given in the text: God knows, hears, and sees all the words, thoughts, and deeds of humanity. For though Moses was on Mount Sinai, the Lord informed him that things had gotten out of hand on the plain below (vv. 7–8). Yahweh quoted verbatim to Moses what Aaron and the Israelites were saying. (This in itself is another warning that nothing happens on earth without God knowing about it.) God also saw the calf and was aware of their bowing down to it and worshiping it. Nothing is hidden from his eyes. That is the point we will need to come to realize in this whole matter of sin. It is not what we can get away with when those who might censor us would know about what happened or was said; it is what God sees, hears, and records that is at the heart of the problem of sin. It is amazing that the people thought that neither Moses, whom they judged to be dead, nor God, their Lord and provider of the covenant, saw or cared about their partying and gross sin. But while men and women sported on the plain, their conduct was being viewed from above.

God's indignation is clear from his very first word to Moses, "Your people, whom you brought up out of Egypt" (v. 7). It is also clear that God regarded sin as lawlessness, for Israel had turned away from what he had commanded (v. 8). No wonder he referred to them as "stiff-necked" (v. 9), a metaphor referring to young bulls who refuse to have their necks brought under a yoke.

In a striking figure of speech, God is depicted as if he were beyond all remedial discussion due to this great offense against his law and his person. The Lord spoke in such a way as to test Moses. "Leave me alone," he said, "that my anger may burn against them and I may destroy them. Then I will make you into a great nation" (v. 10). What seemed to be a command not to petition God in prayer on behalf of his sinful people was in reality a high testimony to the effectiveness and power of prayer. For if God could see that prayer would be so potent in persuading his offended holiness to exercise mercy, then we as believers had better flee more quickly and more frequently to this retreat. But there is more; God could also see that the man he had prepared these eighty years would do exactly what God in his sovereignty had taught him to do: Moses would besiege the Lord in prayer as a mediator on behalf of these sinners. The situation was as commentator George Bush assessed it:

> The words . . . which seemed to forbid, were really intended to encourage Moses in his suit. They are not indeed a positive command to him to pray in behalf of Israel, but they indicated what it was that would stay the divine hand from punishing; and were equivalent to saying, "if you intercede for them, my hands are tied, and I cannot execute the deserved vengeance."[1]

The counteroffer, to make a great nation out of Moses instead of continuing on with Israel, might have been very tempting to some people. This offer assaulted Moses in the area where most men are vulnerable: his pride. But Moses was totally disinterested. The long years of learning through the experiences of life now paid off. God's man had grown in grace. Moses' previous hot temper and superquick responses to raw injustice and wrong were now tempered by the very patience God had exhibited on Moses' own behalf time and again.

The man God had prepared to be a leader and mediator began to earnestly entreat his Lord. His initial questions in verses 11 and 12 are not expostulations but examples of places in Scripture where the interrogative can be used for the optative mode. Moses made a threefold plea: (1) do not let the Egyptians rejoice over the ruin of those whom they hate; (2) do not forget the covenant you made with the patriarchs; and (3) do not destroy so quickly what you have employed so much power to preserve and bring this far (vv. 11–13). The real goal of his prayer was, as the goal of all true prayer should be, the glory of God.

Meanwhile the people who were the objects of this prayer were casting off all restraint and running wild (Exod. 32:25). It is a curious fact that the same verb used twice in this verse is also used in Proverbs 29:18, which reads, "Where there is no revelation [from God or a proclamation of that word to his people], the people cast off restraint [break loose, become unmanageable, and apostatize]."

Rather than urging individuals and churches to have a five-year or ten-year plan or vision statement (which, incidentally, is a good idea), the verse in Proverbs warns us about the lawless state of affairs that will result when other programs and priorities are substituted for the Word of God. The culture goes berserk and runs wild where the Word of God is not taught and responded to in all of its fullness.

We Risk Facing the Loss of Atonement for Our Sin (32:30–35)

When he saw the sin of Israel, Moses' initial reaction was violent; in fact, in a rage that is not altogether excusable, he heaved to the ground the tablets written by the finger of God. Then, in a call for a division of the house, he summoned all who were on the Lord's side to come over to him (32:26). Only the Levites responded, surprisingly enough—those who belonged to Aaron's tribe. (There is irony for you.)

Next, Moses commanded these volunteers to strap on their swords and to go through the camp, executing all the ringleaders of the rebellion. Three thousand were slain.

On the next day Moses lectured the people about the enormity of their sin (Exod. 32:30). "Great sin" may be a technical name for this type of immorality, for the phrase is found in a few other ancient Near Eastern records and in the attempted seduction of Joseph by Potiphar's wife (Gen. 39:9). One should not, however, automatically rank this sin higher than other sins on a scale of wickedness. It would appear from verse 30 that not all the guilty died with the three thousand of the preceding day. That is why I referred to the latter group as ringleaders. Those who were exempted from death on that occasion were not permitted to draw the false conclusion that their guilt was less serious, for Moses charged them with having sinned a "great sin."

"Perhaps I can make atonement" must have been the sweetest sounding words the heavy consciences of these wild sinners had heard in the previous twenty-four hours. The point of the expression is not that Moses was in doubt whether there was an atonement but rather whether he was the instrument. Again, Bush is most helpful:

> He thought he might perhaps be an instrument of reconciliation; for in no other sense could atonement be properly predicated. . . . He was not without hope, nor yet was he destitute of fear; accordingly his words were calculated to preserve the people in a due medium between desponding dread and presumptuous confidence.[2]

This same mode of address is used elsewhere in Scripture to both encourage sinners and protect them from being overly presumptuous about the grace and forgiveness of God. Amos 5:15 reads, "It may be that the LORD . . . will be gracious" (NKJV); Jonah 1:6 has a similar word, "Maybe [God] will take notice of us"; and Acts 8:22 likewise comments, "Perhaps he will forgive you for having such a thought in your heart." God's forgiveness is free and always available, but we must not trifle with it, cheapen it, or use it in such a way that we become casual about the seriousness of our offense against the command and person of the living God.

God had prepared Moses for this role of being an intercessor and mediator. Both ministries were anticipations of our own deep need of someone who would come from heaven, pray for us, and be our mediator. Already in patriarchal times, Job had cried out for a mediator, a defense attorney who would be his advocate (Job 9:33). Now Moses would fill in this gap on behalf of the Lord as he began to pray in one of the few interjections in the Bible: "Oh, what a great sin these people have committed!" (Exod. 32:31).

The plea of the mediator was that God would forgive. So emotionally worked up was Moses and so deeply affected was he by their sin that verse 32 is an incomplete sentence. He leaves the ellipsis after the alternative, "but if not . . ." This heightens the impassioned and pathetic tone of the prayer. It is as if we, the readers, are being allowed to be in the same place where the sobbing prayer of God's servant is being poured out before God. (See 1 Sam. 12:14–15 for a similar conditional sentence.)

"Nothing is so efficacious," comments Bush, "in obtaining mercy as deep humiliation before God."[3] But we are shocked to hear Moses offer to be "blot[ted] out of the book you have written" (v. 32). The offer sounds very much like the apostle Paul's wish that he could be accursed if only it would lead to the salvation of his brethren, the Jews (Rom. 9:3).

What is the book Moses referred to? Psalm 69:28 and Philippians 4:3 mention a "book of life." Later on, Isaiah 4:3 will refer to being "recorded among the living." So what did the expression mean at the time Moses spoke? Did he wish to die early rather than witness the destruction of his people? Or is he offering to yield up his place as one of the redeemed in order to ransom his people, that is, exchange his life so that the people might be released from the guilt of their sin?

Surely no human life, no matter how valuable or godly, can be sufficient to atone for anyone's sin, much less for the sin of a whole nation. The Egyptians had the practice of recording the names of those who hoped to be associated with the pagan deity in the after-life. Moses, however, must have been aware of the existence of such a record in the divine counsels of God. The expression, then, was a gesture on Moses' part of his deep sorrow for his people and of his recognition that they had no basis on which to plead for the mercy or favor of God. Unless God was moved to exercise his own mercy because of the prayer of his mediator, they would have no hope.

The offer of volunteering his name in exchange for the deliverance of all these people was unnecessary. The theology of individual responsibility for one's own sin was clearly set forth: "Whoever has sinned against me I will blot out of my book" (v. 33). This is the same teaching that would be stated so frequently in that great chapter of Ezekiel 18, "The soul who sins is the one who will die." Everyone is responsible for his or her own sin.

The sin of the people resulted in a major shift. In the past the Lord had led Israel, and Moses had only been there as God's servant (Exod. 3:8; 12:42, 51; 13:17; 20:20). But now Moses and an angel (not the Angel of the Lord, that is, Christ himself, in whom resided the very essence and being, or "name," of God; Exod. 23:20–21) must lead them. So rather than the Lord and his servant, a servant and the Lord's messenger become the guides and leaders of Israel. That was a significant loss.

In addition, a day of judgment when sin would be punished was promised. The phrase, literally, "in the day when I visit" (32:34 NKJV), is probably the first reference to the much discussed "day of the Lord" mentioned so frequently by the prophets. This was not just any old day; it was to be the day of God's visiting, one day that would stand out supreme over all other days. Later revelation would make it clear that this day could be a time of national judgment in the immediate future. However, it also signaled an even greater time of trial, not only for Israel but for all the nations that had turned their backs on the only true God as well. Accordingly, for the calf-worshiping sinners of the exodus, the near aspects of that day commenced when the Lord struck Israel with a plague, much as he had already visited the Egyptians with a plague prior to the exodus (Exod. 7:25; 8:2; 12:23, 29).

How risky it is to try to wait God out with an unrepentant heart. We need his atonement, for how else will we be able to be at one with him?

We Risk Facing the Loss of the Presence of God for Our Sin (33:1–17)

In its most risky feature of all, sin separates us from the presence and goodness of God. What person or community can long exist without his helpful and restraining influence? Yet the presence of God cannot coexist where there is sin, especially gross sin.

Exodus 33:1 is probably more accurately rendered in the past perfect sense, "The Lord *had* said." It is thus a continuation of 32:34, where the Lord was still speaking to Moses. The general effect of the message from God was still the same, for Israel had shown as yet no special signs of repentance. Therefore, the signs and reality of the divine presence were withdrawn immediately. Sin does indeed cut us off from God. In fact, under such sinful conditions, it would have been even more dangerous for the divine presence to remain. This would have increased Israel's responsibility and their exposure to punishment. That is why those of us in the Western nations, who have been so privileged in experiencing so much of the presence and power of God, are all the more vulnerable. We will be dealt with much more speedily and harshly than the other nations, who have not been so privileged.

But thanks be to God, Israel's long-delayed cry for help finally came (33:4). Why is it that we poor sinners are so reluctant to call for help when we know we are drowning? Is it that we are too proud to admit that our basic need is to humble ourselves under the mighty hand of God? The people began to mourn and to strip off (the same verb was used in Exod. 3:22 of Israel's "plundering" the Egyptians; also 12:36) their ornaments. This latter action signified that they had begun to humble themselves under God's hand. Thus the text repeats this significant and most blessed development in verse 6: they had humbled themselves.

Verse 5 may give the appearance that God was in some doubt or perplexity as to what he should do. Again, however, it is only by way of accommodation to our impoverished understanding that he speaks in this way. Truly God is never at a loss as to what he should say or do. His perplexity, if there be such, concerns not whether he should show mercy but how to display it so as to act consistently with his honor. Once Israel humbled themselves in genuine repentance (and not just in attrition, that is, sorrow over the fact that they were caught) for their sin, there was no longer any apprehension over how God might act toward his erring children. Therefore the language of doubt is deliberately used to imply that there was a plan and special design to the mercy of God once mortals repented.

The identification of the tent mentioned in verses 7–11 poses some problems for the interpreter. Possibly it was a temporary tent specially constructed to hold the ark. Or it may have been one that Moses set up outside the camp as sort of a second home and the only place where the presence of God would meet him (the presence of sin in the camp handicapped that function there). One thing is certain: this could not have been the tabernacle itself, for that had not yet been built (Exod. 35–39). Regardless of how we answer this question, the important point is that God had withdrawn his presence, and he had visibly removed himself from their midst. Moses was the only remaining point of contact for the grace of God in their lives. Only he now experienced the presence of God.

Verse 14 is best understood as a question, otherwise it merely repeats verse 17 and is confusing in the context. Accordingly, it should read: "Shall my presence go with you and shall I give you rest?"

The mediatorial role of Moses can be seen. He did exactly what God wanted him to do and what the Lord had trained him for. We must not think that Moses was more lenient and gracious than God. For was it not God who had called Moses and who had patiently trained him?

Therefore, on the basis of Moses' arguments as a mediator and on the basis of the people's repentance and attitude of contrition, these were the progressive steps of mercy and favor witnessed by Israel. First, the Lord relented in the threatened judgment (32:14). Second, the people were allowed to continue on to Canaan with divine guidance, not the presence of the Lord himself but that of a heavenly messenger (32:34; 33:1-2). Finally, in response to Moses' intercession and mediatorial work on behalf of Israel, the Lord himself would once again accompany Israel on their journey to Canaan (33:15-17).

Israel learned that there is no substitute for the personal presence of the living God. How foolish and how risky it is for us to let sin interrupt and finally usurp that relationship. Let us therefore immediately implore the Savior for his forgiveness.

We Risk Facing the Loss of the Goodness of God for Our Sin (33:18-34:7)

Because God was pleased with Moses and because he knew Moses by name, God graciously acted favorably on his previous request. But Moses made yet another request of the Lord. He wanted to be shown God's glory.

The "glory of God" is sometimes treated as a religious term whose meaning is better left unexplained. (It is often spoken with an odd inflection of the voice as it sort of rolls around in the speaker's mouth.) But the glory of God is nothing less than the sheer weight of his presence. At its root lies the concept of heaviness, and only in its secondary derivatives does it come to mean the outsplashing, or radiance, of God's glory.

Thus it happened that Moses witnessed in a new way all the goodness that is contained in the name of God. Moses was not allowed to look directly on God's face—no one could do that and live (Exod. 33:20). But he was permitted to look on the "aftereffects" of the splendorous glory of God (33:23). The word is usually translated "back," but that is certainly inappropriate here. God is incorporeal and does not have any physical form as such (see Isa. 31:3 and John 4:24). However, the term can also refer to that which is behind or what comes after, and that is the rendering I prefer—"aftereffects"—a translation that readily suggests itself, especially in our space age with its rockets and their afterburners and afterglow. God caused all his "goodness," that is, all his attributes, to pass by before his servant, plainly manifesting the sum and substance of what he is before the eyes of his servant. The aftereffect of the radiance was awesome.

Not only did God cause his goodness to pass by Moses, but he also proclaimed his "name." The name of God signifies more than the mere vocable or nomenclature by which he is addressed. The name in Scripture also signifies the person's character, attributes, and nature, the entirety of all that is connected with one's person. This may be seen in phrases like "to walk in the name of the LORD" or "taught them your name," found in certain ethical injunctions and doctrinal teachings. What could have been more comforting in this context of alienated sinners than the rehearsal of all that the divine name means over against the desperate needs of unrevived and ailing men and women? Thus the Lord passed by, and in august and stately terms he trumpeted forth: "Yahweh, Yahweh, the compassionate and gracious God, slow to anger and abounding in grace and truth" (34:6 author's translation).

The name *Yahweh* (meaning, "he is who he is," or "he will be [there]") was in itself another declaration, not only of the self-existence of God, but more directly of the fact that he was God, who would be there to see, act, forgive, and do whatever needed to be done. This name God had patiently explained to Moses in Exodus 6:1–8. Now Moses was just grasping the full impact of what had been mere words.

Five special attributes of God are unfolded in this declaration of his name as he passed before Moses. First, there was mercy or compassion. That is, at the head of the list of the divine perfections stood the benevolence of God. It is this attribute that predisposes our Lord toward us poor, miserable sinners, prompting him to grant us relief, kindness, and clemency. No wonder the psalmist celebrates God as being plenteous in mercy. Connected with the noun for "womb," this word depicts the love of a mother for her baby. It is that same attribute that excited the apostle Paul in Ephesians 2:4–7, "But because of his great love for us, God, who is rich in mercy, made us alive with Christ even when we were dead in transgressions." And likewise the apostle Peter raves, "Praise be to the God and Father of our Lord Jesus Christ! In his great mercy he has given us new birth into a living hope through the resurrection of Jesus Christ from the dead" (1 Pet. 1:3).

The second quality is the graciousness of God. How richly he has acted toward us, granting one unmerited gift after another, especially the gifts of forgiveness and reconciliation.

He is, in the third place, "long of nostrils." This is an anthropomorphism, or description of God in the form of men. Just as anger tends to swell one's nostrils, so the opposite is evidenced here. Bush commented,

> Nothing is more wonderful than the patience of God when we consider the provocations which he continually receives at the hands of the ungodly. . . . Nay to bring the matter home to ourselves . . . [have] we not provoked him to anger every day of our lives? Yet to the praise of his

patience here we still find ourselves, standing on praying ground, and favored with the offers and opportunities of pardon.[4]

The fourth and fifth attributes are treated together: "abounding in grace and truth." That is how John described Jesus in John 1:17, with a deliberate allusion to this statement of Yahweh in Exodus 34:6–7, a statement repeated some ten times in the Old Testament itself. The richness, plenteousness, and sheer bountifulness of God's favor staggers the imagination, as does his unadulterated truth. Truth of every description must take its genesis in the source and Lord of all truth. Likewise, we would not have known grace, God's unmerited favor, unless it had been revealed in him who so freely and bountifully forgave Israel of their outrageous actions, thoughts, and blasphemies in the treacherous incident of the golden calf.

Conclusion

By now God's invitation to us is abundantly clear. Why would anyone attempt to live with the guilt and despair of sin? Why would we wish to risk so much for so little? Why would believers live like spiritual paupers and act with such mediocre results in their own churches and in the spread of the gospel around the world?

Revival would come to America, yes, to any nation of the world, if we obeyed the injunction of Scripture and confessed our sin. How foolishly Israel acted and how stupid she appeared when she did not quickly own up to her sin and seek the Lord's offer of forgiveness. Are we not equally foolish if we also refuse to repent? Look at what the name of God means once again and claim each one of those five attributes for yourself. Enjoy the fullness of every bit of the goodness of God, for he delights to act on behalf of any and all who will take him at his word. Let the great pardoning name of God pass before you and your house this day.

4

It Is Time to Serve the Lord Only

Revival under Samuel
1 Samuel 7:1–13

*I*t was time for revival once again. The state of both the religious and national life had slipped to a new low in the days of the judges of Israel. There had been at least five different respites from the dreary drone of wickedness and evil during those wretched days when "there was no king in Israel; everyone did what was right in his [or her] own eyes" (Judg. 17:6 NKJV; 18:1; 19:1; 21:25). But it is impossible from this distance to document whether a genuine revival took place during any of that period of time.

It is true, of course, that periodically Israel "cried out to the LORD" for deliverance, and he sent them a savior—not once, but repeatedly. But only in the last instance of this monotonous cycle is it recorded that Israel ever acknowledged their sin and bluntly confessed, "We have sinned against [Yahweh], forsaking our God and serving the

Baals" (Judg. 10:10). Again, according to verse 15, "The Israelites said to the LORD, 'We have sinned. Do with us whatever you think best, but please rescue us now.'"

Never is it recorded that there was any evidence of change on the part of the people, except for their prayers of desperation for relief from the trouble their sins had gotten them into. The Hebrew word used for their prayer is connected with the word *cry*, and hence they were prayers born out of distress and deep despair. But they were without any apparent contrition or repentance or a solid renunciation of their former way of life. Accordingly, the spiritual tide had been running out for decades and centuries when God graciously raised up Samuel.

Rarely has immorality, injustice, and corruption of every sort achieved greater freedom. Samples of all of these sins could be found in the priest's own office and home. The high priest Eli had failed both as a leader of the nation and as a father. The offerings to the Lord were distorted, and Eli's sons exceeded every boundary of good taste, morality, and common decency. They insisted on having the sacrifice done to their own specifications rather than God's (1 Sam. 2:12–17), and, worse still, they brazenly "slept with the women who served at the entrance to the Tent of Meeting" (1 Sam. 2:22). Never once, however, did Eli attempt to restrain Hophni and Phineas, and for this ultimately he was rebuked by God (1 Sam. 3:13). Things indeed had become critical when the same evil that society was guilty of was also commonly reported in the household of faith. What then shall that nation or people plead in the day of God's wrath? This sign more than any other barometer of wickedness is the one that sounds the alarm, supposing there are any left who still have enough spiritual discernment to hear it.

But the litany of sins is longer than the few alluded to already. These were days in which "the word of the LORD was rare" (1 Sam. 3:1). As wickedness took hold of lives, the word of God became proportionately scarce. This is another principle that the watchful observer of revivals must note. When pagans and believers alike find it convenient or preferable to substitute almost anything in place of the reading, hearing, and proclamation of the Word of God, beware: trouble for that people is just around the corner.

Not even the oppression of the Philistines had driven Israel to her senses. Nor had the loss of the nation's most sacred treasure caused concern among the people. For by now the ark of the covenant had been out of the center of Israel's religious life for twenty years, and no one seemed to be overly exercised about it or deeply concerned for its return. No, these were the worst of times for Israel, and the tragedy (as it usually is in such times and places) was that few knew it.

Suddenly there was a break in this boring and embarrassing downward march in spirituality. How it came about is not altogether clear. Certainly, twenty long years of continual harassment and the frustration of frequent military incursions must have helped. One clue is given in the Hebrew text. It shows that verses 2 and 3 of 1 Samuel 7 are closely connected. There is no gap between them, for the action of the Hebrew infinitive translated "abode" or "remained" is continued in the five verbs associated with it somewhat as follows: "The ark remained at Kiriath Jearim, and it happened, and the days multiplied, and the days grew to twenty years, and all the house of Israel mourned, and then Samuel said . . ." (literal translation). That is, Israel had mourned a disproportionately long time. Misery had once again earned the first opportunity for the hearing of the Word of God in its rightful authenticity.

The focal point for 1 Samuel 7 seems to be located in verses 3 and 4. There the theme of serving God only appears twice: "Commit yourselves to the LORD and serve him only" and "so the Israelites put away their Baals and Ashtoreths and served the Lord only." Moreover, the chapter contains three challenges from Samuel to Israel and by application to all who would, like Israel, also wish to be revived in their spiritual lives:

1. We must commit ourselves to the Lord (vv. 1–4).
2. We must confess our sin and pray to the Lord (vv. 5–9).
3. We must count on God's help and act boldly (vv. 10–13).

These challenges face all who hunger and thirst after righteousness.

We Must Commit Ourselves to the Lord (7:1–4)

Twenty years of uninterrupted oppression by the Philistines had humbled God's people. Misery had accomplished what blessing could not.

> The revival began as many revivals begin: with loud weeping and mournful lamentation over the heavy load of guilt and its effects. So it was, for example, in the revival of the Indians in the whole area of the Susquehanna under David Brainerd. As he commenced proclaiming the message "Herein is love," John Shearer reported that men fell at his feet in anguish of soul. These were men who could bear the most acute torture without flinching. But God's arrow had now pierced them; their pain could not be concealed and they cried out in their distress, "Have mercy on me." What impressed Brainerd most deeply was that though these people came to him in a multitude, yet each one was mourning apart from the group. The prophecy of Zechariah was fulfilled before his eyes. The woods were filled with the sound of a great mourning.[1]

So it happened in Israel as well: they "lamented after the LORD" (v. 2 NKJV). Suddenly there had come a decided reorientation of the inner life of those who long had sensed no need of God. The pain and grief inflicted by the ruthless Philistine conquerors had done God's office work. "The image," says David Erdmann, describing the force of "lamented," "is that of a child that goes weeping after its father and mother, that it may be relieved of what hurts it."[2] It is a verb meaning "to wail, lament" (cf. Ezek. 32:18; Mic. 2:4), and it connotes sighing and deep sobbing.

But there was another strong force at work during those same twenty years, and many tend to overlook it, both in relation to those times and in the current setting. It was the preaching of God's faithful servant Samuel. Had not the text itself clearly anticipated this development? For in 1 Samuel 3:19 the writer remarks under the inspiration of God that "the LORD was with Samuel as he grew up, and he let none of his words fall to the ground." Graciously God had anticipated the final crumbling of the dam. When the sighing broke out, there was the word of God. It had been there all those twenty years, but the people could not hear it. Sin had deafened them to it. But the prophetic labors, like those of so many of God's present ministers of the word, were rewarded after long years of waiting.

The prophet expressed himself conditionally: "If you are returning" (v. 3), he intoned. The participle *returning* assumes that the people had already started to turn inwardly toward the Lord. Thus the work of God was already underway. Accordingly, we are supplied the context (lamentation) for their hearing this word, the means (preaching) for this obedient response, and the content (what follows in v. 3b) of that word.

The first aspect of this word of the Lord was the same as that demanded of Jacob: "Get rid of the foreign gods you have with you" (Gen. 35:2; cf. also Josh. 24:23). A wholehearted fellowship with the living God is incompatible with any and all competing loyalties.

The second emphasis in Samuel's message from the Lord to Israel and to us is "Fix your hearts on God." If the preceding command was negative, this is the positive side of the same truth. An established, or fixed, heart is the opposite of a wavering, vacillating state of mind, which in ordinary circumstances often marks persons caught in the web of heavy grief and sighing. But here was a deliberate and solid decision to toss every other diversion away and to serve God alone.

The third and central theme of Samuel's message was to "serve him only." It is not enough to empty our lives of all the false crutches and idols that we have brazenly erected there; we must also be willing to have this empty service replaced by glad service to the only true and living God. This again was another positive aspect of his message. And what a privilege to serve so exalted a friend as the Lord of glory.

One more aspect needed to be added, and this fourth element of Samuel's word was the promissory aspect of God's Word to all who from the heart will obey the living God. "He will deliver [them] out of the hand of the Philistines" (v. 3c). Thus, when we turn to God in true repentance, he then will turn to us, and he will remove the terrible source of our anguish. But it has to be carefully observed, yes, even for this Old Testament economy, that what was being asked for here was more than external showmanship or elaborate ritual. No, the response had to be "with all your hearts" (v. 3).

Who said Old Testament religion was more a matter of external religion? Those who take this line of reasoning have no idea what they are talking about. Prior to the flood the Lord read the "thoughts of [the] heart" of that wicked generation that had to be destroyed (Gen. 6:5). "The LORD searches every heart and understands every motive behind the thoughts" (1 Chron. 28:9). Yes, "the LORD knows the thoughts of man" (Ps. 94:11). It ought to be abundantly clear from these samples representing some twenty-five Old Testament texts that a person's inner disposition and motives are clearly read by God. He personally holds us responsible for responding to him with nothing less than a total commitment of our inner beings for revival. The case was no different for Israel, for God was no different then than he is now. Thus the mighty preaching of Samuel set the tone, the agenda, and the conditions for a new work of God in their midst. But there is another challenge we must face.

We Must Confess Our Sin and Pray to the Lord (7:5–9)

It was time for a national assembly, for when the conditions are right a revival is inevitable. All the elements for revival were now in place. Thus, just as atmospheric conditions signal the coming of the next weather system, so the earnestness, repentance, and removal of idols in Israel signaled the presence of the proper conditions for revival. It was in the hands of God as to when and if that revival would be granted.

The called assembly at Mizpah, then, was not the originating cause for the revival. Those conditions were spiritual in nature and had already taken place in the hearts of the people prior to this invitation. As Autrey observed, "It was not really a question of whether there would have been a revival if there had been no assemblage at Mizpeh [sic], but was it possible not to have a Mizpeh?"[3]

Mizpah, meaning "watchtower," has been identified with two sites. The first is with a site connected with the prophet Samuel's name known as Nabi Samwil. It is located just five miles northwest of Jerusalem in the tribe of Benjamin on a hill 2,935 feet high, overlooking the city. The other site is the northern extension of the Mount of Olives known today as Scopus, also meaning "watchman." Preference should be given to the former site, for it was also later honored as the place from which the war against Benjamin was launched (Judg. 20), where Saul was elected king (1 Sam. 10:17), and from which Judas Maccabaeus led his revolt against Antiochus Epiphanes. It could more conveniently hold the masses of people that the text describes.

To this place all Israel came. The time was ripe, and in the fullness of time God visited his people once again. Four things took place here that had a profound effect on Israel. First, there was an act of dedication. In Samuel's call for assembly, he had promised to intercede for the people at Mizpah. Let it be marked down as an extremely important principle that there can be no real, lasting work of God in revival without a genuine work of intercession on behalf of the people of God. Samuel was God's man who would stand in the gap and perform this ministry of a mediator. Verse 6 notes that after the people assembled, "they drew water and poured it out before the LORD." There is no parallel to this act in the Old Testament. The Targum renders this phrase paraphrastically, saying, "They poured out their hearts in repentance before the Lord." Apparently, the significance was that just as water poured out on the ground could not be collected again, so the commitment of their lives indicated a similar desire. But perhaps even more to the point was the later expression in Lamentations 2:19, "Pour out your heart like water," or the one in Psalm 22:14, "poured out like water." Surely this act signaled a deep contrition and humiliation for their sin. The water in this case may have reflected the tears, grief, and misery that their sins had caused them and for which they now were sorry. They wanted to dedicate themselves.

Next, there followed a self-imposed fast. Their sorrow was more than just words; they backed it up with action. Thus they voluntarily afflicted their bodies to do without food in order to physically join in the grief of their souls. There was only one official day of fasting in Scripture (the one commanded for the day of atonement in Lev. 16:29, 31). Other days were acceptable, however, so long as they were not used as substitutes for doing the work of God or talismans for earning the favor of God when obvious acts of righteousness were being avoided, as was the case in Isaiah 58.

Verse 6 also says, in the third place, that they confessed, "We have sinned against the LORD." Because the area of their sin had been public, their confession had to be public, too, to be genuine. Accordingly, although two symbolic acts had set forth their grief over their sin—the pouring out of water and the fasting—it was still necessary to acknowledge their repentance verbally. Of course the point is also well made that all sin is at once directed "against the LORD." Sin is a falling short of, a going beyond, or a straightforward violation of the command and/or Person of the living Lord. At its root it is opposition to the holy will of God. And this is what has blocked the relationship with God and separated all of us from his love and favor.

The fourth feature of the Mizpah meeting was that Samuel "judged the children of Israel" (v. 6 KJV). Although some modern versions shy away from using this expression, it is clearly the meaning of the Hebrew. Perhaps we do not understand that there is a proper consequence for all genuine repentance. We thereby miss the fact that there must also be a work of adjudication to be carried out by God's earthly representative. Certainly God is the only one who can judge us in any real or ultimate sense, but he has also given us his representatives. Samuel was one such representative. He was there by God's design for the purpose of directing and ordering God's people in the administration of justice and righteousness. In accordance with the previous acts of repentance, the reality of their confession must be tested, both the amount of restitution and the alacrity with which it was carried out. Wherever there had been theft, cheating, or other acts of injustice, the sincerity of the nation's confession was somewhat in doubt until there were acts of full restoration or plans for it. God had placed Samuel in the post of leader of this great convocation so that he might exercise the function of "judging."

As Samuel had promised (v. 5), he also entered fully into the work of intercession on behalf of Israel. There is no greater work in a revival than the work and ministry of prayer. Without this most necessary petitioning of the Lord, revivals are dead before they get started. This is the universal testimony of all the revivals in the Bible and in history.

But Israel's concern was that Samuel might cease this ministry of praying on their behalf. Much is said these days about what goes into making a leader and what are good management principles. But few components of either can be as rudimentary for the would-be pastor, overseer, or leader in the church (or any other part of God's vineyard) than praying constantly and fervently for the people over whom God has graciously placed you. So Samuel prayed for all of them. It was the highest purpose he had in the gracious calling of God. He presented the people in prayer as objects of God's mercy, forgiveness, and grace.

But this is never the end of our prayers on behalf of the community of faith. There is always the matter of a right relationship to God and prayer for the growth in grace of these same people. Revival was meant to be a continual reviving of the life.

But there was more. Mark it well: whenever there are deep stirrings of the Spirit of God in the renewing and reviving of lives, there the evil one will also be just as active in attempting to counter all the good work that has been done. His tricks are too many and varied to be listed here, but the people of God would be foolish to overlook them or to be ignorant of them. Accordingly, just as God was stirring the hearts of Israel at Mizpah, the devil was rousing a mistaken judgment among the Philistines: the Israelites had assembled at Mizpah, they reasoned, to launch a national revolt against their rule over them.

When this became clear to Israel, they cried to Samuel, "Do not stop crying out to the LORD our God for us, that he may rescue us from the hand of the Philistines" (v. 8). And there is our sin as well. First of all in leaders: How often do we fail our people by failing to pray for them? If there is any text that is needed for the revival of God's leaders, it is this one: God's work is not merely related to the quality and depth of the biblical exposition each week, the number of visits made to new families, the extensiveness of our counseling or discipleship programs, or any similar good and important works; it is most directly related to the quality, endurance, and earnestness of our daily petition to God on behalf of those whom we serve as the flock of God. May we not sin against God by failing to pray continually for his sheep. It is just as necessary to pray for the sheep and their hearing of the word of God as it is to prepare well for the proclamation of that word.

Samuel, in his priestly function, presented the people to God in two ways: by prayer and by the sacrifice of a young (eight-day-old) lamb (see Lev. 22:27). The point is that prayer without a sacrifice is groundless. But thanks be to God that he has provided the final sacrifice that has opened the way into his presence in prayer for all who have accepted his free gift and sacrifice.

It should also be noted that this lamb was given up as a whole burnt offering because the people had resolved to give themselves fully and undividedly to the one who had graciously forgiven them and restored them to new life.

Verse 9 adds so beautifully, but in such stark simplicity: "And the LORD answered him." Later Jeremiah would learn the same lesson. "Call to Me, and I will answer you, and show you great and mighty things, which you do not know" (Jer. 33:3 NKJV). What a challenge to confess our sins and to enter into prayer on behalf of God's people. When our hearts are loosed from all the junk that binds them and holds them captive, we experience unprecedented joy. Why should we who make up the church continue to allow lust to blind our eyes, greed for money and possessions to occupy our pursuits, and ambition to swallow up our hearts? Instead, let us confess our sin and be healed. Let us make full and fair restitution for all that we have taken. Let us enter into prayer for God's work, workers, and people, lest we sin further by failing to pray for one another. Only in so acting can we be prepared for the third challenge this text brings to us.

We Must Count on God's Help and Act Boldly (7:10–13)

If we are to serve God only, then we cannot look at circumstances with too much alarm. They will cripple and immobilize us spiritually, physically, and emotionally.

Thus it happened that God not only answered prayer when the people of Israel decided to confess their sin and serve him only, but he also began to work all things for good on their behalf. For just as the Philistines decided to attack them while they were still in the midst of their revival meetings at Mizpah, God dramatically intervened, striking the enemy with lightning from heaven. As the Philistines attempted to climb the heights of Mizpah, God sent loud thunder and threw the whole assault into disarray (v. 10). In that condition they were easily routed by God's men. In a similar way, God had worked for Joshua in the past (Josh. 10:10), and he will work again for the deliverance of all who call on his name, if they are walking in the light as he is in the light.

Because all of us are prone to forget those times when we were in deep trouble and how God rescued us so wonderfully, it is altogether appropriate that we set up certain memorials to aid our frail memories. So Samuel set up a stone and named it *Ebenezer*, meaning "stone of help" (v. 12). God had helped them when they no more deserved to be helped than we often deserve. But it was also meant to be an encouragement for the new trials of tomorrow. There is nothing to fear when we walk by faith, conscious that our sins have been forgiven and that we serve the Lord alone.

The good word that Samuel uttered on this occasion was, "Thus far has the LORD helped us" (v. 12). That demarcation embraced not only all the victories they had experienced in the past but also the sorrows and defeats as well. How patient a teacher our Lord is. Twenty years of waiting (until Israel finally sensed what the Lord knew from the very beginning) had come to fruition. The result was indeed lasting, for no longer did the Philistines come into Israel's territory as victors. Repeatedly they were repulsed. And this was because of the positive effects of the revival and the prayers of God's servant Samuel. Notice that verse 13b indicates that the protection from the Philistines continued for as long as Samuel lived. Who could miss the connection between the people's request that Samuel should never cease to pray for them and the winning ways of Israel?

Thus a nation was reborn and unified in the joyful service of God. Where there had been division, strife, fruitlessness, and guilt-laden lives, there now was happy service for the living God.

Conclusion

To serve God alone, therefore, is to make him sole Lord. It is to recognize and serve no other master or rival. With a heart fixed unreservedly on him, all forms of vacillation, ambivalence, and doublemindedness are utterly rejected and repented of. We must choose this day whom we will serve, just as Joshua declared he would (Josh. 24:15). And it is time we also confessed with Israel of old and the hymn writer:

> Here I raise my Ebenezer,
> Hither by thy help I've come;
> And I hope by Thy good pleasure,
> Safely to arrive at home.

Has it not been too long since we last saw the fires of genuine, nationwide revival sweep our land? Have we not sensed a yearning for authenticity and wholehearted service for the living God that is devoid of staleness, boredom, and lackluster dullness? It is time for revival to begin in the house of God. The spiritual state of the church is mixed today, but if a generalization may be permitted, in proportion to our numbers the church has been outclassed when it comes to general effectiveness and the production of lasting results. Few in society, government, or crime fear our prayers or sense the dynamic power of the resurrection to the degree they should. Is this not a distressing signal that revival is needed? Therefore, let the fire of God fall freshly on us once again. And may the nations of the earth see one more time that our God is the living God who has spoken accurately and continues to act dramatically to the honor and glory of his own name.

May the Lord of the church come and revive his church again and call each of his own to a new basis for serving him only.

5 It Is Time to Let God Be God

Revival under Elijah
1 Kings 18

*F*ifty-eight years had passed since the kingdom was ripped apart in 931 B.C. At that time the glorious united kingdom, which had lasted for well nigh a full century with all the splendor of the reigns of David and Solomon, was divided into two southern and ten northern tribes. Subsequently things had not gone all that well, especially for the northern ten tribes.

During this relatively brief time, the northern tribes had been ruled over by seven kings: Jeroboam, the installer of the two calves designed to replace the worship of Yahweh (1 Kings 12:28–32); Nadab, who walked in the sins of his father, Jeroboam (15:26); Baasha, who murdered Nadab (15:27); Elah, a drunkard and murderer (16:8–9); Zimri, who was guilty of treason (16:20); Omri, a military adventurer who did "worse than all who were before him" (16:25–26); and finally

Omri's son, Ahab, who did more evil than all who were before him. It was Ahab who married the infamous Jezebel, daughter of the king of Sidon (16:30–31). These were not the best of times politically. Neither were they the best of times spiritually, for the nation had been won over to the worship of the Canaanite gods, especially Baal. The decline of national and spiritual strength was enough to make any God-fearing person weep. But where was that godly remnant?

Elisha raised that same question after the prophet Elijah had been taken up to glory: "Where now is the LORD, the God of Elijah?" (2 Kings 2:14). If ever the nation needed God, it was during these wretched days. Everything was turning to dust right in front of their eyes.

We cannot help agreeing with the significance of this question, not only for that day, but for our day as well. How did God become so small in their eyes and in the eyes of our generation? Only lilliputian minds and hearts would have diminished God to such minute categories as he is often relegated to by our contemporaries as well. Is it any wonder that J. B. Philips wrote *Your God Is Too Small?* Indeed, that is what had taken place in Israel: the need for revival was urgent once again!

Here is a crime that shouts to heaven for relief. We must beg God for pardon and for a new sense of his greatness. How dare we compare him to men, forces, nations, problems, issues, or systems of our own invention? The shout of Isaiah must also be heard by our generation: "Say to the cities [of America, indeed of the world], 'Behold your God!'" (Isa. 40:9 NKJV). We need a whole new view of the living God in all his fullness as the only proper antidote for our poor emaciated categories in which we so pietistically, but incorrectly, operate.

In order to startle Israel back into the realities of thinking biblically about God, the Lord of glory sent a man, Elijah the Tishbite from Gilead. Few could have come from more lowly backgrounds than this man. Gilead was a high, stony region in Transjordan just east of the Sea of Galilee. Furthermore, Elijah was a nobody.

Indeed, the only fact we know about him is the name his parents seemed to have given him, meaning "Yahweh is my God."

Thus, while a nation was going crazy over a nonexisting god named Baal, this man by his very name shouted the reverse to the general eddies of his day. Almost out of nowhere he appeared and took center stage in the palace of Ahab—that henpecked husband and poor excuse for a king. Without fanfare or wasted motion, he bravely announced this divine message to the weak Ahab, "As the LORD, the God of Israel, lives, before whom I stand, there shall not be dew nor rain these years except at my word" (1 Kings 17:1 NKJV). But how could this backwoods rustic fail to be impressed by the presence of royalty and all the splendors and pageantry of the Israelite court? Why was he more impressed with the presence of God than he was with being in the presence of the earthly monarch?

It would appear that Elijah possessed a vision of God that exceeded all the trappings of other mortals. And that is the vision we will need to recapture if we are to experience the reviving power of God once again. Yes, it is high time that we in our day let God be God.

In this the fifth great revival in the Old Testament (1 Kings 18), three works of God demonstrate that he is the incomparable God:

1. He makes us courageous (vv. 1–20).
2. He shows us his power (vv. 21–39).
3. He answers our prayers (vv. 40–46).

In order to capture the attention of a people that had abandoned its exclusive loyalty to their Lord, God removed from them some of the assumed gifts of life. It is only God who can give or withhold rain. And that is what he did in this instance to pull men and women back to their senses once again.

He Makes Us Courageous (18:1–20)

God's second command to his brave new recruit was suddenly given after three and one-half years of absolute drought in which there was neither dew nor rain. "Go," he commanded, "and present yourself to Ahab, and I will send rain" (1 Kings 18:1). We are told, "So Elijah went."

How did Elijah become so bold? Did he not have any sense of self-protection, any desire to live? Had he not heard that Queen Jezebel was putting the Lord's prophets to death by the score? Was he not aware there was a price on his own head, so much so that every neighboring monarch had to swear to Ahab that they had not seen this elusive prophet or given him sanctuary?

It was God, of course, who made his servant so bold. Indeed, it is amusing to note with Arthur Pink that "wicked men are generally great cowards: their own consciences are their accusers, and often cause many misgivings when in the presence of God's faithful servants even though [these servants] occupy an inferior position in life to themselves."[1] There are many illustrations of this truth. "Herod feared John . . . knowing him to be a righteous and holy man" (Mark 6:20), and "Felix trembled" before Paul (Acts 24:25 KJV). Only the Lord can make us bold and courageous, even when we are facing powerful enemies.

For three and one-half years God tried to let the events of life, especially the awful suffering of the drought, soften the hearts of this royal couple along with their people. However, the reverse had happened. The queen was infuriated to such an extent that she took up killing the prophets of Yahweh as a hobby.

Yet God graciously sent his prophet back to the king. It is interesting that God asked Elijah first to obey by giving an announcement to the throne, and only then would God send rain. The correct rendering of these clauses seems to be "Go . . . and then I will send rain." How important those first steps of obedience are for the great and climactic moments of success later on.

Thus it came about "in the third year" that God finally was ready to confront his people with their serious vacillations and to place the option of a revival in front of them. It is true that Luke 4:25 and James 5:17 both record the drought lasted for three and one-half years. But it might well have been that the prediction of 1 Kings 17:1 came six months after the first normal dry season. Josephus reported a severe drought under the Syrian king Ithobal, usually considered to be a contemporary of Ahab, for the lack of any rain or dew was area wide and therefore affected the neighboring countries as well.[2] It must have been embarrassing for Ahab to acknowledge to these kings that the reason for the drought was because of his nation's sin against the God of heaven and earth according to the declaration of one of his prophets named Elijah.

But it is also most disappointing to see how slow they were to respond to this act of severe love. As Jeremiah put it later on, "O LORD, . . . you struck them, but they felt no pain; you crushed them, but they refused correction. They made their faces harder than stone and refused to repent" (Jer. 5:3). Probably some were more disposed to write the whole tragedy off as a freak event in nature than to see in it the divine hand of judgment. A spirit of hardness and defiance had counseled the people to stick it out, for it had to start raining soon. It could not go on like this forever—or so they reasoned in their own sinful state.

Eljah was not only bold in facing the enemy, he was courageous in rebuking fellow believers as well (1 Kings 18:3–15). The believer we have in mind here is Obadiah, Ahab's "secretary of state." We are told straight out that Obadiah was a devout believer, for he "feared the LORD greatly" (v. 3 NKJV). Now some fault him for holding a position in Ahab's government, but we do not agree. How can he be faulted for holding a position of influence in a corrupt government, so long as it did not lead him to personally compromise his own principles? On the contrary, he could offer valuable service to Yahweh in this office, as in fact he did. Still many commentators complain that he was a compromiser and therefore out of the will of God at this time. Some will accuse him of faults: (1) he gave no evidence of delight in seeing a fellow believer; (2) he resented being told to go tell Ahab that Elijah had returned; (3) he was self-centered and concerned only for his own protection and not for the welfare of the kingdom of God; (4) he distrusted Yahweh's words and rather feared that God would take Elijah away by the help of the Spirit of God; (5) he was overly defensive about his actions from his youth on and wished to brag about his rescue mission for the hundred prophets of Yahweh.

Now there is no doubt that Obadiah was fearful, but so was the prophet Habakkuk in the midst of his own turmoil of soul in Habakkuk 3. But we cannot agree that Obadiah gave any evidence of compromising, for verses 3 and 12 contradict that view. His reference to his daring deeds was not a boast but was rather a means of attesting his sincerity. Nevertheless, Obadiah still needed a gentle rebuke from the prophet Elijah. Elijah settled all of Obadiah's fears with a strong declaration in the name of the Lord (v. 15). And so Obadiah obeyed willingly without any further debate. The prophet's word was as certain as the fact that the Lord of hosts was living.

But the Lord also empowered his servant Elijah to rebuke the wicked (vv. 17–20). At last the long-sought confrontation was taking place. The first words out of Ahab's mouth were to shift the blame from himself to God's messenger. Indeed, how quick the wicked are to distort the facts and to foist the burden for the state of things onto the shoulders of those who merely announce or proclaim the divine judgment for these sins.

The gods of Ahab and Jezebel specialized in rain, dew, and thunder. Yet they had not raised even a drop, much less a good downpour, in all the three years since Elijah had announced to Ahab the awful news that Yahweh would send a drought. The smarting hearts of this royal duo saw that their only defense was to rouse sympathy for themselves and to shift the blame onto God's minister. Why could they not see that these were just games they were playing?

God's servant was once again more than a ready match for this weak defense: "I have not made trouble for Israel. . . . but you and your father's family have" (v. 18a). And the root of the problem was not to be found in the symptoms but rather in the real cause: "You have abandoned the LORD's commands and have followed the Baals" (v. 18b).

Obviously Ahab was in no position to complain, protest, or bargain. The real person in charge now was God's man. Therefore, in a most extraordinary move he ordered the king to summon all of Israel to Mount Carmel for a showdown. The state-paid 450 prophets of Baal and the 400 prophets of Asherah were likewise to appear. What could Ahab do? I wonder if he even dared to tell Jezebel what he had been ordered to do, for her absence on Mount Carmel is conspicuously noticeable. So Ahab sent word out to all Israel to gather at the assigned place (vv. 19–20).

How marvelous are the works of God through the intrepid Tishbite. But this was only the beginning, for God had an even greater work in store for all those despisers of genuine religion.

He Shows Us His Power (18:21–39)

If there ever was a lonely man in the history of faith, Elijah was that man. But one person plus God is always a majority, and Elijah believed that implicitly. His view of God had been forged and strengthened during those long days at the brook Cherith/Kerith, penned up with no place to go, and then in a suburb of Sidon named Zarephath, the very backyard from which the Gentile queen, Jezebel, had come, where her father was king. Three years of prayer and meditation on the Word of God were no small part in the preparation of this prophet for one grand afternoon of work. But we must be careful not to think that it all happened spontaneously, without any agonizing of heart or soul. That is a very narrow view of spiritual preparation.

Immediately, without any wavering or waffling of position, Elijah seized the initiative and bluntly challenged the people with this question: "How long will you go limping [wavering, tottering] with two different opinions? If the LORD is God, follow him" (v. 21 RSV). The word *limp* is the famous word used of the Passover. It refers to people who are not walking uprightly but who are like intoxicated persons. That is, the people were fickle, inconstant, and broadly syncretistic in their faith. Moreover, the people were double-minded fence-sitters who wanted to retain full loyalties to two opposing opinions at the same time. They were like the Republicans in 1884 who were humorously called mugwumps because they, too, like Israel and many candidates for revival today, had their mugs (i.e., faces) on one side of the fence and their "wumps" (i.e., the seats of their trousers) on the other. God, however, "hates double-minded men" (Ps. 119:113).

Who then was on the Lord's side, clearly and without any equivocation? asks our text, even as Moses had asked during the golden calf episode recounted in Exodus 32:26. Jesus warned that "he who is not with me is against me" (Matt. 12:30) and that if we were neither hot nor cold, he would spit us out of his mouth (Rev. 3:15).

What does a person say to this? What is there to say when the Word of God unmasks us for what we are? The Israelites did what we need to do as well; they "said nothing" (v. 21). "O for that plain and faithful preaching," exclaimed A. W. Pink, "which would so reveal to men the unreasonableness of their position . . . that every objection would be silenced and they would stand self-condemned."[3] The power of God had certainly demonstrated itself in the challenge of Elijah. But the most awesome display of the power of God was yet to come.

The choice of fire to evidence the power and authenticity of the claims of God is in itself a study in theology. Surely when the land, beasts, and all humanity were languishing, the answering of their prayers with rain rather than fire might seem much more appropriate. But God had Elijah choose fire both to show God's power and God's acceptance of the sacrifice. On three previous occasions God had sent fire from the heavens to light the fires under a sacrifice. The first was at the dedication of the altar of the tabernacle in Leviticus 9:24, the second when David dedicated the altar on the future site of the temple in 1 Chronicles 21:26, and the third when Solomon dedicated the newly built temple in 2 Chronicles 7:1. On each of these occasions, God's fire marked his acceptance and approval of the sacrifice offered. The theological point, then, is this: before the mercy and favor of the rains can return to the drought-stricken landscape, there must intervene a sacrifice, a substitute for sin, that is acceptable to God. That is precisely what our theology of the cross argues for: Jesus himself became our substitute so that we might be forgiven.

With the appearance of fire often came the revelation of the divine name (e.g., Exod. 3:15). It was, in fact, a declaration of the glory of God, that is, his presence, even as it was at the burning bush (Exod. 3:2). Even the restoration of the altar by Elijah had theological significance, for he took twelve stones, not the politically safe ten representing the ten northern tribes of the nation where he now ministered, thereby deliberately alluding to a similar situation in the history of Israel when Jacob and his family of twelve sons had to be called back from their idolatry. As Elijah challenged the idolaters here to get rid of their false gods, so had Jacob in an earlier revival in Genesis 35. The informing theology was obvious, and his refusal to legitimize the nation's sinful division into the ten northern tribes and two southern tribes for these fifty-eight years was also pointedly clear. Elijah, as the expression goes, had a lot of skin on his nose. Or was he just functioning with the boldness of an accredited messenger of Yahweh? At any rate, he clearly had in mind that earlier occasion when the ancestors to these same people had to be similarly challenged.

What took place as Elijah allowed the Baal contingency to go first is at once both humorous and pitiable. From six in the morning until three o'clock in the afternoon these devotees cried, shouted, and cut themselves with swords and knives, all to no avail. Meanwhile, Elijah rested on the mountainside (as I would picture it), perhaps staring down at the Mediterranean Sea and thoughtfully chewing on a piece of straw. (The text does not tell us that he did these things but it says so in the margins of my Bible. I must warn the reader, however; there are very wide margins in my Bible, and the notes I put there are *perspired*; only what is in the text of Scripture is *inspired*.)

If you were ever tempted to laugh out loud while reading the Bible, here is one of the places you might wish to do so. How sincere and yet how pathetic and misdirected were the worship and the prayers of these prophets. Elijah decided to have a little fun and offered some free advice as to how they might get a response from their erstwhile nonexistent god, as if he were in sympathy with them or in hope that they might be able to call down fire. The truth of the matter was that he knew there was no chance at all for them to succeed. So Elijah mockingly suggested that they might wish to shout louder (v. 27). He taunted with great mirth that Baal might even be sleeping—it is reported in the Canaanite religious tablets discovered at Ugarit that Baal sometimes went on trips and also frequently took naps. And these stupid fools took the advice seriously and increased their frantic activity of calling Baal's name, cutting themselves with their swords and the like, hoping to attract Baal's deaf ear and eye. But should they not have known? Was it not clear to them that the Lord, the God of Israel, was God and there never was and never would be any other competing God anywhere in the whole of creation? And if Baal was the god of dew, rain, and thunder, why had he not shown his stuff prior to this—three whole years, no less? That should have said it all. But how slow we humans are to get the point. Can you imagine how ravaged their economy must have been at this point in time—an agricultural economy? Where were they getting their daily sustenance?

Now at exactly the time when the evening sacrifice would be offered at the temple in Jerusalem, where the two southern tribes worshiped, Elijah began the service for sacrifice on the twelve-stone altar (vv. 30–31). By so doing, he again reminded the Israelites of northern Israel of their original position before God. He also specifically referred to the previous revival (under Samuel) and attempted to awaken in their memories an earlier occasion when they had to be rebuked by God for the same thing. Again using the informing theology of Genesis 35, he said, "Your name shall be Israel." So their very name was based on the occasion when God had cleansed his people of their sin and had renamed them in the earliest revival recorded in the Old Testament.

Elijah's prayer was a masterpiece in simplicity and directness. In approximately sixty words in the original Hebrew text, he appealed to the God of Abraham, Isaac, and Jacob to let it be known on that day that he was God and that there was no other (vv. 36–37). There was no need for a wearisome or drawn-out prayer. He had fervently prayed in his closet for over three years. Now it was time to witness the power of God.

Verse 38 bursts on the page of Scripture with the joy characteristic of the mighty God of the resurrection: "Then the fire of the LORD fell." This was no ordinary fire. For those who wish to speculate that it was the result of spontaneous combustion, traceable perhaps to the sword dances of the Baal dervishes, there are the three drenchings that the altar, the wood, the sacrifice, the stones, and the surrounding ditch received. And if it be protested further that this is an impossible feature to the story because there was supposed to be a shortage of water, I merely point out that there was plenty of salt water at the base of Mount Carmel. How glad I am that God led Elijah to take these additional steps, almost in anticipation of our modern skeptical age. It surely has saved us from reading and responding to some two dozen doctoral theses advocating some variation on the spontaneous combustion theory. Such proposed solutions to the mighty demonstration of the power of God are all wet!

And was there revival? Were the people convinced? Verse 39 affirms that "when the people saw this, they fell prostrate." I think I would, too, if I had been there and had witnessed such a mighty display of the presence and power of God. Indeed it is a fearful thing to fall into the hands of the living God if we are not prepared to meet him. And Israel certainly was not prepared. They had acted as if he were merely one more god on the god-shelf along with the others. But now the people's spontaneous declaration was "Yahweh, he is God! Yahweh, he is God!" (v. 39). And so he is, without any rival at all. Why are we forever trying even today to demote God and to place other loyalties alongside of him?

He Answers Our Prayers (18:40–46)

The final work of God observed in this chapter is that evidenced in answering prayer. If we have seen Elijah in public prayer on the top of Mount Carmel, we are now given a view of his ministry in private prayer in the closet.

It is no wonder that Scripture uses Elijah as an example of prayer in James 5:17–18. "Elijah," James assures us, "was a man just like us. He prayed earnestly that it would not rain, and it did not rain on the land for three and one-half years. Again he prayed, and the heavens gave rain, and the earth produced its crops." What a great encouragement to pray, and what a great encouragement to come to God to be revived again.

This portion of Scripture can be very helpful in teaching us what to pray for in revival and how to pray for it. Some have erroneously remarked that if God wishes to do something, it is none of our business. He probably does not need us interfering with his plans, so why should we pray? (This argument is especially convincing when it would appear that God has promised a certain outcome.) Again, if God needs any assistance, it is objected, why would he ask us merely to pray? But the promises of God were not meant to inhibit or to discourage us from praying. The plan of God is 180 degrees opposite of that kind of thinking. This is reinforced when we compare verse 1 of chapter 18 with verses 42–44. Had not God promised Elijah that if he would go and announce God's message to Ahab, the Lord in turn would send rain? In fact, we translated it as a result, or purpose, clause: "Go and present yourself . . . so that I may [or, *and then I will*] send rain" (v. 1). And so Elijah, fully persuaded of the fact that rain would come, nevertheless went to God in fervent, private prayer.

Too frequently we moderns have hidden behind the doctrine of the sovereignty of God as the reason why we are hesitant to pray fervently and persistently for revival. Scripture will not tolerate such a conclusion any more than it would have Elijah just sit and wait after the great immediate crisis was over. May Elijah's example (and remember, he is cited as our model of proper prayer technique in James) rebuke our poor excuses, and may we be taught that the promise of revival and showers of blessing in the good providence of God were not meant to say that we have no part or responsibility in this work.

We must note the following characteristics of Elijah's private prayers. First, he withdrew from the crowd and went into the privacy of his own thoughts with God to petition him precisely for what the Lord had promised to do. Second, he prostrated himself in prayer before God, for he bowed his head between his knees, demonstrating in his body the state of his heart and soul. Of course there is no preferred or recommended posture for prayer in the Bible, but it is always proper for the whole person to enter into prayer if it is to be a Spirit-led exercise of the whole person. Third, he was persistent in prayer, for he sent not just once but seven times to see if the answer was on the way. Fourth, he was fully confident and expectant that God would answer his prayer. Finally, he based his prayer, as we have already argued, on the promises of God.

Each aspect of this truth teaches us that God is God and that he delights in answering prayer. This work of God is just as significant as his work of making us bold or of showing us his power.

Conclusion

Our conclusion must be one of renewed admiration for the fact that God is the only Lord of history. The truth that Israel should have realized in that moment of great disclosure is that the Lord is God and there is no one like him in all the universe.

How shameful Israel must have felt. How cheap they must have seemed when the prophets of Baal failed so dramatically and so miserably. But then, how can we in our generation throw stones and criticize them? Have we not been just as guilty of substituting all sorts of schemes, programs, personalities, and prior commitments in the place that should have been rightfully occupied by God alone? Is it not time that we, too, came to know that God is God? Why have we likened him so much to that which is unreal, false, and ephemeral?

Surely we are ripe candidates for revival when there is competition for the attention and support of God's people on Sundays by such things as national football games televised during church services or Superbowl Sunday in January. There is nothing wrong with legitimate leisure activities, such as times of pleasure at the symphony. But how the people of God complain when the allotted sixty minutes for worship is exceeded. One would never believe that these were the same people who would later on sit for hours on hard bleachers without backs to watch a ball game or who would clap for four encores at the musical event of the year. But sixty minutes is all they can spare for the living God! Shame on us! The contrast in our attitudes shouts to high heaven that we, too, need to come to know what it means to come face to face with the only true God.

May God bring us a new vision of himself and of the majesty of his person. Let us be done with artificial and inauthentic representations of God. And may he revive our hearts even as he did for Israel in Elijah's day.

6   It Is Time to Seek the Lord

Revival under Asa
2 Chronicles 14–16

God is not limited. He can work in all times, and the revival under the Judean king Asa proves that he can work in times of prosperity as well as adversity. In the fifteenth year of this monarch, a great revival took place, but it was certainly different from any that we have investigated thus far in the Old Testament. Ernest Baker pinpointed that difference this way,

> It did not follow a period of religious decline, but a period of reformation. Neither was it occasioned by national adversity, causing the people in despair to turn to God; but it came after a season of increase and prosperity; and after a great national victory and deliverance. During the two preceding

reigns, the worship of Yahweh had been pushed into the background, and the erection of idols and places for their worship had proceeded with the active support of the rulers. Upon Asa's accession to the throne, ecclesiastical reform was immediately effected. The state policy was reversed. The people were commanded to observe the law of God, and an active campaign against idolatry was instituted.[1]

In the majority of the revivals in history, it takes tragedy to finally arrest the attention of an apostatizing people of God, but in this case the background for the revival was a reformation. Instead of a time of spiritual famine and religious decline, we are given a surprising exception in the revival under King Asa.

Now a reformation must not be confused with a revival. Reform may begin when God's Word forms the basis for all action, thinking, and living. It leads to a time of moral living and righteousness in the land. But revival begins in the heart and leads to deep contrition and repentance for sin, with a willingness to change, make restitution, and live differently from that time forward.

The reform movement of the southern Judean king Asa continued for fifteen years before revival came. That would place the Judean revival prior to Elijah's revival, which came to the northern kingdom almost twenty-five years later. Asa's revival occurred thirty-five years after the collapse of the united kingdom at the death of Solomon, that is, in 896 B.C., while Elijah's came in 875 B.C.

During the reformation period, however, Asa was actively pursuing all that was good and right in the sight of God (2 Chron. 14:2). He energetically assailed all pagan idolatry with a vengeance. Down came the foreign altar installations, sacred stones, and enigmatic, cultic Asherah poles (vv. 3–4). The land also experienced a time of unusual prosperity. There was a tremendous amount of building going on. Asa put up walls, towers, bars, and gates and secured the land on every side (vv. 6–7). Towns were remodeled and repaired, and public works were promoted.

Generally, it is said that cycles of prosperity follow, rather than precede, revivals. But again, the Asa revival is an exception to this observation. It is not always necessary for God to send trouble to get our attention. Sometimes his very goodness forces us to realize that we are the recipients of abundant favor that we do not deserve. In times like these we are ripe for the persuasive work of God's gracious Holy Spirit.

America may be experiencing one of these eras of reformation. Although there are plenty of reasons for decrying the growth of wickedness, evil, and injustice at almost every level of our society, there is also a more positive side. For example, just a few years ago hardly anyone spoke out against the terrible crime of abortion. Recently, however, some even in the executive branch of our government and others in our evangelical churches have closed ranks in an unprecedented way to forge one of the strongest alliances for righteousness this country has witnessed in years. Still, one swallow is not enough to declare that summer has arrived. However, there are other indicators as well. A whole host of social and moral crimes are under serious attack by these and other groups. Among them are child abuse, wife beating, pornography, drunkenness, gambling, and war. Seldom has this writer seen such a rallying of the forces of good. Furthermore, according to reliable estimates in the late 1970s, more than twenty-five percent of America's college and university students claimed to be born-again believers. This is something like 2.5 million believers out of a total student population of 11.5 million. In the gracious providence of God, could it be that we are in the vanguard of a revival that God would grant if we, who know Christ, would only go further and meet the conditions? Our prayer is that this reformation might be strengthened in its depth, fervor, and effectiveness and that it would eventually, but quickly, lead to a full-blown revival.

One other factor that led to revival in Asa's day should be noted here. During the fifteen years of his reformation, Asa had been equipping the army for any exigency. But when the challenge came, in the threat posed by Zerah from Ethiopia, he was vastly outnumbered. However, Asa gamely called on the name of the Lord and stated flatly that he relied on the Lord and on his name to extricate Judah from this ominous circumstance. And God granted a national victory in the face of overwhelming odds, which ordinarily would have signaled certain defeat. But it was this victory that God used to show once again how the goodness of God often leads us to repentance (Rom. 2:4) and, in this case, revival.

Therefore, the key to Asa's importance is to be found in a single phrase: he sought the Lord. Thus in the three chapters (forty-eight verses; the parallel account in 1 Kings 15:9–24 has only fifteen verses) dedicated to his life in 2 Chronicles, the writer used the verb phrase "to seek [the LORD]" nine times (14:4, 7 [twice]; 15:2, 4, 12–13, 15; 16:12), showing that he meant it to be used paradigmatically. This is especially significant in light of the fact that the occurrence of the verb in 2 Chronicles 6–7 is so programmatic in its appearance there. In the introduction to this book it was pointed out that four verbs from chapters 6 and 7 form the programmatic outline for the rest of 2 Chronicles. That is, nearly one-half of the thirty-six chapters of 2 Chronicles are occupied with the five reigns that exhibited some of the greatest revivals in history, and each of these five accounts seems to focus on one of the four verbs mentioned. The first and the fifth account share the same verb, thus bracketing or framing the argument.

It is true that "to seek" God is a favorite expression of the writer of Chronicles. He used it twenty-nine times altogether, whereas the parallel accounts in the books of Samuel and Kings used it only twice. The contrast can be seen by comparing 2 Chronicles 7:12–14, our controlling text in this study of revivals, with 1 Kings 9:2–3:

> The Lord appeared to [Solomon] at night and said:
>
> "I have heard your prayer and have chosen this place for myself as a temple for sacrifices. When I shut up the heavens so that there is no rain, or command locusts to devour the land or send a plague among my people, if my people, who are called by

my name, will humble themselves and pray and
seek my face and turn from their wicked ways, then
will I hear from heaven and will forgive their sin
and will heal their land."

2 Chronicles 7:12–14

The LORD appeared to [Solomon] a second
time, as [He] had appeared to him at Gibeon. The
LORD said to him: "I have heard the prayer and plea
you have made before me."

1 Kings 9:2–3

From this point on the Kings material resumes and parallels
Chronicles word for word.

But though the words *seek*, *pray*, *humble yourselves*, and *turn*
can be found in the speeches, prayers, and narratives of Chronicles,
they particularly abound in the material that reports the five revivals
that highlight this book. Therefore, this section, especially the
description for the way to get back to fellowship with the living
God, was indeed programmatic.

Within thirty-five years of the division of the kingdom, and almost
twenty-five years before God sent Elijah to the northern ten tribes, God
had sent three prophets: Shemaiah (2 Chron. 12:5, 7–8), Azariah
(15:2–7), and Hanani (16:7–9). Shemaiah, of course, was earlier and
ministered to King Rehoboam. He emphasized the phrase "Humble
yourself" (12:6–7 [twice], 12). Next, Azariah emphasized the theme of
Asa's day, "Seek the LORD." Finally, Hanani expressed the same truth
in another phrase, "Rely on the LORD" (16:7 [twice], 8).

Thus this episode announces to present-day readers that it is
time for us to seek the Lord. There are three results that we will
experience if we are willing to do that:

1. We will experience a time of peace (14:2–7).
2. We will experience God's presence again (15:1–7).
3. We will prevail over our foes (14:9–15; 16:1–10).

We Will Experience a Time of Peace (14:2-7)

The prophet Shemaiah had set the stage for this section of the text. He warned Judah's first king following the rupture of the kingdom in 931 B.C. that because the king had abandoned God, God would abandon him (12:5). That sobered the king, and the text says repeatedly that he humbled himself (12:6, 7 [twice], 12). There was more going on here than meets the English reader's eye, however, for the Hebrew text has a wordplay going on between the term for "humble oneself" and the term for "subdue" (13:18).

Of the thirty-six times the term that lies behind this wordplay is found in the Old Testament, eighteen of them are found in Chronicles, and of those eighteen, fourteen are used in a religious sense. But it is the appearance of this term in its religious sense in 2 Chronicles 7:14 that sets the pattern and the program for the rest of the book of Chronicles and for a significant theology of revival.

When we come to Asa's day, we find that a reformation is under way, even though it is not a revival. Already some of the good benefits of what God was going to do were being realized. For here was a man who commanded Judah to seek the Lord, the God of their fathers, and to obey his laws and commands (14:4).

What does it mean to seek the Lord? What it did not mean is seen in Leviticus 19:31, that is, to seek out mediums or wizards and to be defiled by them. But positively, it did mean to "seek the LORD and His strength; seek His face evermore" (1 Chron. 16:11; Ps. 105:4 NKJV). To "seek the LORD" and to "seek his face" probably meant the same thing, unless the later expression had more of the nuance of searching for the companionship and comfort of his presence continually.[2]

"Seeking Yahweh" can be used to define who is qualified to be a true member of the community of faith. "Not seeking Yahweh" disqualifies a person from full fellowship or any participation in that community. But if one is to judge by the words with which this expression is paired, seeking involves "knowing," "serving," and "being found by" God. Indeed, "the idea of 'seeking God' is so complex and so general in the Chronicler's historical work that one must consider the possibility that when all is said and done it denotes nothing other than the Chronicler's typical ideal of piety."[3]

In its prophetic use, the expression appears to be equivalent to a summons to repentance. Thus, Amos 5:4–6 urges, "Seek me and live." Likewise, Jeremiah 29:12–13 says, "You will seek me and find me when you seek me with all your heart" (cf. Isa. 55:6–7). This same concept of wholeheartedness is idiomatic for the writer of Chronicles as well. He urges individuals "to devote [their] heart . . . to seeking the LORD" (1 Chron. 22:19; 2 Chron. 11:16; or with the combined expression of the "face" instead of the "heart" in 2 Chron. 20:13). Another construction is to set, or establish, one's heart to seek the Lord (2 Chron. 19:3; cf. 12:14; 30:19). There can be no half-hearted relationship or search for God. Neither can one's repentance be halfhearted. We must enter into this commitment with all our heart and with all our soul (2 Chron. 15:12–13, 15).

Seeking God involves (1) voluntarily and wholeheartedly turning to God, (2) an inner attitude of devotion to serve him, (3) a decision to turn away from all evil, (4) a decision to fulfill his will, and (5) a commitment to go to him in fervent prayer. Furthermore, it is the chief means of averting evil (Amos 5:4, 14), the evidence of true humility (Zeph. 2:3), and the basis for sensing the presence of God (Hos. 5:15). All true repentance, communion with God, service for him, prayer to him, and spiritual growth in him revolves around truly seeking the Lord.

When Asa tore down the pagan installations, smashed the sacred stones, and cut down the sacred groves of an Asherah, he not only demonstrated how sincere his search for God was, but he also acted on the basis and in the spirit of the Word of God commanded in Deuteronomy 7:5; 12:3; and 16:21–22. He also demonstrated what Proverbs 14:34 says: "Righteousness exalts a nation, but sin is a disgrace to any people." Indeed, that is what Jeremiah put into the alternative prospects for judgment or blessing on any nation in 18:7–10.

> If at any time I announce that a nation or king-
> dom is to be uprooted, torn down and destroyed,

and if that nation I warned repents of its evil, then I will relent and not inflict on it the disaster I had planned. And if at another time I announce that a nation or kingdom is to be built up and planted, and if it does evil in my sight and does not obey me, then I will reconsider the good I had intended to do for it.

When the nation Israel sought the Lord, he gave them rest from all their enemies: "The land is still ours, because we have sought the LORD our God" (2 Chron. 14:7). The connection is not accidental, nor was it meant merely as a casual comment. It was theology in its most real and practical form. Thus, it is both amusing and sad to see the mania of modern nations. They maintain a high state of military readiness but usually neglect the preparations of the hearts of their people to meet the high standards of the government of heaven. Of what use is the most sophisticated or unique weapons system on the face of the earth if that nation has flaunted righteousness, justice, and mercy or failed to walk humbly with the one true God?

For those who truly seek God, there is a second result that will follow.

We Will Experience God's Presence Again (15:1–7)

Once again God used a prophet to stir up the hearts and consciences of the people and king. This time he sent Azariah, who spoke as the "Spirit of God came upon [him]" (v. 1). Azariah's challenge was, "The LORD is with you when you are with him. If you seek him, he will be found by you, but if you forsake him, he will forsake you" (v. 2). Every other ambition, feeling, longing, and urge has to be set aside in favor of searching for the living God if we have any hope of being found by him.

The presence of God was not to be regarded lightly. Even though the king had just returned flushed with unbelievably great success on the battlefield, he must not be any more presumptuous than we ought to be when the goodness of God deals with us more gently than we have a right to expect.

The text urges us to come into a deeper knowledge and fellowship with the living God. The Lord has been with us on many an occasion when we deserved it far less than Asa, in whose heart God had begun a reformation prior to a revival. Is it not time that we seek out the Lord with a new sense of hunger and thirst for righteousness? Oh, to know the joy, quietness, confidence, nourishment, and power of the abiding presence of the living God.

Azariah did not cater or pander to the ego of the monarch. He did not congratulate him on a splendid victory, nor did he try to worm his way into the higher echelons of government by indulging in unnecessary flattery over the crushing defeat of the Ethiopian king. Instead his message was one of going forward in spiritual growth.

We are never so vulnerable as when we have had unusual success, for our heads are in danger of being turned by the headiness and extravagant praise such situations sometimes bring. Then, more than ever, we are in special need of being reminded that it is time we sought the Lord. His very goodness should lead us to a new sense of repentance and a deeper quest for the presence of God in our lives.

The informing theology of this truth may be found as far back as the word Moses delivered in Deuteronomy 4:29: "If from [the exile] you seek the LORD your God, you will find him if you look for him with all your heart and with all your soul." This principle is now reinforced by a review of history in verses 3–6 of 2 Chronicles 15. It is amazing that there is no main verb in the Hebrew of verse 3, thus three periods could be intended here: *the archaic past* in the experience of the judges of Israel, *the present condition* of the kingdom, and *the future* under the Assyrians, Babylonians, Greeks, or Romans. Apparently the writer was being deliberately ambiguous so his statement could be principlized for all times—such as our own! That is, its truth fits all times in a type of generic wholeness that embraces the common condition of all people apart from the presence of the Lord.

The price of our godlessness is as high today as it was yesterday for Israel; they were "without the true God" (v. 3). All attempts to live life apart from God lead to atheism, either real or practical. Acting as if God does not matter in some areas of life or as if we can handle things on our own until we get into trouble is to live without the true God. "But the LORD is the true God; he is the living God, the eternal King" (Jer. 10:10). The accent in this clause is on the adjective *true,* for there is no truth apart from the author and maintainer of truth in all its forms.

A second price is in the absence of a teaching priest (v. 3). The priests in the Old Testament functioned as the community's teachers (Lev 10:11; Deut. 33:10). But this is a most dangerous situation as well, for "where there is no revelation [proclamation of that word], the people cast off restraint [become ungovernable]" (Prov. 29:18; cf. Exod. 32:6).

And thirdly they were "without the law" (v. 3). How then shall we live? If there is no path to walk in, how shall we judge by what standard we are to make ethical, moral, or practical decisions? The psalmist was especially glad for the help the law of God gave him. It was more to be desired than honey and the honeycomb (Ps. 19:7–11).

Tragically, these three indictments summarize our day and the experience of many believers. The great human need, both past and present, is to "turn" (v. 4) and repent, for whenever people turned in the past, they found God. Without revival, our cities and streets will remain unsafe for travel, one nation will unjustly rise up against another (vv. 5–6), and one crisis after another will be precipitated: economic, domestic, international. Herein lies something more basic and necessary than the Geneva talks on disarmament. We have failed to seek God's solution. By not taking the gospel into the city, it has come to pass that we cannot even take our cars there and park, for fear that they will be stolen or vandalized.

The price for refusing to be renewed by the Spirit of God is very high. The nations themselves shall be put into a confusion (v. 6) as our Lord allows one nation to discipline another. Thus nations rise and fall according to the signal given from God.

Asa was instructed not to give up. He was to "be strong," for his work would be rewarded (v. 7). The admonition is reminiscent of those given to Joshua, and the plea "do not give up" would be reflected later in Zephaniah 3:16, as would the promise about reward be reflected later in Jeremiah 31:16. It seems ridiculous for a man who had just had such a huge success to be challenged in this way. But his need is no more ludicrous than our own in similar circumstances. Often it is easier to face a hostile nation or army than it is to face evil and sin squarely in our own lives and that of our nation. No doubt the writer of Chronicles uses the conscious exaggeration of hyperbole when he paints the picture of the past in such negative totalities in verses 5 and 6. But by putting it in such identifiable terms, readers through the centuries have recognized his formulation as having a great element of truth for describing their own circumstances and then for constructing their own view of the future.

In sum, we must "come near to God and he will come near to [us]. [We must] wash [our] hands, [we] sinners, and purify [our] hearts, [we who are] double-minded" (James 4:8). This is one search we cannot afford to give up on.

There is one more result from our wholehearted search for God.

We Will Prevail over Our Foes (14:9–15; 16:1–10)

There are two examples to illustrate our point, one positive and one negative, unfortunately. When Asa depended on the Lord and sought him with all his heart, Asa's testimony was, "LORD, there is no one like you to help the powerless against the mighty" (14:11). The incomparability of God exceeds everything known to men or women. Asa's prayer in those early days was, "Help us, O LORD our God, for we rely on you, and in your name . . . do not let man prevail against you" (14:11). Even that word *rely* is important in this context (it also appears in 16:7 [twice] and 8). All other reliances are false and ultimately hopeless when compared to the God who exceeds everything we can think or imagine. So let us raise our own *Ebenezer* and mark it down that no man or force can prevail against God or his people. He springs to the aid of those who themselves are powerless. And when it comes time to act, they act, think, and pray in his name (14:11). God will never abandon his people, church, or Word. But whether a nation or a denominational group will continue to experience that favor may be a different sort of question. The name of God will never lack for devotees or successful representatives to carry it around the world. On the other hand, God is not stuck with America, evangelicalism, or our special methodologies. He could raise up from the former Soviet Union or China a whole new cadre of men and women who would rely on him implicitly. No, it is not his cause that hangs in the balance; instead, it is we who are being weighed and found wanting if we do not turn to seek him with all our hearts.

The Ethiopian army of Zerah was crushed before the army of Asa. The victory, as it always does under these sorts of circumstances, belonged to the Lord (vv. 13–14). As in those real contests of life, we must anticipate in our spiritual warfare more evidence of the power, victory, and success of the Lord's cause and name. It is embarrassing to realize that for almost one and one-half millennia the church has made little or no impact on the Islamic world. The church once flourished in North Africa. And what shall we say about so many other "hidden peoples" that have not yet been reached with the gospel? If there is no one like our Lord, and if we only need to turn to him, seek him with our whole hearts, and rely on him alone to help the helpless, then why do we remain where we are? With the apostle Paul we shout, "Therefore . . . be steadfast, immovable, always abounding in the work of the Lord, knowing that your labor is not in vain" (1 Cor. 15:58 NKJV).

I wish this were the end of the chapter, but unfortunately Asa's life has another segment. He forgot, as we all too quickly tend to forget, the lessons he had learned earlier in his career with the Zerah incident. Faced with an unprovoked attack from northern Israel, he decided to "rely on the king of Syria" (16:7 NKJV) to put some pressure on Israel by attacking them on their northern border. The idea was that while they were thus occupied, Asa would be able to recoup his resources on Israel's southern border and build up the fortifications. But what often makes good logical sense is not always good theological sense, especially if it runs directly counter to God's Word. In appealing to Ben-hadad, king of Syria, Asa introduced a military conqueror over his own relatives in the ten tribes to the north. Furthermore, by purchasing this military favor, he also tacitly recognized that he was weaker than, and therefore politically in subjection to, the Syrian ruler.

But God sent another prophet named Hanani to roundly rebuke him for his false reliance on human powers in preference to the Lord. All such reliances spell disaster. This includes all of the self-help emphasis of our day and all sociological and psychological explanations that do not have a realistic view of guilt, sin, or God. It is lethal to lean on another nation, philosophy, or methodology as a substitute for the living God.

When Asa had relied on the Lord, chided the prophet Hanani, God delivered the enemy into Asa's hand. Why had he suddenly thought better of that? Did he not know that "the eyes of the LORD range throughout the earth to strengthen those whose hearts are fully committed to him" (16:9)? The omniscient eye of God still searches for those who are completely given over to him. In the hands of God, ordinary, weak individuals who trust in the Lord with all their heart and soul suddenly become God's choice instruments, and they do mighty exploits for the Savior because God shows himself strong on behalf of those who rely on him.

There were three marks in Asa's decline. First, he allied himself with the Syrian king, Ben-hadad. Next, he angrily threw the prophet Hanani into prison for rebuking him. Finally, he relied on physicians for healing rather than relying on God. This third sin will trouble some in our modern culture who, of course, see nothing incongruous with their testimony and seeking help from medical doctors. But we must be careful not to translate our contemporary conception of physicians back to the ancient world. The physicians of that day depended not on scientific procedures but on incantations and magical remedies. To turn to them was tantamount to turning away from God. Thus Asa did do a very "foolish thing" (16:9). No longer was his heart "fully committed to the LORD" (15:17), and therefore no longer could he or Judah rejoice (15:15).

What a waste after so many years of wonderful reformation and then times of great revival. More than ever we ought to be warned that it is not the person who begins the race who should boast but only the one who takes off the equipment after the contest. It is always proper to seek the Lord.

Conclusion

The past decade and a half have been unusually good years in America. They should have led us to seek God in a way we have never done before. How can we explain the unusual strength of the dollar against other currencies? How can we explain the sudden and dramatic drop in our own double-digit inflation while other countries around the world continue to have soaring rates, sometimes reaching as high as several hundred percentage points per year? Again, against the best prognostications of the experts, how can we, simultaneously with these other features, have a drop in unemployment figures? And why should our gross national product, interest rates, and the stock market be holding so well for so long against all normal expectations? Are all of these factors pure accident? Or are they due to the human sagacity of the current government administration? No, God is speaking to us through his kindness. The very goodness of God is leading us to repentance. There is also the moral minority, that remnant for whose sake the rest of us are being given further opportunities to seek the Lord.

As the deer pants for the water, let our souls pant for the living God. "Such is the generation of those who seek him, who seek your face, O God" (Ps. 24:6). May Christ's church be revived and search for him as never before. May we know a new communion with the King of kings and Lord of lords. May we know what it is to serve, obey, and know him in an altogether unique way, for if we seek him, he will be found by each one of us.

7   It Is Time to Pray to the Lord

Revival under Jehoshaphat
2 Chronicles 20

Some individuals, who are basically well meaning and who strive to do what is right, are often also very naive and easily misled. King Jehoshaphat fit squarely into this category. For even though he was a pious and successful monarch, he nevertheless had to be repeatedly censured by God's holy prophets. Four of them rebuked and corrected him when he became entangled in ungodly alliances and relationships. Jehu, the son of Hanani, charged him with helping Ahab and those who hated the Lord (19:2). Eliezer, the son of Dodavahu, charged him with being unequally yoked in a shipping venture at Ezion Geber (20:36–37). Micaiah, son of Imlah, roundly rebuked him for joining with Ahab to venture against Ramoth Gilead (18:16). And the Levite Jahaziel encouraged him as he went out to battle against the eastern nations (20:14–17). But for all of Jehoshaphat's sins and weaknesses of character, he mastered the discipline of prayer. And few chapters in the Bible can better illustrate the effectiveness and power of prayer than 2 Chronicles 20.

If 2 Chronicles 7:14 serves as the paradigm for the whole book, as I have argued, then chapter 20 and the events narrated from the life of Jehoshaphat focus on an important component of all revivals: prayer. The preaching of the Word moves men and women to humble themselves under the mighty hand of God and to turn from their wicked ways and seek God's face in a renewed way. Prayer moves God to graciously pour out the blessing of heaven on sinners, undeserving as we are.

The writer of Chronicles clearly wanted to lift high the kingdom of Israel under David and Solomon as the model and the forerunner of the messianic kingdom. Although the latter kingdom was already realized in principle, from his perspective it was also still future in the two advents of Christ. Therefore, all the successors on the Davidic throne were likewise subjects of great interest, for each was a transmitter of that ancient promise and the heart of its present manifestation. Accordingly, the role they play in worship, their responsiveness to the proclaimed Word of God, and the leadership they give to the things of God will be very determinative in the life of the people. Jehoshaphat was most instrumental in leading his people into a new experience of the power of God through prayer.

This is not the first time the chronicler expressed an interest in prayer. He had inserted the brief, plaintive cry of Jabez to God even in the midst of rehearsing the genealogies (1 Chron. 4:9–10; God's response was also recorded: "And God granted his request."). Then there was Solomon's prayer for wisdom (2 Chron. 1:8–11; 9:22), which God also granted most generously; Asa's prayer for deliverance in the midst of the crisis precipitated by Zerah the Ethiopian (2 Chron. 14:9–15); and Hezekiah's prayer for a lengthened life (2 Chron. 32:24–25). But the prayer that forms the best model for our praying is that of Jehoshaphat in 2 Chronicles 20.

This raises the question of what it means to pray. Briefly, when we pray we make our request known to God by the help of the Holy Spirit; in the name, authority, and mediation of our Lord Jesus

Christ; with faith, fervency, and submission to the will of God; and with sole reference to his honor and glory. Each part of this rather elaborate definition is important and plays a role in our entering into prayer.

First, the efficient cause of prayer must be the Holy Spirit. James 5:16 translated literally teaches us that it is the "prayer worked in by the Holy Spirit that is effective." Thus all prayer that is not prompted by the Word of God or worked in (i.e., energized by) the Holy Spirit is just so much howling in the ears of God. But if it be objected, as it surely will, that the Spirit of God was not present in the Old Testament or that he did not so function, then consider David's request in Psalm 51:11 that the Holy Spirit not be taken from him. Also note the rebuke that Jesus gave (prior to the cross) to Nicodemus for his ignorance of the ministry of the Holy Spirit in the process of regeneration (John 3); the Lord was horrified that Nicodemus could be a teacher and still not know about that ministry of the Holy Spirit. So there is a strong case for the work of the Holy Spirit in the life of the believer in the Old Testament.

The only proper object of prayer is God. Thus the aim of our praying ought to be the glory and honor of his name, and our requests ought to be in accordance with his will. That is why many believers end their prayers with a statement like "all these things we ask in Jesus' name." This is not a magical password or a talisman. It says that we wish for nothing that is not in accordance with the high and holy will of the living God. "This is the confidence we have in approaching God: that if we ask anything according to his will, he hears us" (1 John 5:14).

Moreover, our prayers must be offered in faith, "with no doubting" (James 1:6 NKJV), and we must approach the throne of grace believing "that he exists and that he rewards those who earnestly seek him" (Heb. 11:6). Also our prayers must be with fervency (James 5:16). There can be no prayers of incense offered up without any fire.

Prayer then is the great means the Father has opened up for making our requests known and for joining in the work of ministry around the world. Prayer is God's sovereign medicine and remedy for the afflicted mind. Being able to approach God is one of the inestimable privileges we have as believers, a gift won for us by the death of Christ.

But God already knows our wants and desires, so why pray? The answer is that we pray not so much to inform God as to draw our own affections toward him and the holy things for which we plead. But is it not vain to pray, some might argue, especially because our prayers cannot alter the providence of God? The answer is no, it is not fruitless and a waste of time and energy. The same providence that orders the end orders *the means* by which that end is obtained; and part of that means is our prayer. Therefore, just as God has decreed the blessing, so he has decreed that the blessing should come by prayer. Hence prayer is not an optional, spiritual luxury; it is a must.

How then should we pray if we wish our prayers to be acceptable to God? Here are some suggestions. First, if we want God to hear us, we must begin by hearing him (Prov. 1:24–28). Second, we must deeply desire what we ask for, for "he who asks coldly, begs only a denial." Third, we must come with sufficient resolve to wait for the answer. Fourth, we must not pray for things that are purely selfish and only for our own gratification (James 4:3). Finally, we must stress praying for some grand purpose and avoid a narrow provincialism that sees only one's immediate household, friends, or church as the object of prayers. An example of a grand prayer that lifts us beyond narrow, myopic prayers is the one that focuses on the need for revival in our day.

2 Chronicles 20 gives us five reasons to pray, each of which adds fresh incentive to this most holy exercise of the soul:

1. God rules over all kingdoms of the nations (v. 6).
2. God delights to do what he promised (vv. 7–11).
3. God judges all who oppose his work (v. 12).
4. God delivers us from our distresses (vv. 14–17).
5. God upholds those who have faith in him and his Word (vv. 18–30).

When King Jehoshaphat had been confronted with an army of huge proportions, he resolved to take the matter immediately to the Lord in prayer. In fact, he gathered the entire population of Judah, including the men, wives, and little ones (20:13). The people came from every town in Judah to seek the Lord's face (20:4). It was on this occasion that the king stood up and led them in this most instructive prayer. He begged God to intervene on their behalf, and in the process he gave these five reasons to pray.

God Rules over All the Kingdoms of the Nations (20:6)

In the way he addressed God, we learn with what confidence Jehoshaphat came to the Lord in prayer. That confidence is instructive, teaching us that God is the same God who has given us the same promise he gave to the patriarchs Abraham, Isaac, and Jacob. He rules the world on the basis of this ancient but ever-renewing promise-plan, which he began to disclose shortly after the fall. Furthermore, God's authority extends over all of heaven and earth. It is as Nebuchadnezzar learned by hard experience: "The Most High is sovereign over the kingdoms of men and gives them to anyone he wishes and sets over them the lowliest of men" (Dan. 4:17, cf. v. 25). It is no wonder, then, that no one ever has or ever will successfully resist or block God's will.

For this reason we must never regard prayer lightly. Among all the potentates and controllers of power-blocs in the world, none comes even close to equaling the Lord's authority, might, and ability to rectify things. Let us therefore come boldly as we approach his throne of grace for mercy and seasons of refreshing. Once God has been pleased to move in times of revival, who or what can withstand him? May God grant us a new vision of his incomparable greatness. This is the best cure for our faintheartedness. If we have not because we have not asked, let us pray to the Lord, who owns and runs the universe. Down will come all the strongholds and deep pockets of resistance to the gospel when we storm the gates of heaven and pray that our Father would vanquish these heavily ensconced foes.

God Delights to Do What He Promised (20:7–11)

Founding our prayers on the promises of God is not meant to teach us to pray timidly, as though worried about asking for anything not explicitly written in the Scriptures. It is rather an important exercise in learning to pray in accordance with God's will. Furthermore, these promises were not given to excuse us from praying but to teach us what to pray for and how to pray for it.

The promises on which Jehoshaphat based his prayer dealt with the gift of the land to Israel forever (Gen. 13:15; 15:18). By extrapolation the situation of an unprovoked enemy attack fell within the boundaries of these promises and offered great grounds for the king to ask for their defeat (2 Chron. 20:7).

Also, at the dedication of the temple, the Lord had promised Solomon that God would hear the prayers of his people, whether Jewish or Gentile (2 Chron. 6:14–42; 7:15). He said, "My eyes will be open and my ears attentive to the prayers offered in this place."

The Lord expects us to obey him as Abraham did and thus Abraham was called the "friend" of God (20:7; James 2:23). Jesus said, "You are my friends if you do what I command" (John 15:14).

Furthermore, when we are in distress—and God anticipated we would be at times—we should take our situation to him in prayer. This was anticipated in Solomon's request in 2 Chronicles 6:28–30 referred to by Jehoshaphat (20:9). Jeremiah also said it well: "You will seek me and find me when you seek me with all your heart" (Jer. 29:13). This latter verse was used in the life of a young lawyer who was studying for the bar. But God had other plans for him, and Charles G. Finney was soundly converted and called into a ministry of evangelism and revivals. According to his own testimony, God used this verse as one of the most significant challenges in Finney's own life.

The promise of God is that he will hear and be found by all those who search for him with all their hearts. Now that has to be one of the greatest inducements that has ever been given to a ministry of prayer. As Luke's Gospel puts it, "If [we] being evil know how to give good gifts to [our] children, how much more will [our] Father in heaven give the Holy Spirit to those [of us] who ask him!" (Luke 11:13 NKJV). Why do we not ask?

God Judges All Who Oppose His Work (20:12)

In many ways the word *judge* epitomized the message of Jehoshaphat, whose name means "Yahweh will judge." But it is also a recognition of our own impotence: God must judge, not we. Asa realized that he, too, was powerless in this situation (2 Chron. 14:11), but God delivered him because he relied on the name of the Lord. Thus, when we, like Jehoshaphat, "do not know what to do" (20:12), we should do what he did and turn "our eyes upon [God]" (v. 12).

Wisdom has been promised to those who lack it, and this text is another example of such. The psalmist testified, "My eyes are ever on the LORD, for only he will release my feet from the snare" (Ps. 25:15), and, "As the eyes of slaves look to the hand of their master, as the eyes of the maid look . . . to her mistress, so our eyes look to the LORD our God, till he shows us his mercy" (Ps. 123:2). Finally, he said, "But my eyes are fixed on you, O Sovereign LORD; in you I take refuge—do not give me over to death" (Ps. 141:8).

There is no need to keep score or to worry if might will make right in a world where God is the final and only real judge. Though we may be buffeted by enigmas and distresses, we can fly to our Lord in prayer and seek his help. Surely he knows how to right the wrongs and to silence the unprovoked attacks. He is the supreme judge of all the earth.

God Delivers Us from Our Distresses (20:14–17)

In this paragraph we are introduced to another specially prepared individual who was enabled by the Holy Spirit to do what

God wanted him to do in ministering to Jehoshaphat. His name was Jahaziel, the son of Zechariah. This Levitical singer and fifth generation ancestor of Mattaniah was just as much filled with the Holy Spirit as the New Testament apostles.

Through him the Lord answered Jehoshaphat's prayer of distress. His main word, which is repeated twice and is therefore an inclusio, or frame, for his message, is "Do not be afraid" (vv. 15, 17). How many times does the Lord need to remind us that we must forgo our phobias? Repeatedly the Bible urges us to "fear not" and then usually quickly adds "for I am with you." And that is the promise attached to the prohibition here (v. 17).

The encouraging word was, "The battle is not yours, but God's" (v. 15). Thus the theology was the same as that of 1 Samuel 17:47 in the David and Goliath situation: "All those gathered here will know that it is not by sword or spear that the LORD saves; for the battle is the LORD's, and he will give all of you into our hands." Later on, Nehemiah would comfort his badly shaken workers by saying, "Don't be afraid. . . . Remember the Lord, who is great and awesome" (Neh. 4:14). In his case, too, the battle was to be most unusual, for Israel would not be required to fight at all because the Lord would fight for them.

There were things to do, however. The Israelites were to "position [them]selves, stand still, and see the salvation of the LORD" (v. 17 NKJV). The command was reminiscent of the one given to Moses at the Red Sea, when Pharaoh's army was closing in and Israel was trapped by the mountains, the sea, and the enemy; every word is the same except for the additional phrase "stand still" (Exod. 14:13). This was one of those occasions when all frantic human activity was to be of no avail. It was time to trade business for worship.

To those who come to God in earnest prayer, he will grant deliverance, regardless of the odds. How slow we are to capitalize on this fact of spiritual life. Too frequently we assume that deliverance rests in our hands. But just one moment of serious reflection should tell us that such is not the case. Nor was it so on this occasion, for God worked mightily on Israel's behalf.

If only we would learn how to be strong and not be afraid. If only we would realize what a difference the presence of God makes in every testing or opportunity of life. Haggai reminded the people of his day of this fact (Hag. 2:4–5). Indeed, the little preposition *with* appears over a hundred times in conjunction with the promise of the real, powerful, comforting presence of the living God.

God Upholds Those Who Have Faith in Him and His Word (20:18-30)

Jehoshaphat's response to Jahaziel's ministry of the Word of God was to lead the people in bowing their heads and falling down in worship. And then, surprisingly, some of the Levites stood up and broke out in praise. The revival was on. How God's people love to praise him when their burdens have been lifted. How spontaneous is the gift of doxology and music when our guilt, concerns, and sins have been cast on the burden bearer. Verses 18–19 are among those select passages of Scripture in the Old Testament that show us that every great once in a while God's people can and do respond beautifully to the call of the Word of God. And how wonderful it is when this happens. May our own hearts long to own up to a similar confession, and may the joy of our lives be the high honor of raising our voices in the praise and magnification of the God of gods and Lord of lords.

Early the next morning, the king addressed the people with a summons to a new display of faith in the Lord. In fact, he used a play on the same words that the Holy Spirit used later when speaking through the prophet Isaiah to King Ahaz in the very famous virgin birth passage (Isa. 7:9). The king said, in a wonderful pun, "Have faith in the LORD your God and you will have staith" (2 Chron. 20:20). The Hebrew term translated "faith" and "staith" is the word we have anglicized into "amen." Thus he urged, to put it in other words that attempt to capture the pun in English, "Be sure in the Lord and you will be secure" or "Affirm the Lord and you will be confirmed" or "Stand firm in your Lord and you will be stood firm."

How cowardly we act when we put our trust in ourselves, our institutions, money, growth, political pull, intellectual analysis, or our own resourcefulness, rather than putting our trust in the Lord. It was Isaiah who announced this principle best: "You will keep him in perfect peace, whose mind is stayed on [the Lord], because he trusts in [the Lord]" (Isa. 26:3 NKJV). Also he added, "The one who trusts [in the Lord] will never be dismayed" (Isa. 28:16). We ask in surprise, "What, never be dismayed?" No, we will never be dismayed when our hearts are garrisoned about by a vital trust in the living God.

In verse 20b Jehoshaphat commended the word of the prophets to our trust as well, for we must trust the Word of God just as much as we trust the Lord. For how will we ever know how to live or think if we do not have the Word from God's holy prophets and apostles? Indeed, without such a faith in the Word of God, we shall be denied every opportunity for success and for a genuine revival in our day. Our cry must be, "Back to the Book, the Word and the testimonies of our Lord." More than anything else, we need an end to the awful famine of the Word of God in our day. Too frequently we have settled for talking about the Word of God without a patient listening to it, the whole context, the whole counsel of God from Genesis to Revelation proceeding line after line, verse after verse, and paragraph after paragraph. This can only lead to spiritual malnutrition and, as Amos described it, "a famine of hearing the words of the LORD" (Amos 8:11).

Much of the blame for this state of affairs must lie at the doorstep of the ministry—not all ministers, mind you, but all too many in our day. We must painfully reflect on this phenomenon. In the words of Charles G. Finney,

> And ministers ought to know that nothing is more common than for spiritual Christians to feel burdened and distressed at the state of the ministry. I would not wake up any wrong feelings towards ministers, but it is time . . . that their souls are kindled up. . . . When a minister has gone as far as his

experience in spiritual exercises goes, there he stops; and until he has a renewed experience . . . [and] his heart is broken afresh . . . he will help them no more.

He may preach sound doctrine . . . but, after all, his preaching will want that searching pungency, that practical bearing, that unction. . . . However much intellectual furniture [he] may possess, [he remains] in a state of spiritual babyhood. . . . [He] needs to be fed [rather] than to undertake to feed the Church of God.[1]

When both of these objects of trust were understood and held in proper balance, the people broke out into song. Thus, singing was not restricted to the temple, but was just as at home amid the dangers of life as it was in the quiet sanctuary of God. Like Paul and Silas, who sang at midnight in prison at Philippi (Acts 16:25), the Israelites sang when faced with evil forces.

The praise of God is directed toward the beauty of his holiness (v. 21). The phrase probably refers to the summation of all God's attributes and the dazzling array that his Person cast on the scene where he was present. The invitation to worship God in the beauty of holiness is frequently given (e.g., 1 Chron. 16:29; Ps. 96:9; and in part in Pss. 29:2 and 110:3). Accordingly, the phrase also involves the element of the spiritual character of God's people as they come to worship him. Our outward and inward attire is not an inconsequential matter when it comes to appearing before the living God.

In most of the revivals known to us from Scripture, there is the thrill of the great joy that accompanies the genuine revival of God's people. Verse 27 tells us why: "The LORD had given them cause to rejoice." Moreover, a holy terror and fear that originates from God overtakes the hearts of those who raise their fists against the living God (v. 29). But the peace of God is reserved for all who trust in him. Thus verse 30 says that "God had given him rest on every side."

Conclusion

Rather than stressing the doctrine of prayer by repeating the word *pray* over and over as in the revival of Asa (and as in the next two revivals in 2 Chronicles), the chronicler demonstrated the effectiveness and necessity of prayer by illustrating how effective it was in the life of King Jehoshaphat and his times.

If prayer carried the day for these people, then we ought to learn to make our appeal to heaven as well. There is no higher court of appeal or avenue of influence among mortals. Let us therefore let our prayers begin to flow to heaven. May they find their authority in our Lord's promises, and may they find their poignancy in our current needs for cleansing and genuine revival.

Prayer must be the hallmark of our Christian lives and the ministry of the church. It must become our number one priority if we are ever going to be more than a minority band exercising selective holding actions until the Lord returns. Such minimalistic goals are a weariness to God and a bother to mankind in general.

One more observation: our prayers must enlarge in their scope. All too frequently we ask only for ourselves and for our immediate environment. Where are the worldwide concerns that our Lord taught us to have? Where is the passion for the success of the Lord's cause around the face of the globe and in every people-group known? As Charles G. Finney observed: "A backslidden heart . . . reveal[s] itself in praying almost exclusively for self . . . or friends. . . . It is often very striking and even shocking to attend a backslider's prayer meeting. . . . Their prayers are timid and hesitating and reveal the fact that they have little or no faith."[2]

Is it not time that we begin to pray and to pray in the biblical manner? And has this passage not taught us why we ought to pray? May our God mercifully lead his church once again into a ministry of prayer.

8 It Is Time to Turn Back to the Lord

Revival under Hezekiah
2 Chronicles 30:1–9

*E*rnest Baker, in his pioneering study of Old Testament revivals, began his remarks on the revival under Hezekiah with this arresting assessment: "The revival in the time of Hezekiah is amongst the most sudden of those recorded in Scripture. Hezekiah began a work of reformation during the first month of his reign, and within two months the whole land was swept with a wave of spiritual enthusiasm."[1] It is not always possible for us to say why there is such a sudden response as the one under Hezekiah. Surely it is finally due only to the Spirit of God moving on the hearts of men and women. But what secondary causes, if any, were present and specially used by the Spirit of God in this situation are not directly stated.

One factor can clearly be ruled out, and that is any positive influence that may have come from Hezekiah's father, Ahaz. On the contrary, the period under Ahaz, king of Judah, was the epitome of evil. For the sixteen years just preceding the revival, he had done little more than poison the spiritual life of the people (2 Chron. 28:1–27). Everything Ahaz did led the people further away from God. The chronicle of his deeds reads like a litany of woes, for each act was another nail in his coffin and contribution to the spiritual doldrums of the nation.

To mention a few, we note first of all that he "made cast idols for worshiping the Baals" (2 Chron. 28:2), mixing the worship of the various Baal idols with his worship of Molech (v. 3). To this he added the burning of incense in the Valley of Hinnom and on the hills and under every spreading tree (vv. 3–4). But worst of all, he also burned his children as a sacrifice to the god Molech (v. 3).

Such unspeakable carnality, sensuality, and cruelty is reprehensible enough in the eyes of good and decent men. Imagine its effect on the living God. The unbridled licentiousness that accompanied much of the Canaanite worship of Baal and his consorts is well documented from the oldest discovered alphabetic script in the world, the Ugaritic documents found at modern Ras Shamra in Syria. My doctoral dissertation was on the Ugaritic pantheon, and I can testify that modern pornography seldom exceeds the debauchery to which these gods and goddesses and their devotees gave themselves. It is no wonder that the next statement that follows in verse 5 reads, "Therefore the LORD his God handed him over to the king of Aram [Syria]."

Do not miss the point here, for this is no odd instance from a bygone day with which we have nothing, or very little, in common. We, too, can be caught up in sensuality. In fact, the modern entertainment industry by and large panders to our thirst for and adoration of sensuality. Many theaters, nightclubs, movies, and television programs go straight for the fleshly heart when they glorify lewdness, indecency, and immorality and generally flaunt every law of God. Such foul corrupters of the spiritual life are every bit as effective as the ancient worship of Baal and Molech in distracting hearts and minds from that which is pure, holy, beautiful, and true.

Even the abominable practice of offering live babies to Molech by placing them on the arms of the hollow-bellied furnaces that served as replicas of the alleged deity has its modern counterpart. Then the priestly drums rolled and the clamor of song and the noise of music ascended to heaven as these little ones rolled gently down the arms of idolatrous monstrosities and into their brimstone bellies for an offering to Molech. But how much different is the same act repeated in the sterilized environment of an abortion clinic or a hospital today? If we continue to destroy one and one-half million babies a year by abortion, will not God also hand us over into the hands of our enemy? Our greatest threat is not the former Soviet Union or any other nation; our greatest threat is ourselves. If we do not soon repent and turn back to God, we are going to face some of the most difficult times we have ever faced as a nation.

Verse 19 of 2 Chronicles 28 is startling. It says that the Lord "humbled Judah because of Ahaz, . . . for he *cast off all restraint* in Judah and had been most unfaithful to the LORD" (author's translation). The remarkable fact about the words in italics is that they translate the same verb that was used to describe the enormity of Israel's sin in the golden calf incident (Exod. 32:25). It is the verb meaning "to make naked," "to let the reins loose," or "to become unbridled, lawless, or ungovernable." Wilbur Smith once asked,

> Can you think of any single phrase of four words [cast off all restraint] which would more perfectly describe our modern civilization than these? It seems as though economically, socially, domestically, in the home, in business, in the nation, throughout the world, men have thrown aside all restraint, and live, and act, and think, and plan, as though there were no universal law of recompense, as though men would never be punished for breaking the law of God, as though the future would take care of itself, and as though we should live only for the immediate present.[2]

As a result, Judah was plagued with a host of problems. Such wickedness cannot go unbridled without the love of God suddenly calling that people to justice. Therefore, there came a period of severe military weakness. A number of the people were carried away captive to Syria (28:5). Moreover, the northern kingdom inflicted a devastating defeat on Judah, carting off in naked disgrace upwards of two hundred thousand women, sons, and daughters, as was the habit in that day (v. 8). Other nations repeated the same feat, for Ahaz also had trouble from the Philistines and the Edomites. But rather than call on God for help, he appealed to the king of Assyria. Instead of the expected help, however, he was further insulted and robbed by the king he had hoped would be his ally (vv. 16–21).

For most of us this would have been enough trouble to force us in humility to a confession of our sin, but not Ahaz. "He became even more unfaithful to the LORD" (v. 22). He now sacrificed also to the gods of Syria, the very nation that had defeated him. If these gods had helped Syria, he must have reasoned, then he would fall down to them, and perhaps they would help him also (v. 23). It is tragic to see how sin corrupts the reasoning powers, common sense, and wisdom of those who refuse to turn back to God, but who instead continue on their reckless path of destruction. The chronicler curtly concluded, "But [the gods of Damascus] were his downfall and the downfall of all Israel" (v. 23).

From this point on Ahaz's evil knew no sane boundaries. He "shut the doors of the LORD's temple" and took all the furniture and implements from the temple and cut them up (v. 24). He built altars for pagan worship in every town in Judah (v. 25). His wickedness was so extravagant that there was no hope of anything but more evil. The time was long overdue for the nation and its leadership to turn to God. And this was the ministry that God gave to the young son of Ahaz.

How did this evil man produce such a godly son as Hezekiah? Surely the fact is that Hezekiah is one of the best refutations of the oft repeated but badly understood warning that the sins of the fathers visit the children to the third and fourth generation. That is only true when the children agree in the evil of their fathers and decide to walk in their footsteps. However, in this case, Hezekiah saw the wickedness of his father and refused outright to imitate it, and God blessed him. He could not beg off having any responsibility for his situation by using the excuse of those to whom Jeremiah and Ezekiel later prophesied. Those rebels said in effect, "The 'old man' has sinned, and therefore there is no use fighting city hall" (Jer. 31:29; Ezek. 18:2). Even in those days, however, these two prophets had to protest vigorously that "the soul who sins is the one who will die" (Ezek. 18:4).

Hezekiah is a man who began to practice what he preached before he commended it to others. Without any immediate influences for good that we can detect from a human point of view, Hezekiah opened the closed doors of the temple and inaugurated services of worship and sacrifice once again. His words were bluntly to the point:

> Our fathers were unfaithful; they did evil in the
> eyes of the Lord our God and forsook him. They
> turned their faces away from the Lord's dwelling
> place and turned their backs on him. . . . Therefore,
> the anger of the Lord has fallen on Judah and Jerus-
> alem. . . . This is why our fathers have fallen by the
> sword. . . . Now I intend to make a covenant with
> the Lord, the God of Israel, so that his fierce anger
> will turn away from us. My sons, do not be negli-
> gent now.
>
> 2 Chron. 29:6–11a

But a revival does not only depend on the open doors of the house of worship or on the existence of divine services. More is needed than these outward acts of piety. There must be a turning around. That turning is twofold: it is a turning from sin, the first ninety-degree turn, and a turning toward God, the second ninety-degree turn, to make a complete about-face.

The informing theology of Hezekiah's revival can be found in that great parting word of Moses, uttered just before he passed on to glory in Deuteronomy 30. Three times (vv. 2, 8, 10) Moses urged Israel to return to the Lord if ever they were tempted to wander away from him.

The Hebrew word "to turn or repent" is pronounced *shuv*. And in every one of the 118 instances where the word occurs with a religious significance, God was trying to give his people a *shove* in the right direction. The earliest prophetic use of *shuv* is found in the revival that took place under Samuel (1 Sam. 7:3). All the prophets, both in word and deed, referred to it and to the activity of repentance as the quintessence of their ministries. Therefore, it is probably the one expression that summarizes the whole prophetic ministry. In Zechariah 1:4, Zechariah, the next to the last prophet, chides, "The earlier prophets proclaimed: This is what the LORD Almighty says: 'Turn [i.e., repent] from your evil ways and your evil practices.'" Likewise 2 Kings 17:13 agrees: "The LORD warned Israel and Judah through all his prophets and seers: 'Turn from your evil ways.'" Accordingly, the word appears ten times in Isaiah, twenty-eight times in Jeremiah, twenty times in Ezekiel, seven times in Hosea, five times in Amos, and three each in Zechariah and Malachi.

The word appears thirteen times in 2 Chronicles (6:24, 26, 37–38; 7:14, 19; 15:4; 30:6, 8–9; 36:13) but five times in 2 Chronicles 30:6–9. This is probably due to the influence of 2 Chronicles 7:14, and therefore its use in chapter 30 reflects a thematic declaration. Thus, the keynote for this passage is the doctrine of repentance.

In this short selection from the four chapters dealing with the marvelous years of this monarch's reign there are four alternatives. Each one is a call to turn from wickedness and sin, as that programmatic verse of 2 Chronicles 7:14 had specified. The four alternatives are:

1. Turn to God with an unqualified trust, or he will not turn to us (v. 6).
2. Turn to God with a wholehearted obedience, or he will make us despicable to all (v. 7).
3. Turn to God with glad service, or he will not turn his anger from us (v. 8).
4. Turn to God with unceasing prayer, or he will withdraw his presence and favor from us (v. 9).

And just as Hezekiah announced under the inspiration of the Holy Spirit some seven centuries before the first advent of Christ, it is time again to turn to the Lord. We, like those Judahites of old, must turn from our sin and turn to God if we wish to enjoy the fullness of the new life in Christ. Therefore, we are faced with the same four alternatives that Hezekiah set forth to the people of his day in the letter he sent by couriers throughout Israel and Judah (30:6).

Turn to God with an Unqualified Trust, or He Will Not Turn to Us (30:6)

Turning to Yahweh demands an unqualified and unconditional trust in him and an equivalent renunciation of every other coalition, secret love, or means of support. The totality of this commitment is the central issue. As Jeremiah evaluated the situation, he concluded, "We will come to you, for you are the LORD, our God. Surely, the idolatrous commotion on the hills and mountains is a deception; surely in the LORD our God is the salvation of Israel" (Jer. 3:22b–23). The fact that there is no one else to turn to beside the Lord is the point also made by Hosea: "Assyria shall not save us, we will not ride on horses, nor will we say anymore to the work of our hands, 'You are our gods.' For in You the [righteous] find mercy" (Hos. 14:3 NKJV).

The fact that we are being bidden to return to the Lord implies that we are in a backslidden state. At first all of us will attempt to deny this strong assertion or implication. Like the men and women of Malachi's day, we will retort, "Who, us? We are to return?" (Mal. 3:7). But backsliding is one of our key diseases. It consists of taking back our consecration to the Lord, leaving our first love for God, abstaining from the regular and wholehearted devotion to God in worship and prayer, and maintaining the outward forms of religion without the realities. Briefly stated, "The backslider in heart will be filled with his own ways" (Prov. 14:14 NKJV). Thus, like the church at Ephesus, many of us have left our first love (Rev. 2:4). If some of us believe that the message to repent is misdirected when it is aimed at the church, we need only to examine the opening of the book of Revelation a little closer. There the apostle John called at least four of the seven churches to which he wrote to repent (Rev. 2:5, 16, 21; 3:3).

As has been mentioned already, there are two aspects of repentance. Forty-eight of the 118 religious uses of the word (which incidentally is found altogether some 1,056 times) appear with the preposition *to* or *unto* and usually with the Lord as the object. That is the positive aspect of repentance. But it must be preceded by a negative aspect in which we "turn from" evil and sin. Consequently, *turn* or *repent* appears 40 times with the preposition *from*. Both actions are needed. In fact, "turning," or "conversion," as it is known from the Latin root word, is the whole process whereby we turn from sin and to the Lord. The first action, which involves godly sorrow for sin, is called *repentance*, and the second action, which reaches out to receive what God has given to us, is called *faith*. That is how we come to faith in Christ, and that is how we continue to live by faith as well.

The promise that God would hear his children when they come to their senses in their state of backsliding is as old as Moses. He advised: "When you are in distress and all these things have happened to you, then in later days you will return to the LORD your God and obey him. For the LORD your God is a merciful God; he will not abandon or destroy you or forget the covenant with your forefathers, which he confirmed to them by oath" (Deut. 4:30–31). And that is the same promise-plan in which we are still sharing.

The object of our affections must be none other than the God of Abraham, Isaac, and Jacob. The incomparably great God is the base of all true religion, and the promise-plan is the central plan by which the Lord has been operating the universe since the experience in Eden. But when our hearts are sold out to other coalitions, loves, and priorities, then we are entrapped by our own sin. As Hosea said, "Their deeds do not permit them to return to their God. A spirit of prostitution is in their heart; they do not acknowledge the LORD" (Hos. 5:4).

The alternative of 2 Chronicles 30:6 is this: "Return to the LORD . . . that he may return to you." How else can we experience once again the full power and presence of the living Lord? One of the saddest texts in Scripture is Hosea 5:15: "I will go back to my place until they admit their guilt. And they will seek my face; in their misery they will earnestly seek me." Consequently, instead of enjoying the Lord's countenance as requested in the Aaronic benediction of Numbers 6:24–26, we feel separated, powerless, ashamed, bored, and let down. But if we turn from our wicked ways, we will once again sense that God is gracious, making his face to shine on us and giving us peace.

The great hope of Scripture, and of our Lord, is that "perhaps [we] will listen and each [of us] will turn from [our] evil way. Then [God] will relent and not bring on [us] the disaster [he] was planning" (Jer. 26:3). We must make the first move if God is to normalize relations between us and we are to have his favor turned full force on us again. O let us turn for his name's sake and for our own good.

Turn to God with a Wholehearted Obedience, or He Will Make Us Despicable to All (30:7)

We are likewise urged to turn from our deadening obsession with failures of the past. Too frequently we assume that we are heirs of an irreversible situation, and thus we are excused for not taking any direct or personal action to turn around. But this defeatist's mentality only falls into its own trap. It insists on following the sins of the fathers or in saying that since the fathers have sinned, what can we do? But Hezekiah avoided that trap. Few have ever had as godless an example to follow, and yet few have excelled as well as he. He refused to settle for the performance level of the past or present generation. And we must come out from hiding behind our contemporaries.

Of course that generation was sinful, and of course we may be in as difficult straits morally and ethically as they were. But the judgment of God will not always tarry, and we cannot presume upon his patience forever. It is high time we acted. Each generation and every individual in it must answer to God. The alternative is the horrifying prospect of national disgrace. Unfaithfulness ultimately has a very high price, even for a secular culture. If we continue in it, we will then slide from the dizzying heights of being regarded as the most favored among the nations to the status of utter contempt, for that is what God threatened in this passage, if Hezekiah's people did not turn from their sin, just as we must.

There are those who feel that we began to experience some of this in the 1960s. It became popular then to take potshots at United States citizens abroad, calling them "ugly Americans," for instance. The vice president was pelted with rotten fruit, eggs, and verbal abuse. Even those nations that had received millions of dollars in aid from the United States of America, and those to whom we responded when they were surrounded by enemies, joined merrily in the new game of denouncing the "imperialistic" Americans. What is certain, however, is that if we continue to turn our backs on God, he will turn his back on us and make us despicable among the nations.

The word *unfaithfulness* and its associated terms appear frequently in Chronicles and always in passages that have no parallel in the books of Samuel or Kings. As it is used by the chronicler, unfaithfulness is evidenced by worship of pagan deities, lack of purity in the heart, and lack of obedience to the Word of the Lord. Hezekiah's father, Ahaz, we have seen, promoted wickedness (2 Chron. 28:19), and "in his time of trouble King Ahaz became even more unfaithful to the LORD" (28:22).

Such unfaithfulness regularly invited punishment, usually military defeat or exile and the like. Israel had been taught this harsh lesson as early as the reign of its first king, Saul. But modern nations must not think that the ground rules have changed or that God has eased up on his requirements for fellowship and favor. The truth of the matter is that we, if anything, are more vulnerable today than ever before, because we have so much more knowledge and have been exposed to so much more of the favor and graciousness of the plan and salvation of God. Where grace abounds, so does responsibility.

Turn to God with Glad Service, or He Will Not Turn His Anger from Us (30:8)

Three commands are given to those who are willing to turn: "submit to the LORD," "come to the sanctuary," and "serve the LORD your God" (v. 8). By observing these injunctions, we shall avoid being "stiff-necked," as the previous generations were.

To submit is literally "to give the hand to the Lord." This same expression found in verse 8 is used in 1 Chronicles 29:24, "All the [leaders] pledged their submission to [literally, "gave the hand under"] King Solomon." Thus the hand is given (i.e., raised) as a pledge of fidelity (cf. 2 Kings 10:15; Ezra 10:19; Ezek. 17:18). The condition of being stiff-necked, on the other hand, is a permanent condition of the unregenerate, who resist the Holy Spirit (Acts 7:51). How could believers remain permanently poised against their Lord? Let us therefore raise our hands in pledge of our loyalty and fidelity to God and serve in full submission under his lordship.

We must also come to his sanctuary, for it is impossible to turn to God without also turning to the place where we corporately meet him. God has consecrated the sanctuary concept in both Testaments, and we only defraud ourselves when we forsake the assembling of ourselves together, as is the habit of some (Heb. 10:25). We must mark it well that low churchmanship is low Christianity, and low Christianity is a mark of low fidelity. When the church has to beg, entice, and compete on a popularity scale with the multitude of recreational or leisure options for the attention and faithful attendance of her constituency, then we are in a heap of trouble. And the church is currently in that battle, even though church attendance is said to be at one of its highest levels in history. The question is this: where is our primary affection? Where are we the most comfortable: in the house of God? Or at one of our own pursuits?

The reason for this anomaly is to be found in the third command, "serve the LORD." The problem with much of our contemporary churchgoing is that most prefer a larger church where they can get lost in the once-a-week crowd. It also has the advantage that our chances of being asked to take on a regular assignment are minimal.

Most would not like to be tied down. But true service to God must replace the empty lip service of heartless worship offered only occasionally or even once a week. When other loyalties and interests usurp the place owed solely to God, then Baal worship exists just as surely as it did in Hezekiah's day. Some people's gods are their bellies; others, their jobs, families, books, friends, leisure time, vacation homes, television programs, sport teams, or ambitions (cf. Phil. 3:19).

If we persist in refusing to submit to the Lord, in taking lightly our need to come to the sanctuary, or on insisting on serving our own self-interests ahead of serving God, then his fierce anger will break out against us corporately. It is a fearful thing to fall into the hands of the living God. We can ill afford to have God angry at us.

Turn to God with Unceasing Prayer, or He Will Withdraw His Presence and Favor from Us (30:9)

In a clear echo of Solomon's dedicatory prayer in 1 Kings 8:50 (a verse that had been omitted in the parallel account of this same incident in 2 Chron. 6:39), Hezekiah urges all of Judah to pray for the forgiveness of God. Once again, now for the fourth and fifth times in this short passage of four verses, he uses the verb *to turn* as the burden of his message.

This role of an intercessor who acts as the mediator between God and one's community, church, family, institution, or nation is amply illustrated in such passages as Exodus 32–34, where Moses intercedes on behalf of his people, or even more dramatically, in Daniel 9:14–19. In the latter instance, Daniel used the first person plural, *us, we, our,* at least thirty-nine times in his short prayer, signifying that he identified with his people as he confessed the sin of the whole group. Too frequently we have learned to pray only for ourselves, our families, and those closest to us, much on the order of the individualistic American who believes in looking out for number one. But who will pray for the larger groups if we do not? And how can we disassociate ourselves from the sin of the group?

Is it not, as Daniel prayed, our sin and our confusion that have grieved God? We should learn to pray more in a corporate mode, as well as a personal mode, of confession of our own sin.

One important aspect of turning, then, is the return to prayer, not only for ourselves but also for the forgiveness of others, in an ever-widening circle. And the promise of God can be found in his very name, as he announced to Moses in Exodus 34:6–7: The LORD will be gracious and compassionate. We ought, therefore, to plead for his mercy.

Not only should our corporate praying be aimed at God's forgiveness, but we must also pray for restoration as well. Habakkuk prayed, "In wrath, remember mercy" (Hab. 3:2). So in addition to our returning to God, we must ask that he would return his favor to us. Only as God returns to his people, his church, and his ministers, evangelists, and missionaries will we see the true dynamic for which we were created. But this will not come unless we make a complete reversal of directions and pledge ourselves, our hearts, minds, emotions, wills, and energies totally to his service. We must "repent. . . . [and] produce fruit in keeping with repentance" (Matt. 3:2, 8). It must involve letting "everyone who names the name of Christ depart from iniquity" (2 Tim. 2:19 NKJV).

Even those Ephesian believers who were seated with Christ in the heavenlies needed to hear the shout "Awake, you who sleep, arise from the dead, and Christ will give you light" (Eph. 5:14 NKJV). What an astonishing evaluation of the spiritual condition of that church. But can any more be said about the condition of the contemporary evangelical church in the West?

If repentance is the condition of all of God's blessing, then we must do as Jeremiah urged, "Return, [you] backslid[er]. . . . Only acknowledge your iniquity that you have transgressed against the LORD" (Jer. 3:12–13 NKJV); and Joel, "Return to me with all your heart. . . . Rend your heart and not your garments" (Joel 2:12–13); indeed, the Lord himself through the prophet Malachi demanded, "Return to me and [then] I will return to you" (Mal. 3:7).

History will not be kind to those who demonstrate that they learn nothing from the past. The 1960s can and will be repeated if we do not return to God. I believe God has mercifully given us the years of tranquillity and peace in the 1970s, the 1980s, and on into the 1990s with an unprecedented rise in the stock market, low inflation rates, and almost full employment of the country—perhaps directly related to the obedience of a few in the body of Christ. Parachurch groups and some God-given evangelists have been responsible for picking up where the local church had all too frequently defaulted—especially in the areas of evangelism, and now in the declining rate of full-time workers both in the ministry and overseas. There was a mighty sweeping of literally thousands into the family of God in the 1970s and 1980s because the witness was faithfully and prayerfully given in the power of the Holy Spirit. But that avenue of ministry on campuses and in major crusades does not appear, for the moment, to be as fruitful as it once was in the United States and in Canada. The ball, as it were, is being bounced back again into the court of the local church. True, it was the local church, or at least many of its members, who cheerfully and extravagantly gave funds for the success of these parachurch and evangelistic ministries. But it would appear that the next decade will belong to the gathered church in accordance with God's original design.

Conclusion

It is high time that we turn from our sin. It is time that we turn toward the Lord and espouse his service, his sanctuary, and submit to his name as the highest cause we could own.

Do you not long for authenticity and for the full power of the Lord in your life and in the ministry of the church throughout the world? We have thrilled to every glimmer of success that the gospel has had so far. And yet, is it not time for "the hidden peoples of the world" (including those in the United States) to be found and exposed to the full light of the gospel? Is it not time that the truth-claims of the major world religions were exposed for what they are? Where is the God of Elijah? Is he not our God as well? And will not every religious leader need to appear before the tribunal of the living God in that final day? Where is the fear of God? Where is that boldness that comes from knowing the living God?

May a whole new wave of repentance and turning to God lead to a veritable downpour of his Spirit. And may this revived vitality lead to such widespread obedience that many will be swept into the kingdom of God in unprecedented numbers.

9   It Is Time to Humble Ourselves before the Lord

Revival under Josiah
2 Chronicles 34:1–33

If the Spirit of God did not periodically send revival, this world would be in extremely sad shape. It is alarming to see how frequently the lessons learned by one generation are totally forgotten in another. But thanks be to God, he will not let his fallen children roam about in spiritual fatigue forever. Based on this marvelous record of intervention, there is always the hope and expectation that God will step into the present order of things, no matter how bleak and adverse the circumstances seem to be. Thus, all believers should have a deep expectation and a firm belief in the possibility of revival for their day.

It is true, of course, that some of the Old Testament revivals emphasized the means that God was pleased to use to hasten revival. Care must be taken not to place too much emphasis on that word *means*, however, for it signifies little more than that God holds humanity responsible for such things as prayer and repentance. Means are not meritorious in and of themselves; revival is the work of God from beginning to end. Moreover, his Word also functions as one of the divinely designated means that God uses to drive individuals back to himself. But it is not fair to pit that Word against him in the heavy debates that tend to rage over the real source of revivals. All the work of reviving is the work of God, regardless of whether he is pleased to use means or not.

It is to be regretted that this debate has consumed so much of the energy of the believing community—energy that could have been invested in the work of revival as called for by Scripture. This is said neither to condone anti-intellectualism nor to imply that theology is unimportant—or even that there is not an important theological question involved in the debate. There is indeed a theology of revivals that has yet to be tackled, if it is to be hoped for by our generation. But there is no place for the kind of armchair theology of revivalism that refuses to put the discussion in the context of a working ecclesiology and an involved professorship, clergy, and laity.

Theology was meant to be the servant of the church, not her uninvolved lord and dictator. Therefore, a theology of revivals will not only tackle questions about theology proper (doctrine of God) and soteriology (doctrine of salvation), but it will also root itself in an exegesis of the major teaching passages on the great revivals of the Bible. It will thereby help to bridge the gap of aiding practical theology, missions, and evangelism in working out strategies for putting that theology of revivals into practice.

It is time that our academies (colleges, seminaries, and Bible schools) and churches said a firm "No!" to the kind of abstract theologizing that refuses to dirty its hands with either the hard issue of interpreting the "chair passages" (*sedes doctrinae*) on revival throughout the Bible or the practical concerns of the ministry of Christ's church around the world. It is this hiatus more than any other factor that has made so many in the church suspicious of the abiding contributions and worthwhileness of the research of the academy. As one who has spent most of his life in the academy and who loves it, I call on my colleagues to move immediately in true biblical humility to rectify this suspicion (whether it is altogether accurately launched against the academy and church, or not) by involving ourselves beyond the comfortable boundaries of the traditional range of our disciplines.

Now among the revivals that seem to lack human means that stress the individual's reception of the sovereign ministry of the Spirit of God, there is the revival under King Josiah. Prior to this revival there were no services at the sanctuary. Furthermore, the Bible itself had been lost (among the people of the book!), and hence little instruction could have been expected from that source. Was someone praying somewhere? Had someone memorized the Word of God, and was that person teaching it to children, among whom was to be found the young prince Josiah? It is impossible to decide for certain among these alternatives. But what is certain is that few of the traditional means are readily evident for inspection and promotion here!

There is only one ultimate source for all true revivals, and that is God himself. For just as we should not be frightened by the preparatory means that God has ordained to achieve revival—his Word, prayer, repentance, seeking his face, turning from our wicked ways, and humbling ourselves—so we should not be shy in affirming the sovereignty of God in this whole work either. Without that doctrine, we cannot even get started in our discussion of revival.

Revival Requires Humility

But Josiah's revival has another noteworthy feature. It seems that this revival was especially recorded by the inspiration of God to highlight the requirement of *humbling ourselves* as one of the conditions of revival. The Hebrew verb translated "to humble ourselves" occurs in the Old Testament some thirty-six times, with half of the instances being secular and the other half being sacred. The secular use spoke of subduing or being subdued by an enemy, whereas the sacred use referred to bringing oneself low before God. It is interesting that the books of Samuel and Kings, which often contain material parallel to that in Chronicles, have only three examples of this verb. Two are connected with the external act alone, such as ripping one's clothes in grief, wearing sackcloth, or weeping and fasting. The only one of the three that overlaps material from Chronicles, however, is 2 Kings 22:19 (cf. 2 Chron. 34:27). Chronicles, on the other hand, accounts for fourteen of the total eighteen occurrences of this word used in a religious or sacred sense.[1] Furthermore, as pointed out earlier, it is this expression that figures prominently in the paradigm verse of 2 Chronicles 7:14. Clearly, then, it represents a distinctive concept in the theological formulation of the chronicler.

This is not the first time the concept of humbling oneself has been featured with the turnabout of a king, however. It would appear that the sequence of revivals we have been looking at in 2 Chronicles was bracketed by the chronicler by means of an *inclusio* that featured this term in the early days of the history he reports, just after the division of the kingdom from King Solomon. Thus, Rehoboam, the first Judean king after Solomon, was warned by the prophet Shemaiah that God had abandoned him to Pharaoh Shishak because Rehoboam had abandoned God (2 Chron. 12:5). And instead of steeling themselves against the truthfulness of this warning, "the leaders of Judah and their king *humbled themselves* and said, 'The LORD is just'" (12:6). Accordingly, "when the LORD saw that they *humbled themselves*, the word . . . came to Shemaiah, saying 'They have humbled themselves; therefore I will not destroy them, but I will grant them some deliverance'" (12:7 NKJV). That is to say, even at this late date, when the invasion was already on, it still was not too late to turn in deep humility before the Lord God, who, in response, granted them a measure of relief. The Hebrew term above translated "some" means "for a little," or the like, and the rendering seems preferable to NIV's "give them deliverance." This view is sustained by the statement in 2 Chronicles 12:12, which repeats our key theological expression: "Because Rehoboam humbled himself, the LORD's anger turned from him, and he was not totally destroyed," adding, most significantly, "Indeed, there was some good in Judah."

What Is Humility?

The concept of humbling oneself is very close to the idea of turning to the Lord. Remember how the leaders and king confessed, "The Lord is just/righteous," when they humbled themselves? Not only did they make themselves low in the presence of God, but also they agreed that what he had done was "in the right" and richly deserved by them.

Again, biblical humility is a modesty that replaces vanity, pride, and arrogance. The person who has humbled himself or herself before God is one who is not wise in his or her own eyes, for so the wise writer of Proverbs counseled: "Do not be wise in your own eyes; fear the LORD and shun evil" (Prov. 3:7). The New Testament concurs: "Do not think of yourself more highly than you ought" (Rom. 12:3).

Third, the humble person recognizes that everything she or he may possess has been given by God. The question that Paul puts to us is, "What do you have that you did not receive?" (1 Cor. 4:7). That in itself ought to be enough to keep us from boasting and flaunting whatever few skills may be ours.

But, finally, something more is required in this area of revival than a mere attitudinal reorientation: we need to turn to God with a contrite heart if we are to understand the biblical injunction to humble ourselves before God. David learned this truth when he cried out, "A broken and a contrite heart, O God, thou wilt not despise" (Ps. 51:17 KJV). Only by means of such a brokenness can God begin to remake us into that new person in himself that we can and should be.

Biblical Examples of Humility

Examples of such humility are available in the biblical text. Moses is cited for his humility in Numbers 12:3, but this was no natural gift or lifetime experience. Nor was Moses what moderns often refer to as a wimp; he had naturally strong passions that needed to be conquered. In fact, his hatred of injustice and maltreatment of the oppressed was so strong that it led to several major sins early in his career, costing him an extension to his stay in God's school of hard knocks. But finally he surrendered his hot temper to God while retaining his God-given sense of fairness and justice for all.

A better example of biblical humility is Jesus. As the servant of the Lord described in Isaiah 53:4–10, Jesus willingly submitted himself to the plan and will of God. Philippians 2:6–8 explains that the glory that the preincarnate Son shared with the Father was willingly given up in order to do the Father's will. In imitation of the incarnate Son of God, Philippians 2:5 urges us to "let this mind be in you which was also in Christ Jesus" (NKJV). This is the same mind-set and frame of reference we must have in ourselves if we wish to see revival.

The apocryphal work Ben Sirach makes this astute observation: "The greater you are, the more you have to humble yourself in order to find favor with the Lord" (Sir. 3:18). This is not an inspired source, of course, but the observation is filled with truth. When we depend on our own wits or skills rather than on God's power, we become little gods to ourselves and to those around us. This is the opposite of the demand laid on us in Christ. It makes us resistant to the work of grace in our hearts, and there is no fertile field for the implantation of God's refreshing winds of revival.

"Humility and the fear of the LORD," says the writer of Proverbs, "bring wealth and honor and life" (Prov. 22:4). Why then do we go about seeking on our own what we cannot and will not obtain apart from humbling ourselves under the mighty hand of God?

What then does it mean to humble ourselves? Franz Delitzsch summarized the matter succinctly when he concluded, "To subordinate oneself to God, and to give honour to Him alone, one must have broken his self-will, and come to the knowledge of himself in his dependence, nothingness, and sin."[2]

The theology of humbling oneself before God had been set in Leviticus 26:40–41. There Moses said: "But if they will confess their sins and the sins of their fathers . . . then when their uncircumcised hearts are *humbled* and they pay for their sin, I will remember my covenant with Jacob." This passage provided the informing theology that lay behind 2 Chronicles 7:14. It must be carefully noted how significant a role both personal and collective, or corporate, confession has as a preparation to humbling ourselves under God. It is not enough for each of us to confess our own personal sin; each of us must also confess the sin of the groups to which we belong. This kind of confession is most scarce today, but it is most vital. Daniel prays this way in his famous prayer in Daniel 9, and so should we, because of our corporate identities and because of the command of the Lord that this must take place.

In accordance with the chronicler's teaching, it is high time that we humbled ourselves before the Lord. And if 2 Chronicles 12:6–7, and 12 showed how this humbling first took place in the life of Rehoboam at the beginning of the new kingdom of Judah, then 2 Chronicles 32:26; 33:12, 19, 23; 34:27; and 36:12 show the results of such humbling or of its delay and outright omission as the kingdom of Judah drew to a close. As noted above, the references form a type of *inclusio*, or bracketing, of the revivals of this book.

From among the final kings of Judah, God raised up young King Josiah to demonstrate the effectiveness of humbling ourselves under God. Accordingly, 2 Chronicles 34 calls on us to make three abasements, which may be stated as follows:

1. We must humble ourselves before our God (vv. 1–13).
2. We must humble ourselves before God's Word (vv. 14–28).
3. We must humble ourselves before God's people (vv. 29–33).

May the Lord grant to each of his own the ability to act with all speed and deliberateness in this important preparatory work of humility. And may the example of this young king's heart so stir us that we, too, would long for the same work of God in our lives.

We Must Humble Ourselves before Our God (34:1–13)

Josiah's reign over Judah began in 640 B.C. He was a mere eight years of age. At sixteen, "he began to seek the God of his father

David" (2 Chron. 34:3). As far as the record goes, Josiah had no examples or guides to follow. A very early influence, prior to his coming to the throne, may have been the prophetess Huldah (34:26–28). But he surely did not have any help from his grandfather Manasseh, who reigned for fifty-five years and led a most disgusting life of wickedness and evil, except for a brief time at the end of his life. Not only did that king set up pagan high places for the worship of strange gods; he also copied "the abominations of the heathen" (2 Chron. 33:2 KJV). Following this weakening of the people, the kingdom of Judah was overrun by the Assyrians, who carried Manasseh off into captivity. Only then did he finally humble himself under God's mighty hand. But God heard his confession and brought him back to Jerusalem after he "knew that the LORD is God" (33:13). A weak reformation followed, but not enough to overthrow and unravel more than fifty years of wickedness. Josiah was approximately six years old at the time.

Next, Manasseh's son, Amon, came to the throne, but he followed the wicked example of his father. The very name of Amon came from one of the gods of Egypt, Amon-Re, the sun god! Thus, after two years of ruling, his palace servants assassinated him. The people in turn ordered that those involved in this plot be put to death, for they were weary of all of the political corruption and intrigue. But no one seemed yet able to realize that their problems were moral and spiritual and had to do with their backslidden condition.

Then the eight-year-old Josiah inherited the throne. He took as his model King David: "[he] walked in the ways of his father David" (34:2). The expression "to walk in the ways" signified a lifestyle—in this case a path of practical holiness and righteousness. Solomon had urged, "Do not swerve to the right or the left; keep your foot from evil" (Prov. 4:27). Josiah took such a straight path; further, his thoughts, actions, and inclinations did not verge into left-wing or right-wing alliances.

It was early in his life that he sought the favor of God; he began in his sixteenth year (34:3). It must be observed that a tender heart is the only kind that can seek God and find him, for hearts filled with sinfulness and indifference will remain impervious to any and all the works of God. The way of the transgressor is hard. But if revival is to come, God looks first of all for the tender, humble heart. This is the condition we must seek above all else if our hearts are to be as tender and open to the Lord as was Josiah's.

Josiah had many obstacles to overcome: his grandfather's long reign of wickedness, the sin and brutal murder of his father, the disrepair and disgrace of a dilapidated house of worship, the total loss of any awareness of the Book of the Law of God, and much else. But he found the Lord in spite of all of them.

We need a revival just as desperately as he did. For though it had been almost ninety years since God had last poured out his Spirit on that people, it has been more than ninety years since God has once again poured out his Spirit on our contemporaries. (The last worldwide revival was in 1905.) What obstacles do we have that Josiah did not? That is answered for us by Ernest Baker:

> But though Josiah had [these obstacles] as a hindrance, there was one great obstacle which he did not have to overcome. He was not confirmed to sin. There is nothing so hardening to the heart, and so blinding to the eyes and so searing to the conscience as sin. "Those who seek me early shall find Me." Men who seek late in life, if they truly seek, will find, but it will not be such easy work for them as it is for the young.[3]

Herein lies the greatest difficulty to seeking God: our sin. No wonder we are urged to seek his face early. This provides no excuse for failing to take up the search in later years when youth has passed us by. The time for that is always appropriate. But it will be more difficult then, for we must humble ourselves and become as open and transparent as children if we wish to enter into the joys of the outpouring of the Holy Spirit.

When Josiah turned twenty, he began a reform that purged the land (34:3b). Every competitor of the real God was liquidated, including all altars to other gods, groves where false worship was offered, all images and molten idols. In like manner we are warned in the New Testament, "Dear children, keep yourselves from idols" (1 John 5:21), and, "My dear friends, flee from idolatry" (1 Cor. 10:14), and finally, "Put to death . . . evil desires and greed, which is idolatry" (Col. 3:5).

Not only did Josiah destroy these pagan installations; he scattered the dust of the smashed idols over the graves of the idolaters. This is significant, for even in death the guilt and horror of their religious desecrations did not leave them. Their works, evil as they were, followed them beyond the grave.

Josiah also burned the dead bones of the false priests on their altars (v. 5). By means of this action Josiah apparently unwittingly fulfilled the prophecy of the man of God from Judah who had pronounced judgment against wicked Jeroboam for his idolatrous altar: "O altar, altar! This is what the LORD says: 'A son named Josiah will be born to the house of David. On you he will sacrifice the priests of the high places who now make offerings here, and human bones will be burned on you'" (1 Kings 13:2). That was shortly after 931 B.C. Its fulfillment occurred some three hundred years later in 628 B.C. Yet in this magnificent prophecy are included: (1) the name of the king, (2) his act of desecrating the bones of these desecrators, and (3) the rebuke for this golden calf installation in the northern kingdom by a Davidic king.

In addition to seeking the Lord's favor in his youth, Josiah also did God's will in his youth (vv. 8–13). When Josiah was twenty-six, he began to repair the temple. (The last comprehensive repair of God's house had been carried out by King Joash some 250 years before.) But even more significant, he moved to cleanse and to purify the land. This need for moral and spiritual cleanness was integral for the work of revival that was to come. The Old Testament doctrine of cleanness must not be confused with general cleanliness or with personal hygiene or the like. It signified the state of being ready or fit for the worship of or meeting with God. Haughty, proud, and arrogant men and women cannot worship, be blessed, or grow spiritually. They must humble themselves. The worship of God is one of the best contexts in which humbling of ourselves can take place.

We must ask ourselves, do we have tender hearts? Are we deeply moved by the moral and religious indifference of the populace about us? "Those that seek me early shall find me" (Prov. 8:17 KJV), says the Lord. That is, our quest for God and for doing his will must become an all-consuming passion.

We Must Humble Ourselves before God's Word (34:14–28)

It was during the repair of the temple that a most unusual discovery was reported: the Book of the Law. Can you imagine? The very people to whom God had graciously given his Word were the ones who had so neglected it that it was completely forgotten, lost from sight and memory. This has to be one of the crowning insults ever done by any people to the Lord. But we, too, "are in error because [we] do not know the Scriptures" (Matt. 22:29). Before we begin throwing stones, we ought to remember: we evangelicals argue long and loud for the doctrine of the inerrancy of the Bible, but in our practice we shout something else.

"I have found the Book of the Law in the temple of the LORD," exclaimed Hilkiah (34:15). And when it was brought to the king and read in his presence, he ripped open his robes in grief (vv. 18–19). More than anything else, this gesture substantiates the self-authenticating power of the Word of God. (Verse 27 tells us that the king also wept at its reading.)

If this Book of the Law was the book of Deuteronomy, as some contend, it could have been read in two or three hours. But if it contained the first five books of Moses, as is more likely, it probably consumed more like ten to twelve hours of the king's time. Imagine a modern audience, even an evangelical one, standing (or even sitting) and listening for twelve hours of Bible reading. But so great was the king's hunger for the Word of God and so frightening were the implications of the wrath of God, which almost certainly was dangling over the nation, that every matter of state was put off in deference to this most pressing situation.

There is more here. There is the matter of the indestructibility of the Word of God. Autrey remarked,

> Despite the fact that God's people were fickle, that the priests and rulers were often godless, and that many of the perils threatened the destruction of the written Word of God, it did not perish. It survived the indifference of its friends, the ravages of time, and the wilful plans of Satan. . . . One would almost be afraid for the Book if he should forget the perils through which the Word has come through the centuries. The Bible will survive; of this we have no doubt. But will the generation that loses knowledge of it? This is our concern.[4]

There is also the power of the Word of God, for the entrance of God's Word gives light. Thus, in spite of the previous reforms that Josiah had already introduced, when the entrance of God's Word came, he gained a greater understanding of what God had already begun to do. The proclamation, reading, and study of God's Word and meditation on it are absolutely essential in the lives of believers.

The basis of all true preaching and teaching of the Word of God is the fact that it has its source in the living Lord. Accordingly, the word of the prophets was "This is what the LORD, the God of Israel, says" (vv. 23–24, 26). Too many in our day pronounce lying words in the name of the Lord that he has not spoken (cf. Jer. 29:23; Ezek. 13:7). There can be nothing more demoralizing than to speak or hear a message that is uncertain or whose authority is doubtful. That is the number one plague of much liberal preaching today. But if we evangelicals teach with the idea that this message has come from God but carelessly or openly refuse to obey it, are we any better off?

What Josiah focused on were the judgments of God. Indeed, the curses of God are just as true as are his blessings. We are taught to say "amen" to both. And if we know by experience that one (his blessing) is true, then we must also believe that the other (his judgment) is true as well.

When the king ordered, "Go and inquire of the LORD for me . . . about what is written in this book" (v. 21), Hilkiah brought Huldah the prophetess to him. Jeremiah had been ministering in Judah for five years, but God used a woman at this time! Three times she assured the king that her authority was to be found only in the Lord himself. The content of her message can be found in six expressions that parallel the contents of Deuteronomy 29. The phrases spoke of an impending disaster if the people did not confess their sin and humble themselves:

v. 24 "all the curses written"	Deut. 29:20–21, 27
v. 25 "because they have forsaken me"	Deut. 29:25
v. 25 "burned incense to other gods"	Deut. 29:26
v. 25 "provoked me to anger"	Deut. 29:20, 23, 28
v. 25 "[wrath] will be poured out"	Deut. 29:23, 28
v. 25 "and will not be quenched"	Deut. 29:20

How massive is the heavy cloud of judgment that hangs over our heads if we do not humble ourselves and repent. But for the person whose heart is responsive to this word of judgment, there is great hope.

How important it is to respond to God's Word and to offer to him a tender heart and receptive spirit. It is not sufficient to know that the Bible is God's Word or to argue for its inerrancy; we must, with a spirit of contriteness and humility, act on the basis of what it says. When we hear the Word proclaimed and applied to our times and people, surely we can sense that something is drastically wrong. Indeed, rather than result in indifference or unconcern, the Word of God will always "overtake" and arrest the humble and tenderhearted person, leading him or her on to obedience. O for more willing, responsive, and grateful hearts, minds, and feet!

God gives grace to the humble, and in due time he will once again exalt them (1 Pet. 5:5–6). Therefore, "Blessed are you who weep now, for you will laugh" (Luke 6:21). May we hear and respond to God's Word as never before, for it is time to humble ourselves under the Word of God.

We Must Humble Ourselves before God's People (34:29–33)

Having abased ourselves before God and his Word, we must ask with our text, what about our abasement of ourselves before God's people? It is interesting that in this section the word *all* appears no less than eleven times in the original text. Every class of people whether great or small had to hear the words of the promise of God, for the Word was read in the hearing of all the people.

The king reconsecrated himself in his sacrifice to follow and to do with all his heart and soul all that God had spoken (v. 31). Leadership was given, therefore, to the people, who now joyously shared the Word as well.

The preaching of the Word produced three different results in the people. Some, like the king (v. 31), responded positively and decided to do all that was written in the law of God. Others took the pledge to act in accordance with that Word (v. 32) but without wholeheartedness, enthusiasm, or even any repentant remorse. What had been said of the king was not said of this group, for they did not agree to follow the Lord with all their heart and soul. They merely pledged, or literally, were "caused to stand" (i.e., as an act of pledging).

The third group also responded positively, and they joined in removing the detestable idols from all their territories. However, they served God only for the length of time that strong leaders were present (v. 33 NKJV). It is noted that "as long as [Josiah] lived they did not fail to follow the LORD, the God of their fathers." How odd that they should so quickly abandon the God of their fathers and, for these Josiah years, at least, their God as well.

But for the moment we may rejoice that the revival had touched all. Standing beside "his pillar," the king had promised in the presence of God to renew God's covenant and to follow him whether anyone else did or not (v. 31). In that sense Josiah humbled himself not only in the presence of the Word of God and the God of the Word, but also before a watching nation. He did everything in his power to lead them back to the full experience of the blessing and joy of the Lord.

The brilliant career of this godly monarch was suddenly halted in one of the strangest episodes in the history of revelation. When he was thirty-nine years of age, he went out to prevent Pharaoh Necho from going up to Carchemish on the Euphrates. Necho warned him that he should stay out of this matter, for he had no military intentions toward Judah or Israel. Furthermore, God himself had commanded Necho to go up to this battle. But Josiah refused to listen, commented the writer of Chronicles under the inspiration of the Holy Spirit, "to what Necho had said at God's command" (2 Chron. 35:22). This is one of those rare moments in Scripture when God also speaks through pagan monarchs as he did to Nebuchadnezzar in Daniel 4. Thus, when Josiah, appearing in a disguise, interfered with the will of God at the Megiddo pass, he was mortally wounded by the archers, and a brilliant, godly career came to an end.

Josiah died in 609 B.C., just before the awful days that began when Daniel and his friends were taken into Babylonian captivity in 606, followed by Ezekiel's being taken into captivity in 598 B.C. The end came when the Babylonians returned for a third time in 586 B.C. and destroyed everything, including Jerusalem and the temple. Not more than a dozen years earlier (621 B.C.), however, God had promised during the repair of the temple and the finding of the Book of the Law that because Josiah had humbled himself before God and because he had humbled himself before God's Word (v. 27), "I will gather you to your fathers, and you will be buried in peace. Your eyes will not see all the disaster I am going to bring on this place and on those who live here" (v. 28). And so it happened just as God promised, for Josiah died prior to those dreadful days, even though the circumstances under which he died were unusual.

If we search for a reason for Israel's final disaster, we may turn to 2 Kings 23:26. The writer, after detailing the marvelous finding of the Book of the Law and the revival under Josiah, remarks that "nevertheless, the LORD did not turn away from the heat of his fierce anger, which burned against Judah because of all that Manasseh had done to provoke him to anger." The destiny of Jerusalem and Judah was fixed, for the cup of their iniquity had filled so full that not even Josiah's reform could ultimately stay the ominous judgment that was sure to come. The most that he could have done was to offer a brief respite from it.

Conclusion

What then is our response? Are we moved at all when we view our sins against the crystal clear character of God? If so, then why will we not abase ourselves in the presence of this wonderful Lord? Again, are we still able to be taught by God's Word, and do we find it to be the source of our every authoritative word from heaven? If so, then why do we not obey its marvelous commands? It is time to humble ourselves in the presence of God, God's Word, and God's people, whom we wish to serve and to stimulate to righteousness, and before whom we live. We have too much pride, arrogance, and haughtiness; we need to humble ourselves under the mighty hand of God.

God searches for those who are "poor in spirit," those who have gone into spiritual bankruptcy so that they might be revived from above and experience times of refreshing from the Lord.

May he grant us the strength of our convictions and mourning for our sin and the sin of our nation. May we learn at the end of such humility of soul and body that "the LORD [indeed] is righteous" (Ps. 145:17).

10   It Is Time to Renew the Work of the Lord

Revival under Zerubbabel
Haggai 1; Zechariah 1:1–6

*F*ollowing the revival under Josiah, God's people had drifted back into degradation and sin, developing the seeds of wickedness planted during the administration of Manasseh. Thus it became necessary for them to learn through adversity what they had refused to learn by responding to the Word of God. Accordingly, Judah spent seventy years in captivity in Babylon, stripped of the comforts of Jerusalem. Mercifully God would once more intervene by putting it into the heart of the pagan king Cyrus to release the people if they so wished and to aid them in reestablishing their place of worship back in Jerusalem. This had been foretold by Isaiah (Isa. 44:28), who predicted not only Cyrus's two great merciful acts (i.e., that he would allow the people to return from captivity, but that he would also provide the materials and give permission for them to rebuild their temple), but also he predicted the exact name of this future Medo-Persian monarch as well.

And so it was that in 538 B.C. the decree was signed and a small band of less than fifty thousand persons returned to Jerusalem after seventy years of captivity. Some estimate that this represented less than one out of every six Jews in Babylon. Even more discouraging, this tiny group returned with very little evidence of a genuine spiritual work in their hearts. Ernest Baker places the first of four postexilic revivals at this point of the return. But frankly, the opening three chapters of Ezra do not indicate any great stirring, either of confession or of the Spirit of God. It is true that they immediately began construction on the temple by laying its foundations in the second month after their arrival, but discouragement quickly set in, and the work ground to a halt. During the next sixteen years, not an ounce of energy was expended on this project, and the people were content to let the matter drop. That hardly seems like the result of a revival. Instead, it is an argument that revival was desperately needed. Finally, 101 years after the last revival under Josiah (104 years had elapsed between the preceding revival under Hezekiah up to the time of Josiah), Haggai and Zechariah both came preaching the Word of the Lord in 520 B.C.

Ezra 5–6 describes the condition of things at that time. Zerubbabel, the grandson of the Judean king Jehoiachin, who had been taken into captivity in 598 (2 Kings 24:15), became "governor" and led the first return in 537/6 B.C. His designation as governor was a reminder of the Babylonian appointment. Even his name was a loan word from Akkadian/Babylonian into Hebrew. That is, Zerubbabel was also known as Sheshbazzar (Ezra 1:8; 5:14), for the same work said to be done by Zerubbabel in Ezra 3:8 is said to have been done by Sheshbazzar in Ezra 5:16.

Zerubbabel belonged to the continuing line of David. The demonstration of this is somewhat involved and not crystal clear at all points, but the main facts are these: Jehoiachin had five sons, who are known to us mainly from the written tablets found in the famous Ishtar gate complex in Babylon. It would appear that they were made eunuchs, and thus the royal line of David was threatened

(Isa. 39:7). Consequently, Jehoiachin adopted the seven sons of Neri, a descendant of David through Nathan, one of Solomon's brothers (1 Chron. 3:5). Thus Solomon's line ceased at this point, failing with Jehoiachin as Jeremiah had predicted: "Record this man as if childless, a man who will not prosper in his lifetime, for none of his offspring will . . . sit on the throne of David" (Jer. 22:30). But Neri's oldest son, Shealtiel, died childless, and so his brother Pedaiah performed the rite of levirate marriage (Deut. 25:5–10); from his loins came the new Davidite, Zerubbabel. Hence Zerubbabel was the legal son of Shealtiel, and thus in David's line, but he was the actual son of Pedaiah and thus also of David.

Suddenly in the midst of Zerubbabel's governorship (520 B.C.), God sent two prophets, Haggai and Zechariah, to rekindle the vision and hearts of the people. It was the sixth month. The season for summer fruits had just ended, and the time of harvest was over. We can almost hear the mournful sigh of Jeremiah, "The summer has ended, and we are not saved" (Jer. 8:20). Surely some must have remembered the famous pun on the Hebrew word for "summer," which also sounds like the Hebrew word for "end," used by the prophet Amos (Amos 8:2; a basket of "summer" fruit was a signal that the "end" had come in more ways than one!). Would this truly be the end for the people? What did God have in mind by sending these prophets at this stage in the year and after sixteen years of no temple, no worship, and no concern for spiritual things? There was enough solemn precedent from the past to alert any who had the least amount of spiritual sensitivity left in their bones.

The message of Haggai, which came first in this new stirring of concern about the fact that the temple project had now been stalled for some sixteen years, as recorded in Haggai chapter 1, emphasized four ways in which the work of God could be renewed in their day if the people would but respond:

1. We must refuse to blame the providence of God (vv. 1–2).
2. We must set priorities for the work of God (vv. 3–6).
3. We must get involved in the work of God (vv. 7–12).

4. We must receive God's enablement to do the work of God (vv. 13–15).

The prophet Habakkuk had once prayed, "O Lord revive Your work in the midst of the years!" (Hab. 3:2 NKJV). The Lord was about to do just that by means of his two messengers. Therefore, Haggai challenged God's people to face up to the weakness of their excuses.

We Must Refuse to Blame the Providence of God (1:1–2)

On August 29, 520 B.C., according to the nomenclature of our calendar, the Lord sent Haggai to challenge the people of God. This was the first time in this postexilic era that the voice of God had been heard through a prophet. It is significant that his arrival is not dated in terms of either the Davidic succession or of the promise that God had previously made to Israel. Rather it was reckoned as occurring "in the second year of King Darius," a ruler of the Gentiles. The times of the Gentiles had arrived.

The message itself was simple and direct. It was what the Lord of Hosts had observed: "This people says, 'The time has not come . . . that the LORD'S house should be built'" (v. 2 NKJV).

The distance that had come to exist between God and his people is suggested by one of the rare uses in the Old Testament of the expression "this people" to describe them. Surely it was a mark of the divine displeasure. Previously, even under the most difficult of circumstances, the Lord had referred to Judah and Israel as "my people." But they had definitely strained their relationship with him, and the demonstrative pronoun indicated that there was a gap of major proportions existing between God and this people as a result of their sin.

Most telling was the lament that the "time" had not yet come to take up the work of rebuilding the temple. Yet the people had found time and materials to effect the rebuilding of their own homes. This lament was only an excuse for delaying the job now for sixteen years. Think of it: one whole generation had been raised without any provision made for the corporate worship of the living God.

Furthermore, when the people used the word *time*, they were saying in effect, "If God had wanted us to rebuild the temple, he should have seen to it that we were better off than we are at the present." That is, the word *time* was only a stand-in word for God, and the people were hiding their own delinquencies behind it. But that was the problem. The reason they gave was a mere pretext for their own laziness and selfish reinvestment of time and interests. Yes, they were going to get around to rebuilding the temple, but not now. There were other things that had to happen first. For example, relations with the Persians had not yet been normalized. Furthermore, they had not yet recovered sufficiently from the long years of the exile. They likewise probably reasoned that they were in a period of economic depression or inflation, and, finally, that these things just took time.

But to the one who wants to do what is right, the time is always present and available. It is we who are ingenious when it comes to inventing excuses or hiding behind our failures to respond to the Word of God. Therefore, we must recognize in the general national situation the rebuke of God. We must refuse to concentrate on the symptoms of the current distresses and go rather to their direct spiritual causes. As Matthew Henry advised, "It is bad enough to neglect our duty, but it is worse to vouch providence [i.e., God] for the patronizing of our neglect."[1] No, the time was more than ripe for doing the work of God, even as it is now for us as well. We, too, must stop making excuses, for how will the reviving work of God ever begin when our hearts exhibit such desperate need of revitalizing?

But there is a second way in which we can renew the work of God in our times and prepare for revival.

We Must Set Priorities for the Work of God (1:3-6)

Again the word of the Lord came to this prophet, and he asked, "Is it time for you to live in your paneled homes?" The point was not that nice homes are a mark of wickedness or that believers would be better served by rejecting all material things and living instead an ascetic life that denies everything material. The Bible clearly teaches a full theology of culture and the proper use of things in all their beauty and mundaneness. But there is the issue of priorities. We must put God's work ahead of our work.

In this case the choice and call for evidencing one's priorities had to do with building the temple. The religious condition of the people's hearts could be seen by their attitude toward this need for a temple. Actually, it could have come in the form of any task for the Savior; this was only the most pressing need of the moment. In fact, the flagrant and patent evidence that Yahweh was not their Lord was the dilapidated state of the temple, which remained as it had for the past sixteen years and for the almost seventy years of their captivity. It was a disgrace and an object of scorn for all who passed by its burned-out ruins. The pagans mocked and hissed with glee over the remains of the place formerly inhabited by the so-called Lord of the universe, indeed, his dwelling place!

To neglect God's house was tantamount to treason against him, for no matter what the verbal level of affirmation of trust in God, the plain fact was that no one cared in the least for what he said. Ultimately this attitude was to invite God's rejection of all their labors.

If times were hard, and there was no denying that they were, why had Judah not cried out to God for help to do this work of building? And furthermore, if they were really so poor, how had they been able to spend so much time and effort on themselves? That was the real point in bringing up their paneled or wainscoted homes. (We are not entirely certain what the adjective means. The Septuagint rendered it "vault-roofed," the Vulgate "panel-ceiled," and the Chaldee "covered with cedar boards." Note Jeremiah 22:14, where paneled homes of cedar were painted with vermilion.)

Meanwhile, the temple of God remained "a ruin" (v. 4). The Hebrew word is similar to the alternative word for Mount "Sinai," which we also know as Mount Horeb. *Horeb* means a "deserted, dry place, or ruin." Therefore, the prophet was making a pointed play on these words in verses 9 and 11 when he quoted God as saying, "Because my house is a 'ruin,' therefore I have called for a 'ruin,' or drought, on your crops." The subject deserved earnest reflection (v. 5) similar to that mentioned in Lamentations 3:40: "Let us examine our ways and test them, and let us return to the LORD." In short, the people were called to assay whether anything was to be gained by trying to outreach God.

It was time for God's people to evaluate where this reversal of priorities had taken them. Were they sowing more and harvesting less? Were they eating more and enjoying it less? Were they drinking more and enjoying it less? Were they earning more and accumulating less? The answer was yes to all four of these questions. But why? In the Hebrew text, the string of verbs in verse 6 is in what is called the infinitive absolute construction. This construction adds force to the timeless aspect of the principle involved: it is universal for all times, seasons, and countries. Simply put, the principle is that no one cheats God without cheating himself at the same time. But the reverse truth is just as clear, "Seek first the kingdom of God and His righteousness, and all these things shall be added to you" (Matt. 6:33 NKJV).

There is a definite connection between the moral and spiritual condition of a people and their material and economic condition. This connection is not only found here in verses 3–6 but throughout the Old Testament. It is unfortunate that many moderns who are familiar with many of the secondary explanations for natural and economic events feel that these are sufficient. But there is also a moral cause for the conditions of drought and plenty. This connection goes all the way back to the fall in Eden, where the ground was cursed for the sake of man. Likewise the world was flooded because of humanity's wickedness, and country after country has been expelled from its land for lack of righteousness and justice. Only when Christ returns will the created order be restored to that for which it groans and travails (Rom. 8:19–22).

It was time for them to renew God's work and for a whole new order of priorities to be established if revival was ever to come. The same is true of us today.

We Must Get Involved in the Work of God (1:7–12)

Verse 7, which again stresses the importance of these matters, is reminiscent of verse 5. The title "LORD of hosts" (NKJV) is never used of deity in the Pentateuch, Joshua, or Judges. Its first appearance is in 1 Samuel 1:3. But it is the favorite expression of the prophets from that time on. Of its 300 occurrences in the Old Testament, 247 of them are in the prophets, and when the size of the books is taken into account, the greater proportion of them appear in the postexilic period. Haggai's little book has 14 examples, Zechariah has 53, and Malachi has 24 for a total of 91 of the prophets' 247 examples. The meaning of "LORD of hosts" (i.e., Master of the heavenly and earthly armies) is that he is the absolute sovereign with invincible might, holding both terrestrial armies (1 Sam. 17:45) and celestial armies of angels (Ps. 24:7–10) at his beck and call.

The purpose of obedience is set forth in verse 8: "so that I may take pleasure in [that work]." Thus it is not that God is pleased or impressed with buildings per se, but insofar as that building represents the attempt to express praise and worship to God, to that degree it brings him pleasure and magnifies his name. Therein lies the true motivation for all acts of service to the living God.

It is a matter of interest that it was necessary for the people of that day to go up to the mountains to cut timber and to bring it down to build the temple. Sixteen years earlier they had been given lumber for this purpose. What had happened to it in the meantime? Had it just rotted in piles when the original project had been abandoned? Or had the people stolen the timber that should have been used for the house of God and used it instead to construct their own homes? Whatever the explanation, they had to replace it if the project was to go on.

In addition to the doxological purpose of our obedience, this section also deals with the costs of our disobedience. When God's work had to go begging for lack of interest, punishment fell, affecting the very ground itself. Once again, Scripture repeatedly underlined the intimate connection between man's performance and nature's productivity. The costs were dramatic. There were shortages in materials, goods, food, and shortages in wages. Furthermore, it was God who called for this drought on the land, according to verse 11. If we mistake this connection in our current assessment of society and its problems, we will miss also in rectifying the situation to any significant degree.

Verse 12 is one of those rare verses in the Bible that indicates that the preaching of God's Word had an immediate and wonderful effect. It celebrated the beauty of obedience, because all the people along with the leadership obeyed the voice of the Lord. The "fear" of the Lord mentioned here is nothing less than an attitude of wholehearted trust and glad submission to the living Lord. It meant turning from evil ("To fear the LORD is to hate evil," Prov. 8:13; cf. Prov. 9:10) and seizing hold of the Lord by faith (Ps. 2:11). Only by meeting these conditions can the work of God break out in our own hearts and in a needy world.

The people believed because God had sent his prophet. May we never forget that the Word of God, joined by the convincing and convicting power of the Holy Spirit, always will be the dynamite of God (1 Thess. 1:5).

We Must Receive God's Enablement to Do the Work of God (1:13–15)

Many will complain in exasperation, "But I am so weary and so unable to do anything more than I am presently doing. How can I receive this challenge to renew the work of God? Already I believe much better than I practice. How will one more challenge help me? Is there no word of comfort in the gospel, other than this repeated emphasis on the need to come clean in confession to God and to have his work renewed in my heart?"

The good news from this OT text is that the enabling power of the Lord was immediately made available to those who responded to the call. The most comforting word for these hurting sinners was "'I am with you,' declares the LORD" (v. 13). Nothing strikes more hope and encouragement into the hearts of God's people than this phrase: "I am with you." It is too bad that we have ruined the statement by our trite use of the preposition *with*. We say to others, "Yes, I am with you," and "I am behind you," but we never say how *far* behind we will be, nor do we make it immediately clear that often we are with them only in a *general* way. But when the Lord uses the word, he means that he is personally, dramatically, and powerfully standing alongside us, no matter what the assignment. There is the real difference. Thus we will never be left to do a solo performance, for there will be two present (e.g., there will be two who teach the class, not just one; there will be two who play the piano or organ, not just one; there will be two who witness, not just one). That is what the Lord means when he says, "I am with you." That is enough to revolutionize how most of us think of Christian service or the prospect of success in any Bible study, youth group, evangelistic mission, or overseas task that confronts the toughest opposition imaginable.

More than this, the Lord also promised to stir up the spirit of the leadership and the spirit of the people so that they together would have a mind to work. And so it was on September 21, 520 B.C.—the people came together to get on with a job that had been sinfully neglected since 536 B.C. How beautiful is the work of God on our hearts when it is received with the kind of joy manifested here!

As if to reinforce this message or to extend it deeper into the population of the community, God sent the prophet Zechariah in November of 520 B.C (Zech. 1:1–6). He gave "one of the strongest and most intensely spiritual calls to repentance to be found in the OT."[2] The prophet pointed out that God was extremely angry with the wicked. Nothing can make this a pretty doctrine. Of course God is a God of love, but we must not conceal the fact that he is also the God of wrath. It is a sure sign of a sickly piety when men and women are willing to hear nothing but the love of God. Verse 2 is very emphatic on this point, for it has a triple emphasis on anger—and the people knew this was so, for after all, what was the exile all about?

However, all was not lost. Repentance was and is the condition for all of God's blessings (v. 3), for when individuals and significant numbers of people in a nation turn to God, he will turn to them. "'Return to Me,' says the LORD of hosts, 'and I will return to you'" (v. 3 NKJV).

Indeed, we are responsible for the lessons taught to us by history. Four times the text refers to the fathers (vv. 2, 4, 5, 6). But even they lived and passed on into eternity, so the point was that no one lives forever on this side of eternity. This question accented the brevity of such spiritual opportunities as Zechariah was offering, and the dangerous situation that they brought (v. 5). Both the ministry of the prophets, whom many thought they would never be rid of and the fathers' longevity were all too short and brief.

But, wonder of wonders, in spite of all this change and transience, the permanence of the Word of God and the invincibility of God's purposes for the ages remain (v. 6). Thus, what the Lord had both threatened and promised, he had done.

Conclusion

It is abundantly clear that we must stop giving to God the scraps of our time and energy. It will do no good to pretend that life has dealt us a raw deal and an unfair turn of events, and therefore we cannot do otherwise than what we are doing now. The truth is as T. V. Moore put it: "The events of life are hieroglyphics in which God records his feelings towards us, the key to which is found in the Bible."[3]

For those who long to fight inflation, blight, crop failure, shrinking monetary values, and spiritual depression around the world, this text urges us to repent and turn back to the Lord and set our priorities straight. We must stop pretending we are too poor or that the time is not quite propitious, for in that day our possessions will have tongues that will wag and tell different stories on us. Now is the time and now is the right moment to call out to God, regardless of how wretched our situation may be.

For those who will respond, the stirring that God wants to effect will lead to a whole new work of the grace of God in their lives. May that work of God come in our lives, and may the life of the nation be renewed once again.

11   It Is Time to Rejoice in the Lord

Revival under Ezra and Nehemiah
Nehemiah 8

*T*his is the longest of all the revival stories in the Bible," commented Ernest Baker.[1] And it belongs to the same general period as the one under Zerubbabel with Haggai and Zechariah.

There were three different groups that returned from Babylon under three different leaders. We have already discussed the first, which was led by Zerubbabel in 537/6 B.C. This was the group that returned to Palestine filled with fervor and a deep desire to blot out the blemish of the desecration of the temple of God. The foundations were laid, but, alas, there was so much weeping about its puny size in comparison with the previous temple and so much opposition that the work ground to a halt. And so it remained for sixteen long years, until God stirred the people with a revival under the preaching of Haggai and Zechariah in 520 B.C.

Eighty years after the first return, the scribe Ezra led another return of exiles in 457 B.C. This return is described in Ezra 7–10. There can be no doubt that Ezra was a godly man. Furthermore, God used him significantly to effect a great change in the lives of the returnees. But it is difficult to say whether this should be counted as one of the great revivals of the Old Testament or as more of a reformation. Ernest Baker argues that it was a genuine revival; in fact, he finds four revivals in this postexilic period where we are only arguing for two.

The key to Ezra's life was that he "had devoted himself to the study and observance of the Law of the LORD, and to teaching its decrees and laws in Israel" (Ezra 7:10). It is no wonder, then, that God used him, for Ezra had made up his mind and prepared his heart not only to enter into a study of the Word of God but also to do what it commanded and to teach others to do the same. That is the mark of a real disciple. Moreover, "the hand of the LORD was on [Ezra]" (Ezra 7:6, 9, 28; 8:18, 22, 31).

When the Medo-Persian King Artaxerxes granted Ezra permission to return to Jerusalem with a group of Jews, he gave him wide-ranging authority to set out on the journey back to Jerusalem unattended by any army personnel, for their trust was in God alone. But when they came to the most dangerous portion of their journey at the river Ahava, Ezra had the people pause for three days in prayer and fasting, for they would now be exposed to wild animals and bands of robbers (they were carrying the silver and golden vessels previously taken from the temple by Nebuchadnezzar weighing about twenty-five metric tons). Because Ezra had testified to the Persian monarch that God was able to protect them, he felt embarrassed to request any protection from his army, despite the fact that Ezra had no trained soldiers or fighters in his group. But they "humble[d] [themselves] before [their] God" (Ezra 8:21), and God answered them by placing his hand on them for his good.

This characteristic phrase of Ezra and Nehemiah, "the hand of the LORD," meant in that day five things for Ezra, and it has the same set of meanings for us: "It guides; and we are obedient to its leadings. It protects, and none shall pluck us out of His hand. It also provides. It brings help to us as required. And it strengthens us for work. It gives us confidence that when guided by Him we shall not fail."[2]

Ezra arrived safely without a military escort. But when he heard about the lifestyle of the Jews who had returned approximately eighty years before under Governor Zerubbabel and how they had by now amalgamated with the pagans in marriage and habits, Ezra was dumbfounded. He sat speechless for a whole day (Ezra 9:1–4). How could the blessing of God be expected on such backsliding?

All who trembled at the law of God joined with Ezra in mourning over the sin of the nation. At the time of the evening sacrifice, he arose and poured out his heart to God, but he asked for nothing. He could only confess the nation's sin, weep over it, and acknowledge that they were embarrassingly exposed to every sort of attack from almost everyone because of it. Then it was that a certain Shechaniah rose to suggest that although it was true that they had broken the covenant and married unbelievers, there still was hope in spite of this (Ezra 10:2).

Three days later the remnant gathered at Jerusalem in a heavy rainstorm, trembling because of their guilt and because of the rain (10:9). When Ezra confronted them with their sin and told them to make confession to God (v. 11), the people responded: "You are right! We must do as you say" (v. 12). Arrangements were made for the orderly disposition of these matters as quickly as possible.

Was this a revival? Possibly so, for it had the elements of humbling oneself, confession, turning from sin, and seeking God's face as revealed in his law. However, it was very limited in the scope of issues that it dealt with: specifically, intermarriage with unbelievers. Generally there is some single pressing issue that presents itself as one of the key reasons for the need for revival. But the factor that decides whether a reformation or a revival has occurred is the effect it has on the whole inner disposition and hearts of the people. It is this latter feature that is strangely missing from the description of this revival. But the point is not worth fighting over, for it is purely a problem in categorization. The main thing was that the people's intermarriage with unbelievers was blocking God from fully opening his hand of blessing on the life of the community. God can be praised for such a uniform resolution of this key issue, which restored the blessing that had been so evidently on Ezra and on those who had trusted God in the matter of their return.

The third and final return took place under Nehemiah in 445 B.C. There is no question that a great revival took place in his days, some seventy-five years after the one led by Haggai and Zechariah (and ninety-some years after the first return)

Nehemiah was not looking for a task, for he was employed already in one of the highest positions in the land, especially for a captive. He was the king's "cupbearer" (Neh. 1:11). This did not mean he was a headwaiter or food taster; instead, his was a cabinet post in the upper echelons of government. But this all changed quite unexpectedly and suddenly when he received a visit from his brother, who brought a most discouraging report about the status of the city walls, gates, and returnees in Jerusalem. Trouble abounded on every hand, and in addition, the walls of the city and its gates had been (apparently) freshly burned once again. The city stood exposed to any and every attack (1:2–3). This was distressing news to Nehemiah, for when he heard this awful report, he sat down and wept and mourned for days (1:4).

He began to fast and pray, beseeching God to remember his promises to the patriarchs (1:5) and to Moses (1:8; cf. Deut. 4:25–31 and Lev. 26:33). Nehemiah's prayer continued constantly from what would be around our Thanksgiving time in November until our Easter in the spring. During this time, God prepared Nehemiah's heart to be part of the solution. Nehemiah was forming a plan to make his plea on behalf of this situation to King Artaxerxes. Even as he made his request to the Persian monarch, however, he offered a quick prayer to God (Neh. 2:4). To the delight of Nehemiah, Artaxerxes granted him his request, and thus the hard task commenced.

No doubt it took a lot of sacrifice to give up the influential position that he, an outsider, had achieved in the government. Nehemiah easily could have argued that it was important for him to stay where he was; indeed, look what this could possibly mean in his representing the interests of his fellow Jews. After all, the problem concerning Jerusalem could be cared for by almost anyone. It affected such a small number of people at the time; surely there was another person just as qualified as he was. But we hear none of these arguments from Nehemiah. Instead, he was moved by the Spirit of God while he continued to call out to the Lord for relief from this open shame of God's city. God pointed to Nehemiah, and he agreed to go and serve.

The story of how Nehemiah returned with a third group of exiles, how he conceived a plan to rebuild the walls, and the opposition he faced is all recorded in the book that bears his name (Neh. 2–7). After he had been in the razed city for only three days (2:11–12), he had formulated a plan by which the task could be carried out. The job was completed in a record fifty-two days (6:15), for nothing can stop God's servants or the work of God when it is done in God's way, using his methods.

Chapters 8–10 occupy a central position in the book of Nehemiah, taking up as they do the issue of the people's spiritual status before God now that they had been given the security of the walls and gates around them, and there was no immediate fear of being exposed to robbers or armies. Indeed, all stood ready at last for dedication, but there was a prior matter to be cared for. More was needed for the sustenance of any nation, especially the weak, struggling country of refugees that Judah represented at this time. They needed a deeper spiritual life. That life could only come from the Lord and could only be mediated through his Word, prayer, confession, humbling themselves before God, and deliberately turning from their wicked ways. Before the people could dedicate the walls and gates of the city, it was first necessary for them to reconsecrate themselves. Here, too, they needed leadership. This leadership also came from Nehemiah when he convened all the people on the Feast of Trumpets (cf. Num. 29:1–6) in a holy convocation.

Nehemiah and Ezra led the people in spiritual renewal just as effectively as they had led them in returning to the land or in giving them administrative guidance. And Nehemiah 8 records one of the most joyful and spectacular celebrations of the work of God known in the Old Testament. This chapter sets forth three ways, exemplified by the exiles who had returned and finished rebuilding the walls and gates, that God's people can begin to rejoice in the Lord:

1. By satisfying our hunger for the Word of God (vv. 1–8)
2. By finding that the joy of the Lord is our strength (vv. 9–12)
3. By uniting to proclaim God's faithfulness (vv. 13–18)

By Satisfying Our Hunger for the Word of God (8:1-8)

More desperate than their need for protecting the walls around their cities was the people's need for a garrisoning of their hearts and minds in the living Lord. Finally, an insatiable hunger, which apparently had been suppressed all these years, broke out with an abandon that seemed as if it would never be filled. People came by the droves—men, women, and all who were old enough to understand (8:2)—to the Water Gate on the east side of town. Their motive was to keep the new moon of the seventh month, the Feast of Trumpets, or Rosh Hashanah, as a feast of thanksgiving for God's gracious assistance and enablement in building the wall. This goodness of God instinctively led them to hunger to hear from God's Word.

A large wooden platform had been constructed (8:4) so that all the people in the assembly could see and hear the reading of the Word. The scene was memorable: There was Ezra in the middle of the platform flanked by thirteen priests, six on his left hand and seven on his right. Acting on the request of the people, he brought the scroll of the law of God (8:2) and opened it in front of all (8:5). Then a most amazing thing happened. When he opened the scroll of the Word of God, immediately all the people stood (v. 5). This was more than a token gesture, for they remained standing for the duration of the reading, which consumed most of the morning, except for those times when they broke into small groups for explanations and questions. The practice is a most God-honoring practice of showing deference to the Word of God. Today, unfortunately, we

tend to rise and remain standing for the singing of our modern cho-
ruses—a practice that may have more to do with something
observed at rock concerts than an attempt to symbolize theology.

In fact, I have often pondered the significance of our present
periods of standing during church services. They seem to be little
more than routine signals, indicating that certain marks have been
reached in the program, or opportunities to stretch our legs in order
to keep us from falling asleep. How much more meaningful this
simple gesture could be if it were connected with a desire to show
thanksgiving, respect, and honor to the God of heaven. We need a
holistic theology of worship that provides a new basis for all acts of
standing in our services. And surely one of the reasons that should
be placed high on the list is to show respect, alertness, joy, and full
attention to the hearing of the Word of God.

Also, too frequently we apologize for any reading from Scripture that requires more than a few minutes of this traditionally hour-
long service. But why should we be so miserly? Should we allow
announcements, hymns written by uninspired human poets, or other
trappings to successfully occupy more time than the Word of God?
Is this not an additional indicator that we need to ask God for a new
hunger for his Word, even as these people exhibited?

Six hours each day were consumed in Bible reading and explanation. Ezra read "from early in the morning (around 6:00 A.M.;
v. 3)" until midday. In the midst of these long sessions of the reading of God's Word, they broke up into smaller groups so that thirteen Levites could explain to the people what they had just heard
(vv. 7–8). Thus it was that the famine of the hearing of the Word of
God finally ended (cf. Amos 8:11, "'The days are coming,' declares
the Sovereign LORD, 'when I will send a famine through the
land—not a famine of food . . . but a famine of hearing the words of
the LORD'"). This famine was not assuaged merely with the hearing
of these words, as if they were somehow magical in their import or
effect, for the hunger persisted until the people understood what
was read. Thus the thirteen Levites followed Ezra's reading of the
law with an exposition of that passage (v. 8).

Some modern interpreters say that the thirteen Levites translated the Hebrew text into the new lingua franca of the exiles: Aramaic. But this view does not make sense in light of the fact that at the same time other portions of the Old Testament were being received in Hebrew, such as Haggai, Zechariah, Malachi, 1 and 2 Chronicles, Ezra, Nehemiah, and Esther. It hardly seems possible that these books should have been written and preserved in the Hebrew script if this was no longer the language of the people. In fact, the Hebrew word around which this debate swirls does not mean "to translate" in Nehemiah 8:8 but "to explain," as it does in the Targums. Accordingly, the Levities "read from the books, from the law of God, *explaining the meaning,* giving the sense of what they read."

What a great formula for success. If only those who teach and preach God's Word today would stick to the text of Scripture with the same degree of intensity and proceed through the Scriptures in the same orderly manner, we too would be able to experience a great revival from God.

As they made their explanations, they pointed to the text of Scripture. For some time now I have been urging my students to "hold your finger on the text" as they preach, so that if they gesture with the right hand, then they should have their left hand's finger on the text, and if they reverse hands for gesturing, so they should also reverse hands for holding the spot in the text they were commending to the whole group of believers to receive.

Too often the Bible is little more than a book of epigrammatic sayings or a springboard that gives us a rallying point around which to base our editorials. But where did we get the audacious idea that God would bless our opinions or judgments? Who wants to hear another point of view as an excuse for a Bible study or a message from the Word of God? Who said God would bless our stories, our programs for the church, or our ramblings on the general area announced by the text? Surely this is a major reason why the famine of the Word continues in massive proportions in most places in North America. Surely this is why the hunger for the teaching and proclamation of God's Word continues to grow year after year. Men and women cannot live by ideas alone, no matter how eloquently they are stated or argued, but solely by a patient reading and explanation of all of Scripture, line after line, paragraph after paragraph, chapter after chapter, and book after book. Where are such interpreters to be found, and where are their teachers? How long will it be before the people of God rise up in holy horror and say, "Enough is enough, already; we will no longer tolerate the few scraps of Scripture that we receive as an excuse for evangelical teaching and preaching."

May God grant to us this kind of hunger, and may he also grant to us this kind of reading and explanation of his Word; for when he does, then the great North American revival cannot be far away.

By Finding That the Joy of the Lord Is Our Strength (8:9–12)

The entrance of God's Word not only gives light, but it also brings great joy. The first joy that it led to in this revival was a joy that came from being forgiven. On hearing the Word of God read and preached with all of its authenticity and power, the people were deeply convicted of their sin. There was much weeping and lamenting (v. 9). Undoubtedly the portions that must have stirred them most profoundly were those deadly serious texts from Leviticus 26 and Deuteronomy 28, which speak of the alternative prospects of blessing or judgment, depending on the people's response to the Word of God. This produced an ominous sense of impending judgment and of God's deep displeasure with them for the failure to obey him.

Weeping is not always a sure sign of true repentance, for many weep over being caught or out of sheer embarrassment; here, however, the people wept because they felt the grief that their waywardness had caused the Lord. And when the holy standard of God's law was set over against their lives, they cried out in repentance to God. Without this repentance and turning from our sin there can be no revival—ever.

Now when the weeping of the people continued for some time, Ezra, Nehemiah, and the Levites comforted the people by urging them to weep no longer. The word from God was, "This day is sacred to our Lord. Do not grieve, for the joy of the LORD is your strength" (v. 10). Only with great difficulty did they quiet the people, for their grief was deep and sustained. Authentic declaration of God's Word joined with genuine repentance produces unremitting joy. This kind of joy is not the cheap imitation of the world; it is a holy and satisfying joy that exceeds all boundaries. It is a joy that has its source in the Lord himself. It is a joy founded on a feeling of being restored and back in communion with him. It is based on God's goodness and patience (Exod. 34:6–7). This joy is a "stronghold," or a "fortress," which acts as a refuge and a citadel into which the believer can enter, no matter what the temperament of the day or the current issues. The Lord himself serves as our rock and our shelter, both in the time of the storm and in the day-to-day enjoyment of his presence.

Such joy and communion with God easily leads to the sharing of it with others, and thus they sent gifts to those who were without the means to prepare a feast-day meal. Those who had themselves been restored and who had reestablished their own relationships with the Lord could now extend a helping hand in his name to others. In other words, their relational theology and their social involvement was an expression of their propositional theology. The hurts and needs of a battered society can only be met by those who have first had the source and communion of their own joy and fellowship restored.

Once again the Bible deals with the spiritual and temporal needs of individuals and society, but it does insist on a priority in these two tasks. Ernest Baker observed in this connection,

> In all healthy spiritual life these two things go together. George Muller was great at prayer, but equally great in his care for the orphans. C. H. Spurgeon preached to the multitudes; but he also built almshouses and orphanages. General Booth

[was] an evangelist of the lapsed masses; but also one who organize[d] relief and rescue works on a large scale. True Christianity is concerned for the people in this world as well as the next. And those who show the deepest concern for the state of the soul are generally those who do most for the people in this present life. The realization of the value of the soul has increased the estimate of the body that enshrines it. We must care for the whole of man.[3]

The joy of the Lord comes, then, because we are forgiven, because we have communion and fellowship with a good Lord, and finally, in verse 12, because we have an understanding of God's Word. So central is this Word for discernment or understanding that it appears six times in this chapter (vv. 2, 3, 7, 8, 9, 12). What greater testimony can be offered for the worthwhileness of faithfully proclaiming God's Word? When God's people understand that Word, there is no containing the holy joy, deep satisfaction, and contentment that overtake the believing community.

The psalmist wrote, "Great peace have they who love your law, and nothing can make them stumble" (Ps. 119:165). Thus, emotional and volitional responses must follow, rather than precede, the understanding of the Word of God. It is sad to see how many programs in the church and in society try to reverse this order. But we will never find any real joy or satisfaction in this search until our hearts come to first rest in the God who made us, redeemed us, and revealed his Word to us. Only then is there going to be any joy in Mudville or any rejoicing in life or in the Lord.

By Uniting to Proclaim God's Faithfulness (8:13–18)

Invariably, the clear teaching of God's Word has as one of its first by-products the whetting of our appetites for more teaching of that Word. So from the second day until the seventh day of the feast, the people sought out Ezra to hear more (vv. 13, 18). As a result, they learned how to observe the Feast of Tabernacles, or Booths (Lev. 23:33–43). Therefore, on the fifteenth day of the month, each family began cutting down branches from the olive, myrtle, and palm trees to form temporary shelters as they recalled once again the deliverance of God from Egypt. Thus they were united in remembering God's faithfulness in the past. Their unity owed its basis to the enduring strength and joy that came from the Word of God.

Not since the days of Joshua a thousand years before had this festival been held—at least on this scale. How complacent the people had grown (v. 17). Now, however, there was true *koinonia*—a new spirit of sharing, of oneness, and a linking of believers that was now possible because of the recent work of God's Word in their hearts brought about by their repentance. Such unity and fellowship exists in its truest form only in the church, or in that group of believers who have united together for the purposes of reading and heeding God's Word. This unity is not the same thing as uniformity, for it still recognizes the diversity of gifts and the uniqueness of personalities. There is no lockstep, cookie-cutter type of regimentation that insists that everyone think or believe precisely as the majority or, worse still, as the leader of the group thinks. This is not a call for conformity or for unanimity on all matters, but it is a call for the softening work of the Spirit of God to unite us around his Word and around himself and thereby to unite us to one another.

Only two days after they finished celebrating the Feast of Tabernacles, they came to the twenty-fourth day of the seventh month, which is the most holy day, called the Day of Atonement (Lev. 16). This day of fasting they also observed before God (Neh. 9:1–38). They confessed their sins in deep humility before God (9:2), listened to the Word of God again for another three hours (9:3), and entered into another three-hour period of confessing their sins before God (9:3). With an exhortation and an invitation for the congregation to enter into praise and confession, Ezra led the people in one of the longest and most moving prayers in the Bible. So ended the record of one of the longest passages about revival in the Old Testament.

Conclusion

So where do we stand today in this matter of spiritual hunger and biblical appetites? Only when this hunger is excited to the heights seen at this time in Judah will we also in our generation begin to experience the first tastes of revival. Our joy will remain incomplete and without full resonance until we experience the cleansing effects that come from understanding and doing the Word of God. No amount of emotional satisfaction can begin to compare with the totally satisfying joy that comes from knowing that we are wonderfully forgiven, that we now have full fellowship with the living God, and from an understanding of his Word. Simultaneously with these good gifts will come the desired unity of believers that we have sought for so long. The scandalous divisions that exist within the body of Christ, not to mention the even more tragic divisions that exist within local churches and Christian institutions, will not be healed until we employ the principles found in a revival such as the one under Nehemiah. We must cry out to God for relief, for much of our efforts to still the troubled waters in the meantime are usually futile.

May our Lord be pleased to visit us with a revival similar to the one he gave under Ezra and Nehemiah. Until then, may all who hunger and thirst for righteousness flee to the full teaching of the Word of God. May they cry out in prayer for God's mercy on our communities, crops, nation, and churches. And may they pray so that revival may come soon in the providence and good hand of God.

12 It Is Time to Prepare for the Lord

Revival under John the Baptist
Matthew 3:1–14

$\mathcal{T}$he record of John's life and labors occupies about 194 verses in the four evangelists (in Matthew, forty-seven; in Mark, twenty-eight; in Luke, eighty-five; and in John, thirty-four). Of these only about thirty report his words; and hardly more than half of these give us distinct and separate utterances, the others being parallel passages in the different writers. Of these eighteen or twenty verses, we trace something more than fifty references to Old Testament statements either in substance or form or both. . . . [and] more than forty are from the three prophets Isaiah, Malachi and Jeremiah."[1] Clearly, John the Baptist's message was immersed in the words and teachings of the Old Testament.[2]

"Nothing is more striking about John than the abruptness with which he is introduced in [Matt. 3:1]. . . . as if the evangelist desired to emphasize his relation to Elijah, who appears in an equally abrupt manner in [1 Kings 17:1]."[3] But there he was! And what is even more amazing is the fact that John suddenly appears after some 400 years of silence, for God had sent no prophets to minister in Israel since the days of the prophet Malachi, about 400 B.C.

John's primary task was "to make ready a people prepared for the LORD" (Luke 1:17b). This work of ensuring that people were prepared for the arrival of Jesus the Messiah had been predicted by both Isaiah and Malachi, some 700 and 400 years earlier. As such, John was to function in a transitional role: he was the *end* of the era of waiting and the *inauguration* of the era of the kingdom of our Lord—"For all the Prophets and the Law prophesied until John" (Matt 11:13).

But what could one man do against such mind-boggling opposition? He was merely "a voice of one calling: 'In the desert prepare the way for the LORD; make straight in the wilderness a highway for our God'" (Isa. 40:3). He could only advise that preparations ought to be made, just as Malachi had predicted: "'See, I will send my messenger, who will prepare the way before me. Then suddenly the LORD you are seeking will come to his temple; the messenger of the covenant, whom you desire, will come,' says the LORD Almighty" (Mal. 3:1). And that was the burden of his message and the heart of his life's work: "In those days John the Baptist came, preaching in the Desert of Judea and saying, 'Repent, for the kingdom of heaven is near'" (Matt. 3:1–2). Merely a voice calling out to a generation that was highly skeptical and more than slightly reluctant to change anything in their lives, much less to trust the Messiah in those days of brutal Roman domination. Nevertheless, John cried out: *The King is coming, we must repent, turn from our sin, and ask God for his forgiveness*.

Even though John's whole ministry probably did not exceed more than six months' time, he relentlessly carried out his mission despite extremely heavy odds against having any type of success. What difference could a mere six months of talking make in such a troubled and sinful world as his? And how could a rustic man of the desert expect to make an impact on the urban centers of Jerusalem and Rome?

If all of that is not enough to make one pause and look for some other way to bring solutions to a world in turmoil, then look at what John got for all his trouble! He had his head cut off by Herod, who did not take kindly to being rebuked publicly for divorcing his wife and marrying his brother's wife.

The Jewish historian Josephus (born in A.D. 37/38 and died about A.D. 100) records how the Jews talked about Herod's army being destroyed by Aretas, the king of Arabia and Petra, in retaliation for Herod's plan to divorce Aretas's daughter (who also was Herod's first wife), so that he, Herod, could marry the wife of his brother instead:

> Now some of the Jews thought that the destruction of Herod's army came from God, and that very justly, as a punishment of what he did against John, that was called the *Baptist*; for Herod slew him, who was a good man, and commanded the Jews to exercise virtue, both as to righteousness towards one another, and piety towards God, and so to come to baptism; for that the washing [with water] would be acceptable to him, if they made use of it, not in order to the putting away [or the remission] of some sins [only], but for the purification of the body; supposing still that the soul was thoroughly purified beforehand by righteousness. Now when [many] others came in crowds about him, for they were very greatly moved [or pleased] by hearing his words, Herod, who feared lest the great influence John had over the people might put it into his power and inclination to raise a rebellion, (for they seemed ready to do anything he should advise) thought it best, by putting him to death, to prevent any mischief he

might cause, and not bring himself into difficul-
ties, by sparing a man who might make him repent
of it when it should be too late. Accordingly he
[John] was sent a prisoner, out of Herod's suspicious temper, to Macherus, the castle . . . and was
there put to death. Now the Jews had an opinion
that the destruction of [Herod's] army was sent as
a punishment upon Herod, and a mark of God's
displeasure to him.[4]

Such was Josephus's account of the character and message of
John and what became of him. From this account it is apparent that
John's summons for a moral and spiritual preparation of the heart
had a great effect on his generation, even though it might have
seemed a most unlikely possibility from many human points of
view.

The call to prepare continues to be raised almost two thousand
years after the first coming of Christ. Individuals and nations are
still advised, by means of this same message given by John the Baptist, to make moral and spiritual preparations for the imminent
appearance of our great God and Savior, Jesus Christ (Titus
2:11–14). There are three preparations that we must make for the
coming King of kings and Lord of lords:

1. We must prepare by repenting of our sin (Matt. 3:1–7).
2. We must prepare by producing the evidences of repentance
   (Matt. 3:7–12).
3. We must prepare by refusing to be offended because of
   Christ (Matt 11:1–14).

We Must Prepare by Repenting of Our Sin (3:1–7)

Six things had been promised about the child, John the Baptist.
He would

1. be great in the sight of the Lord (Luke 1:15a);

2. be a Nazirite from his birth, drinking neither wine nor strong drink (Luke 1:15b);
3. be filled with the Holy Spirit, even from the womb (Luke 1:15c);
4. turn many to the Lord (Luke 1:16);
5. prepare a people for the Lord (Luke 1:17); and
6. many would rejoice at his birth (Luke 1:14).

But above all, he was to be that promised "messenger" that Malachi and Isaiah predicted.

Now the most outstanding characteristic of all the prophets' messages in the Old Testament was the single command, "Repent!" That is how Zechariah, next to the last prophet in the Old Testament line of messengers from the Lord, summarized the focus of all fourteen previous writing prophets: "Do not be like your forefathers, to whom the earlier prophets proclaimed: This is what the LORD Almighty says: 'Turn from [or, Repent of] your evil ways and your evil practices'" (Zech. 1:4).

The word for "repent" or "turn" in the Old Testament is the Hebrew word *shuv*. It appears 1,069 times in the Old Testament to repeat what we have already noticed, and is translated with many different nuances, but the dominant way is to "turn," "return," or to "come back" to the LORD. If a pun will help us to remember it better, the fact is that God wants to give us a *shove* in the right direction—toward himself.

The reason for this clarion call to do a 180-degree about-face is that "the kingdom of heaven is near" (Matt 3:2). Thus, this servant of God, who came in "the spirit and power of Elijah" (Luke 1:17), must, like Elijah, denounce his generation for their sin and failure to trust God. All too common was the idolatry of putting everything and everyone else in the place and ahead of the living God. While it was easy enough to see the idolatry of Baal worship in Elijah's day, it was not always as easy to see the more subtle forms of idolatry in John's day and especially in our own times.

But the sin of John's day and our own surely excites the indignation and wrath of God just as much as it did in Elijah's times. So aware was John of the deep effect that sin had made on every class and on every type of vocation that he would denounce that moral blot on their nation even if it meant that he had to stand alone. Of course, being a child of his parents' older years, he may already have had to stand on his own two feet, for he may have become an orphan well before his thirtieth birthday. Moreover, his Nazirite vow may have tended all the more to have separated him unto God.

Isaiah had indeed pleaded, "Comfort, comfort my people, says your God" (Isa. 40:1), but that comfort could only come where there was a "voice." And that comfort could only come when unrighteousness and moral decline had been faced and confessed to God (Isa. 40:3–5). All too frequently it is assumed that the best way to comfort and minister to hurting folks is to help them with their self-image and to put them with a recovery group that will let them know that others face the same problems they faced. But that method affords little lasting comfort if it does not focus on the God of all comfort and the forgiveness that he can give when we honestly repent of our sin.

We must plead with our generation to turn each one of us from our evil ways and practices. If we do not turn from our sins and confess them to God, we can be sure that there will be very little comfort for heartsick men and women in our day. Neither will we see the glory of God revealed (Isa. 40:5). Once again, the revival fires will pass us by, and we will be left in our sins and misery.

We Must Prepare by Producing the Evidences of Repentance (3:7–12)

John's declaration to his day and ours was that this is the era of the rule and reign of God. Everyone was coming out to hear this unusual messenger, even the Pharisees and the Sadducees, even "though John [had] never performed a miraculous sign" (John 10:41).

Just as the prophet Isaiah had addressed another evil generation, so John began: "You brood of vipers! Who warned you to flee from the coming wrath?" (Isa. 59:5; 10:3 in Matt. 3:7). Surely the question was more than an idle one. Exactly what was the motivation of these religious leaders in taking the time and trouble to go way out into the wilderness of Judea to see what John was saying and doing?

But others were coming out to hear the Baptist as well. All, however, were treated without fear or favor. The tax collectors were reproved for their overcharging, their cheating, and their covetousness. Soldiers were denounced because they had not gotten right with God, and because they were violent, discontent, and guilty of all kinds of extortion. Religionists, such as the Pharisees and the Sadducees, were reproved for their pride of place and character and their loving the eminence and reverence among the people. They were also denounced for their pride over the fact that they taught the law. Few classes, if any, escaped this messenger's warnings about the wrath that was to come if they did not repent of their sins.

All at once the desert was no longer a solitary place; instead, the throngs were coming from every village and hamlet. But this brief opportunity for an insertion of a word from on high was not wasted by John. On the contrary, he warned that no one must take shelter in the fact that they were the descendants of Abraham. Indeed, they had trifled for generations from father to son with their privileges and responsibilities as children of Abraham and the people of the promise and the Book. What proved that the alleged shelter was false and empty was that they had refused to obey Abraham's God (Matt. 3:9a).

God was not trapped by his unconditional covenant with Abraham, as some thought. He could, at any moment, raise up a whole new line of descendants to Abraham (v. 9b). This spirit of triumphalism, of course, is not limited to John's contemporaries; we evangelicals are just as susceptible to its dangers when we think that we, too, have arrived and that God is stuck with us. In fact, in comparison to how bad everyone else appears in our culture, God must, we sometimes falsely reason, be mighty happy to have the likes of some of us church people around as a counterbalance to all that evil!

But how wrong they were in John's day—and how wrong we are in our day—to think and act so poorly when measured by the standard of the holiness of God's own character! Did they, or do we, know that "the axe is already at the root of the trees" (v. 10a)? Doesn't anyone recognize the fact that "every tree that does not produce good fruit will be cut down and thrown into the fire" (v. 10b)?

Israel had been wrapped up in the expectation that there was a coming kingdom for Israel and that God was to be their king. But they had lost sight of the fact that there was something more definite, something more immediate, and something more spiritual. It was a new realm into which the kingdom of heaven extended: the realm of the heart, the spirit of the truly repentant person. Here was the realm in which the kingdom of God would also manifest itself and for which there had to be just as genuine preparation as there was for all the other aspects of God's rule and reign. Hence, the necessity of issuing a serious call to repentance—a turning away from sin, resulting in real evidences of that transaction (v. 8) by the way they lived.

True, there had been washings and purifications previously. These had been for the removal of uncleanness of cups, vessels in the sanctuary of God, and for lepers and for the priests' hands and feet prior to their serving in the temple. But now came the revolutionary thought that even a Jew circumcised on the eighth day, who observed the ordinances and was ceremonially clean, needed to be washed; indeed, had to be washed before God would accept him. Such an open declaration of repentance was a new thought, previously unknown in Israel: it was the baptism of repentance (v. 11).

While John's baptism was merely one of water, the Person that he was announcing and calling people to prepare for would one day come and baptize with the Holy Spirit and fire. The grand event of Pentecost demonstrated what John meant by the baptism of the Holy Spirit (see Acts 2 and the interpretation of that term subsequently given in 1 Cor. 12:12–13), but woe to those who waited to see what the Master meant by the baptism of fire (vv. 11b–12). In that final judgment day, God would thrash the grain, separating the chaff from the wheat, in order to deliver over the chaff to a fire that would never be extinguished! The torments of hell would last forever; no one was to imagine that there would be any kind of last-minute repeal of the rules of the game in a soft-hearted move by God. Now was the time to repent and to turn to God to appeal to him for his forgiveness.

That call for producing the evidences of repentance has not grown any less in our day. It is still too easy to put off God's call for holiness of life in every sector of acting and thinking by pointing to a much more sensate and wicked culture than we as a believing community practice. But that never was the point; the measurement of holiness was the character of God. So, what will we do about our phoniness, our failures, and our flimsy record in the area of righteousness? God wants to revive us and to see the fruit of the Spirit in our lives. The question is, Are we ready to turn and to start producing the fruit that is in keeping with righteousness?

We Must Prepare by Refusing to Be Offended Because of Christ (11:1–14)

Suddenly, the ministry of some six short months was now ended. Then it was that the ministry of Jesus began (Matt. 4:12, 17). Had it been worth it all? A whole lifetime just to minister for six short months?

What had brought John's brilliant and meteoric career to a screeching halt? It had been John's stirring sermon that had dared to rebuke every class of individuals, including the king. John had publicly rebuked Herod the Tetrarch and Herodias his wife. Well, actually she had been Herod's brother's wife, who had eloped to take up with Herod, not many miles away from where her real husband was living.

Infuriated by John's bold call for holiness and righteousness in every sphere of the nation's existence, Herod imprisoned John in the castle called Macherus. Ironically, Macherus had been given to Herod by the father of his first wife, King Aretus in Arabia and Petra. There it was that John found himself—as some might incorrectly infer—as a reward for all the good he had done.

When John heard from prison that the One he had announced was performing miracles and declaring the same message that he had preached—that the kingdom of heaven was near—John sent his disciples to ask Jesus, "Are you the one who was to come, or should we expect someone else?" (Matt. 11:2). John also heard by now that Jesus was teaching that he had come to open the prison door to those who were bound. And wasn't he, John, bound up in this prison? Had he been forgotten? Was he, after all, mistaken about the One who was to come? Who can imagine what must have gone through the mind of John during these days?

The Savior's response was to plunge even more deeply into the work while the disciples of John joined Jesus' disciples, closely observing and following all that he did and said. Then Jesus responded, "Go back and report to John what you hear and see" (v. 4). And, added Jesus, "Blessed is the [person] who does not fall away on account of me" (v. 6).

But how did all of this help John—or us, for that matter? The point was that there is always a temptation in God's work to be offended. At times, God's ways seem so mysterious; his methods seem so contrary to our wisdom. But the finer the gold, the longer it is kept in the fire. One of the last items we wish to submit to God and to turn over to him is our questioning intellects. But here was the crowning mercy that the Baptist was to learn in his last test of faith. Before being welcomed into heaven, he had to learn that there is a blessing for every soul that does not become offended by God when he or she does not immediately understand what God is up to when he takes a certain line of action that is thought of as either incorrect or incomprehensible. Not all of God's works can be fathomed or anticipated. There are some cases where we must simply trust him, and that is that! If he has proven himself faithful in the moments of sunlight in our lives, can we not trust him during the darkness? One former president of Wheaton College, V. Raymond Edman, was fond of saying, "Never doubt in the darkness what God has told you in the light."

Jesus' estimate of John, including this latest bout with doubt, was astounding: "I tell you the truth: Among those born of women there has not risen anyone greater than John the Baptist" (Matt. 11:11a).

But Jesus went on to affirm in the very same context, "Yet he who is least in the kingdom of heaven is greater than he."

Conclusion

John came in the Spirit and the power of Elijah the prophet. But all who will turn from their sins, act the way persons who truly have repented ought to act, and do not get offended at what they do not agree with or understand about the ways of our Lord will be greater in the kingdom of God than even John was—and he was the greatest of all those up to that point in history! What an incentive to holiness, righteousness, and genuine moral and spiritual preparation for the coming Kings of kings and Lord of lords.

Let the rule and reign of God's kingdom begin in your heart and mine immediately. Begin producing the fruit of "right-ness." Pray that God's church might be revived again with a fresh anointing from his Holy Spirit as a new wave of repentance and a turn from wickedness and evil sweep the cultures of the world as a result of the church's getting right with God and demonstrating the reality of the gospel in our lives.

And should adversity arise, let us refuse to be offended by it, regardless of the path of glory or suffering that he chooses for us. For our song will be:

> Lead on, O King Eternal,
> The day of march has come.

13   It Is Time to Embrace the Gift of the Holy Spirit

Revival under the Apostle Peter at Pentecost
Acts 2:1–47

---

*E*rnest Baker accurately depicted the significance and impact of the revival that took place on Pentecost:

> The revival at Jerusalem on the day of Pentecost is the greatest of all time. In every respect it occupies the first place. No revival was ever so sudden, none so tremendous in its immediate effects, and none so lasting in its results. One hundred and twenty disciples of the Lord Jesus were suddenly baptized in the Holy Spirit. Their characters were wonderfully enriched. New gifts of

speech, insight, and argument were conferred upon them. A great accession of zeal, and love, and devotion was added to their motive powers. Within a few hours 3,000 men and women were converted. The Christian Church was constituted. Every day conversions took place; sometimes scores, hundreds, and even thousands, were added to the ranks of the disciples. The work continued for years in Jerusalem itself. It was not the event of a season. It also spread abroad. The revival created missionaries, who went out in all directions. Revivals in other centers followed. Every city of any considerable importance in the Roman Empire felt the influence of the movement during the next few years. This revival made the Apostles, it created the Church, it caused its expansion, it inspired the Epistles, it spread Christianity throughout the whole known earth. The influence of it has reached to our own time.[1]

Such were the effects and results of the revival at Pentecost.

It will be remembered that John the Baptist had earlier predicted that a baptism would come that was "more powerful" (Luke 3:16) than his baptism with water: it would be a baptism with the Holy Spirit. And so it happened fifty days after Passover (*pentakostos*, "fiftieth"), the "day after the seventh Sabbath," that the Holy Spirit came in a mighty downpour on the church.

This eighth (i.e., the first) day of the week was declared in the original "Feast of Weeks" to be just as holy and sacred to the Lord as was the seventh day, or the Sabbath. In fact, this festival was also known as the Festival of Firstfruits. It was another prophetic pointer to Christ, who would also be known as the "Firstfruits" of those who will rise from the grave (1 Cor. 15:23). Pentecost celebrated the period that began with the offering of the first barley sheaf as the barley harvest commenced during the Passover celebration and concluded fifty days later with the wheat harvest (Lev. 23:15–16; Deut. 16:9–12). That is why it was also known as the Feast of

Weeks: it came after a period of seven weeks of harvesting. By the time the first Christian century arrived, however, Pentecost was considered to be the anniversary of the giving of the Law at Mount Sinai (as deduced from Exod. 19:1). It was one of the three great pilgrimage festivals (along with the earlier Passover and the Feast of Tabernacles that would come four months after Pentecost) when all Jewish males would assemble in Jerusalem to worship God. That is where many in Israel were when suddenly what had been promised happened, as described in Acts 2!

The coming of the Holy Spirit at Pentecost was highly significant, both theologically and practically. While the arrival and the presence of the Holy Spirit did not necessarily imply that sensory evidences would accompany that event, God was pleased to give such evidences. And there may have been other reasons why an external manifestation of the Holy Spirit's coming was necessary. Even though the Holy Spirit had been present and working during the Old Testament era, he must now come visibly with unforgettable evidences—just as Calvary was the necessary visible enactment of the benefits that had been received prior to the crucifixion. As Goodwin explained, "[The Holy Spirit] must have a coming in state, in a solemn and visible manner, accompanied with visible effects as well as Christ had."[2]

It happened this way: "When the day of Pentecost came," wrote Luke in Acts 2:1–4, "they were all together in one place. Suddenly a sound like the blowing of a violent wind came from heaven and filled the whole house where they were sitting. They saw what seemed to be tongues of fire that separated and came to rest on each of them. All of them were filled with the Holy Spirit and began to speak in other tongues as the Spirit enabled them."

It should not surprise us that *wind* was a sign of God's Spirit, since both the Greek and Hebrew words for *spirit* also can mean, depending on the context, "wind." In Ezekiel 37:9–14, the prophet had prophesied that wind, as the vitalizing breath of God, would come over the dry bones scattered in the valley in order to fill those bones of the house of Israel with new life at the conclusion of history. But so also would the vitalizing wind and Spirit of God act on the day when God's Spirit would usher in the final days of the Messianic era, which began when Christ appeared the first time (Heb. 1:1–2).

Fire also was a symbol of the divine presence, as many will recall from the numerous Old Testament allusions to such things: the burning bush (Exod. 3:2–5), the pillar of cloud by day and fire by night that guided Israel in their wilderness experience (Exod. 13: 21), the consuming fire on Mount Sinai (Exod. 24:17), and the pillar of fire that hovered over the tabernacle in the desert (Exod. 40:38). God was once again present among his people in a mighty way.

There are four features of Pentecost that will encourage believers today to be prepared for a similar outpouring of the Holy Spirit when God graciously sends revival to the churches and nations of our time:

1. The gift of the Spirit is the fulfillment of God's promise (Acts 2:14–21).
2. The gift of the Spirit brings assurance of God's power over everything, including death (2:22–37).
3. The gift of the Spirit is the reason why we must repent (2:38–41).
4. The gift of the Spirit is the basis for the continuance of those who were revived (2:42–47).

Clearly, the outstanding feature of this revival in Acts 2 was the gift of the Holy Spirit: that is the point Peter emphasizes in this memorable message given at Pentecost.

The Gift of the Spirit Is the Fulfillment of God's Promise (2:14–21)

Despite the scoffing and perplexed questions of many who were present in Jerusalem for this event, Peter addressed the crowd with such a newfound boldness that it was a 180-degree reversal of the intimidated, swearing, and frightened disciple who denied his Lord less than two months previously at Jesus' trial.

"These men are not drunk!" thundered Peter; anyway, it was too early in the morning for them to have gotten drunk (v. 15). "No," continued Peter, "this is what was spoken by the prophet Joel" (v. 16). God had not forgotten the word he had given to his prophet Joel some eight hundred years previously. Even though centuries had rolled by, God's promise still held good.

Unfortunately, all too many all too quickly took up the chant, "Where is this 'coming' he promised? Ever since our fathers died, everything goes on as it has since the beginning of creation" (2 Pet. 3:4). But God never forgets, no matter how great the lapse of time. Indeed, Jesus himself revived the memory of prophetic word as he taught his disciples God's Word. In that sense, then, every revival is simultaneously a unique work of God and a fulfill-ment of the Word of God. And every revival comes when desperate men and women lay hold of those promises and trust that God will do exactly what he promised he would do.

What was it, then, that God had promised through his prophet Joel in the ninth century B.C.? There were three basic items that were promised by Joel 2:28–32: (1) the distinctiveness of this out-pouring of the Spirit, (2) the extent of this outpouring on all flesh, and (3) the results of this outpouring.[3]

While no believer in the Old Testament had been completely without the aid and work of the Holy Spirit,[4] what happened at Pen-tecost was both climactic and effusive. This new, outward, and evi-dential coming of the Holy Spirit in state would be extremely abundant in comparison with what could only now be regarded as the previous scarcity of his work and ministry. Joel, under the inspi-ration of God, carefully chose from five separate Hebrew verbs, meaning to "pour out," the one that would easily link up with the one Jesus would use: the "rivers of living water" that would come on all who believed (John 7:38–39)—indeed, a veritable baptism of the Holy Spirit (Matt. 3:11; Mark 1:8; Luke 3:16–17). If this con-nection with the text in John 7 is correct, as we believe it is, then there was something else unique about the ministry of the Holy Spirit that first occurred at Pentecost, and then in Samaria and in Caesarea. Now not only was a believer regenerated by the Holy

Spirit and indwelt by him to some degree; all who believed were simultaneously baptized by the Holy Spirit by being made a part of the one body of Christ (1 Cor. 12:13).

This did not mean, of course, that there would be no other ultimate and final downpour of the Holy Spirit in the end times in connection with the restoration of Israel to her land, as the prophets Isaiah (32:15; 44:3) and Ezekiel (11:18–19; 36:26–28; 37:12–14; 39:28-29) had predicted. As with many of the Bible's prophecies, there is an inaugurated eschatology; that is, there is both a "now" and a "not yet" to many of these predictions. Pentecost and the present age of the church is surely the "now" aspect of this promise, even though there will come more to this same promise that is "not yet."

The extent of this downpour would be nothing less than "all flesh." This expression, "all flesh," (or as the NIV somewhat incorrectly translated it, "all people," thereby leaving open the question whether Joel meant Jews or Gentiles, or both) "occurs 32 times in the entire Old Testament. In 23 of these 32 instances, the expression refers to the Gentiles alone."[5] Surely the preponderance of usage favors the meaning of "all humanity."

But Joel's promise was even more explicit, for it indicated that the Holy Spirit would come on all without distinction or favor: without distinction of gender ("sons and daughters"), age ("young men . . . old men"), or race and ethnic origin (literally: "and even on men servants and maid servants"). The last of these three pairs was the shocking one, for it began with the doubled exclamation "and even," or "even also." The Greek translators, apparently, could not believe their eyes when they made the Septuagint translation of the Hebrew Bible for the Greek-speaking world. They deliberately changed the expression "men servants" into "my servants," (as did the NIV), implying the servants of God. But in Jewish homes, the servants were not persons from Israel; they were Gentiles. That is why Joel warned us that he meant "all flesh" when he started this section. And neither age, gender, nor race made any difference in the eyes of God: his Spirit would come on all without showing any kind of favoritism. Females would "prophesy" right alongside males. No one could despise dreams or visions of others because they were either too young or too old. And just as surely, no one could castigate the work of the Holy Spirit in the lives of Gentiles who had been outside the covenant. Thus it was that Peter invited the Gentiles to receive the Holy Spirit (Acts 2:38), for the promise was just as much for "all who are far off" (that is, for Gentiles) as it was for Jews (cf. Acts 10:45; Eph. 2:13, 17; Isa. 57:19).

The results were these: everyone would immediately and personally know the Lord. It also meant that the last days had been inaugurated already: history was in its final countdown, beginning with the first advent of Jesus.

Note how God's Word was the norm by which everything that was happening was judged. Where the experiences of those who celebrated Pentecost on that day when the Holy Spirit dramatically visited them was below the norm of the Word of God, they had to be corrected and leveled out to that Word. So it must be in all revivals since that day. God's Word, not my experience, guides my estimate of myself and of what is happening.

The fulfillment of the promise of God's Spirit is the best response that we can give to doubt. The poor band of disciples that had suffered such doubt during the hours of the crucifixion—and for some, even up to Pentecost itself—were suddenly awakened to an inexplicable transformation by the gift of the Holy Spirit. All kinds of intellectual doubts and emotional blockages burst open them before the convincing presence of the Holy Spirit. Consequently, we can affirm without fear of contradiction that the greatest argument for the reality and effectiveness of revival and renewal in the church is the majestic work of the Holy Spirit in lives that only recently had been filled with everything but the power of God.

The Gift of the Spirit Brings Assurance of God's Power over Everything, Including Death (2:22-37)

Peter waxed even more eloquent and bold as he took as his second text the Old Testament passage, Psalm 16:8–11. If the skeptical crowd at Pentecost was still mulling over what they had just witnessed—the overwhelming downpour of the Holy Spirit—they could just as well also reflect the words of the former King David. Had not David, by the same Spirit, testified that the Messiah who would come from his line would not be left in the grave but would be resurrected? And had not David, since he was a prophet (Acts 2:30), seen ahead of time that God would raise Christ from the dead in the future, thereby giving all who wondered what would happen after death more than enough strong reasons to believe that they, too, could be raised?

And if the exalted Christ was raised to the right hand of the Father, and he surely was, then the promised Holy Spirit could be poured out in abundant measure, as indeed they all had just witnessed (v. 33). Why, then, would anyone have wished to crucify this one whom God has demonstrated to be both "Lord and Messiah" (v. 36)?

If this assurance about the ultimate triumph of Christ over death and the grave gave David such joy and assurance, how much more can the gift of the Holy Spirit likewise produce at least the same assurance in us? Nothing, not even death, can stop those enabled by the Holy Spirit.

The Gift of the Spirit Is the Reason Why We Must Repent (2:38-41)

When the Holy Spirit comes, he changes people. Consider what the 120 disciples had been before Pentecost. Even the twelve did not seem to thrive all that well during the three years of our Lord's teaching and influence.

But look at the same group of disciples on this day of Pentecost. Peter, who could not confess his Lord even before a servant girl, much less soldiers gathered around a fire, is now facing thousands of scoffing, jeering, and hostile men without one hesitation or apology. How can we account for such a remarkable turnabout except for the changing work of the Holy Spirit when persons repent?

That is what Peter proclaimed as he preached, "Repent and be baptized, every one of you, in the name of Jesus Christ for the forgiveness of your sins. And you will receive the gift of the Holy Spirit" (v. 38).

Peter had another command: "Save yourselves from this corrupt generation" (v. 40). Peter would not be pleased with the flippant excuses and rationalizations of our day. We complain that it is too difficult to resist the trends of today's sensate and rotten culture. The tides, we explain, are running against any kind of drastic call for repentance and massive changes in lifestyles and habits. But those excuses would never get by the apostle Peter (or our Lord)! His generation and ours were both crooked and exceedingly wicked. And if we do not soon do something to extricate ourselves from its clutches, the end of all of us will be all too sad to describe in detail. The words of Acts 2:19–20 from Joel 2:30-31 give us enough of an idea of the terror of those final days before our Lord's second coming to motivate the hesitant.

The gift of the Holy Spirit will give us the power we need to be saved from the evil generation, thus making us different from the ordinary run of men and women.

The Gift of the Spirit Is the Basis for the Continuance of Those Who Were Revived (2:42–47)

Many revivals in the Old Testament and in modern history were brief. Some would last for a few weeks, while others would last for a year or two. But so decisive was the work of God on this occasion that it has continued to affect the church, and in some cases even the culture itself, right down to the present moment.

The fellowship the believers enjoyed is remarkably described in verses 42–47. High on the list of priorities was a whole new appetite for hearing and acting on the teaching from God's Word. In our day, the hunger for God's Word is about as low as it can get. Rather than pushing the pulpit to give more of the apostles' teaching, or indeed the whole counsel of God, the pressure in most groups of believers is to hear less from the full canon of Scripture and more about ourselves, our needs, and our recovery groups. Isn't this a sign that we are ripe candidates for revival? Isn't Peter's word a word that the twenty-first-century church needs to hear?

Those earliest Christians also espoused the high value of breaking bread and of praying together. It is difficult to continue taking the Lord's Supper while we violate the terms of that ordinance of God by not confessing our sins to one another when we have grudges against one another.

Only when we are clean before the Lord and before each other can we expect what the early church saw by way of the supernatural manifestation of the power of God. What characterized these revived Christians was the song on their lips, gladness in their hearts, and praise for their Lord. No wonder, then, that the Lord added to their number each day those who were being saved (v. 47). And so it has ever been: when the people of God get right with him and with each other, the number of new converts that are won under these revived and renewed conditions exceeds anything seen in any other period of history.

Conclusion

The gift of the Holy Spirit is a divine gift; it is not a gift that is there for the taking, or a power that a person can acquire, seize, or somehow capture on one's own. Our trust must not be in our capacity to receive such a gift, but only in God's power to give it.

This gift, as every other study of revivals in the Bible has taught us, depends on the initiative and grace of God. There may be conditions that we must meet, but in the end we place all our trust in what God can do. That is why it is proper and altogether necessary for God's people to cry out, "Will you not revive us again, O Lord?"

Until we see how poverty stricken and wretched we are, despite the abundance of much of our materialistic secular culture in the

West, we shall never cry as we ought for this most gracious act of God.

Pentecost was preceded by days of Bible study and prayer among the disciples (Acts 1:14–16). Should we do any less?

14   It Is Time to Ask for a Change of Heart

Revival under Philip at Samaria
Acts 8:1–25

---

*S*amaria was the first place outside Jerusalem to experience revival fires after Pentecost. The Samaritans were regarded by the Jerusalem Jews as "half-breeds," both racially and religiously. This was a result of what had happened in 722 B.C. when the Assyrians invaded the northern ten tribes of Israel, destroyed the capital of the northern tribes of Israel known as Samaria, and forced the Jews who remained in northern Israel to integrate with Gentile exiles from other Assyrian conquests.[1] Samaria, then, would be the place where the third great revival of the New Testament would take place.

At the heart of this revival seems to be verse 21. Simon the sorcerer from Samaria (who wanted to purchase the gifts that he saw the apostles exercising) was told that his "heart [was] not right before God." This revival announced that it was time to seek a change of heart. There were three areas in which this change of heart would (and must) evidence itself:

1. a change of heart about suffering (8:1–3);
2. a change of heart about witnessing (8:4–8);
3. a change of heart about empty professions of faith (8:9–25).

A Change of Heart about Suffering (8:1–3)

It took a set of adverse circumstances to help speed the church on its way to accomplishing the mandate issued by their Lord before he left this earth. Acts 8:1b notes that "all"[2] the believers in the church at Jerusalem, "except the apostles," "were scattered throughout Judea and Samaria" because of the "great persecution" that had been unleashed against the church at Jerusalem.

In particular, a ferocious enemy of the church, one named Saul, later to become the apostle Paul, was systematically going from house to house in order to drag men and women off to incarcerate them for their faith. Clearly, his aim, and that of the Jewish leadership in Jerusalem, was to destroy the church (v. 3).

But God used this act of barbarism against his church to help the believers get on with the task of carrying this good news to the ends of the earth, just as he had urged several years earlier. The martyrdom of Stephen was the final straw that scattered the church far beyond the confines of Jerusalem (v. 2). This was to be a story often repeated in the church's history, for the blood of the martyrs became the seed of the church.

"Godly men" (the same words used of the Jews who received the message at Pentecost, Acts 2:5; and the word used to describe the "devout" but aged Simeon, Luke 2:25; and the priest Ananias of Damascus, Acts 22:12) "buried Stephen and mourned deeply for him" (v. 2). Yet out of this immeasurable grief and heartache, God brought something that more than made up for these temporary losses.

The persecution that hit the fledgling church was undoubtedly from the devil. But the evil one could exercise only limited power; all things had to come under the direct sovereignty of God. This was true in the case of Job. Satan had to get permission to act against Job's property, his family, and ultimately, against Job himself. But God was allowing this to demonstrate that Job loved and served the Lord for more reasons than just the fact that God had blessed him and made him a wealthy man. Job said that he would still trust in the Lord even if he slew him (Job 13:15)!

Others were permitted to experience trouble for reasons that God set. Joseph concluded that the unfair dealings of his brothers and the raw deals he experienced in Egypt were motivated by the evil intentions of humans, but God meant them to be for Joseph's own good (Gen. 45:5–7; 50:20).

Ernest Baker made the point so deftly that few can improve on it:

> There are troubles that are the works of ene-
> mies, of evil men, of the devil, of death itself, for
> death is an enemy; and they are intended to harass
> us in the work of God, to wean us from it, to embit-
> ter us against Him, to reveal to the scoffing, unbe-
> lieving world that faith is a matter of circumstances
> and sunshine, but that it withers in the storms, and
> cannot help us in times of trial; and God gives lib-
> erty for all these to come to us because He can make
> all these things serve an opposite purpose. He can
> turn all the devil's weapons against himself.[3]

The battleground of the great conflict is the heart. We can say whose purpose shall be fulfilled. By allowing troubles to sour us we can incline victory to the devil; by allowing them to enlarge our sympathies, and to make us cling to God for help, we can give the victory to God.

The spectators are the men and women of the world; and, by the spirit we allow to rule us, we are furthering doubt or faith in other minds. But God is standing ready to aid us, and to enable us to be his witnesses in storm as well as calm.

Surely that is the result God intends in the midst of suffering for his name's sake.

A Change of Heart about Witnessing (8:4-8)

One of the places to which the dispossessed band of believers fled, because of the persecution of the young church, was Samaria. Perhaps the fact that both the old residents of Samaria and these new immigrants likewise shared the calamity of being dispossessed from their original homes may have provided the first threads of commonality that some Jews ever had with this mixed race of Jews and Gentiles at Samaria.

The point was that the scattered church became the witnessing church as it "preached the word wherever [it] went" (v. 4). Perhaps as a direct result of this witnessing, the believers called for outside help. So it was that Philip, the second of the seven deacons named in Acts 6:5, came down to Samaria and "proclaimed the Christ there" (v. 5).

Consequently, the preaching of Philip in this polyglot population of Samaria formed a kind of bridge in Luke's depiction of the advance of the gospel around the world: a bridge between Jerusalem/Judea and the ends of the earth. His preaching also carried out the plan that our Lord laid down just before his ascension into heaven when he commanded, "But you will receive power when the Holy Spirit comes on you; and you will be my witnesses in Jerusalem, and in all Judea and Samaria, and to the ends of the earth" (Acts 1:8).

Philip did not mince any words about it, for it was evident that the gift of the Holy Spirit was still empowering the Church to act and witness with a holy boldness previously unknown in their midst. Philip "preached the good news of the kingdom of God and the name of Jesus Christ" (v. 12). For him, there was no separation between the message of the gospel with its good news about the death, burial, and resurrection of Jesus Christ and the message of the kingdom. The rule and reign of God had already begun in the hearts of all who believed, even though it would not be concluded until the final day of Christ when he returned once again.

Since the Samaritans accepted the Pentateuch (the five books of Moses: Genesis, Exodus, Leviticus, Numbers, and Deuteronomy) as their inspired Scripture, and since they looked for a coming messianic Restorer (the t^eb), whom they incorrectly thought would be a resurrected Moses, Philip no doubt used Deuteronomy 18:15, 18–19 (as Peter and Stephen had done in Acts 3:22 and 7:37) to prove that Jesus was "that prophet" who had come as Moses had promised.

As at Pentecost, God backed up the preaching of the word with many other signs and miracles in which demoniacs, paralytics, and cripples were healed. Even the evil spirits came out of possessed persons with shrieks (v. 7), all of which must have frightened and amazed the listening crowds in Samaria. The word of God and the works of God reinforced each other as the gospel blazed new paths where it had not gone before.

Indeed, it did take a change of heart for these displaced Jews to begin witnessing and inaugurating the missionary movement in their day. If it was unnatural for them to take the message of a Messiah from Nazareth, called Jesus, to their own countrymen, what must it have taken to go a half step beyond that to preach to the Samaritans—and a full step more to go to the Gentiles later on?

This is what it took: a series of divine interventions in order to convince them that the gospel had to be carried to others. Thus, God used persecution, originating in the hearts of wicked men, to scatter his church and to make them witness all over the Roman empire.

The initiative for sending out these witnesses was solely God's own. Accordingly, it was an angel of the Lord that told Philip to go south on the desert road to meet up with the Ethiopian eunuch (8:26–29). And it was the Lord himself who appointed and commissioned, but now converted, Saul to go to the Gentiles (9:15). Luke seems to stress this aspect of God's sovereignty when he begins the Book of Acts by commenting, "In my former book, Theophilus, I wrote about all that Jesus began to do and to teach" (Acts 1:1). The inference was that this second volume by Luke would now continue the story by showing what Jesus continued to do through the gift of his Holy Spirit, which he had poured out on the church. Even though the Lord would use the instrumentality of a scattered church and the deeds of the apostles, it would be the Lord who would be adding to the church all those who were being saved. It was his name that made men whole in spirit and in their bodies. Yes, even in their calamities, such as Paul's shipwreck, it was none other than the Lord who stood by him (Acts 27:23).

The campaign that our Lord gave to this first group of Christians continues to this very hour. Evangelism and missions must never become optional for the believer: they are at the heart of our commission, for they were at the heart of our Lord's concern for the world. But even if our Lord cannot be seen, he is the one who will inaugurate our witnessing, and he is the one who will stand alongside us as we go in his name. And it will not be our persuasiveness, our logic, or our ability to demolish proud arguments that rear up against the clear case made for the Lord who visited, died, and rose again for us; it will only be the powerful name of our Lord that accomplishes all the work! May our Lord grant us a revived outlook that involves a change of heart about witnessing for, by, and under him.

A Change of Heart about Empty Professions of Faith (8:9–25)

While Philip was preaching in Samaria, he came across one of the city's famous (or as it turned out, infamous) citizens—Simon the sorcerer. So effective were the results of Philip's crusade in Samaria that persons both high and low on the social ladder stopped following Simon the sorcerer and became believers in Jesus Christ. Eventually, even Simon himself "believed" (v. 13) and was baptized, but his "heart was not right with God" (v. 21).

Scripture used this case as an illustration of the fact that it is possible to make an empty profession. Such professions are without lasting effect and without the reality of the power of the gospel. This case alerts us that not everyone who says "Lord, Lord," will be converted and changed.

What exposed the sham in Simon's profession of faith was his desire to buy the power he saw Peter and John using. Peter and John had joined in the revival going on in Samaria under the auspices of Philip. It would appear that God providentially withheld the gift of the Holy Spirit temporarily in order to allow Peter and John, representing the apostles, and perhaps the church at Jerusalem, to lay their hands on the Samaritan believers so that there would be no suspicion of the reality of what God had done in converting them. Neither would it be possible to reduce them as "second-class" citizens in the household of faith because they came from Samaria, or perhaps because this, too, was another aberration that did not represent the same work of God as was being witnessed in Jerusalem.[4] But Simon figured that fame, power, and skills were all available for the right price. He had been able to amaze the city of Samaria with his sorcery (v. 9), receiving acclamations of being a divine power with great abilities (v. 10). Whether the title "the Great Power" (v. 10) meant that he claimed to be God Almighty or not cannot be known for sure. At the very least, he claimed to be the Grand Vizier of God Almighty.

When Simon saw that after Peter and John had placed their hands on people that they, in turn, had received the Holy Spirit, Simon offered to buy this power (v. 19). But Peter sternly rebuked Simon for both his pretentiousness in claiming to be a follower of Christ and for thinking that everyone has a price. "May your money perish with you, because you thought you could buy the gift of God with money!" (v. 20). "Repent of this wickedness," urged Peter, "and pray to the Lord. Perhaps he will forgive you for having such a thought in your heart. For I see that you are full of bitterness and captive to sin" (vv. 22–23). But no, he did not repent. His "heart was not right before God" (v. 21b).

The church fathers remembered Simon the sorcerer as Simon Magnes, the leading heretic in the early church. Justin Martyr (died c. A.D. 165), who himself was a Samaritan, claimed that all his countryman revered Simon Magnus as the highest god.[5] Irenaeus (about A.D. 180) declared that Simon Magnes was the father of Gnosticism and attributed a sect of the Simonians to him.[6] But even more damaging is the second-century *Acts of Peter* with its extensive descriptions of how Simon Magnes corrupted Christians in Rome by his heresies and how he repeatedly was able to show off his magical powers to the disadvantage of Peter's ability to match him. Simon played with spiritual things and thought that a mere external and formal confession was all that was needed. However, God does not look at a person as humans do; he looks at the heart.

Worldly ideas cannot be brought into the work of God expecting that God's blessing and affirmation will automatically be on them. If it is not the Lord who is sending his messengers to witness—convicting their hearers of wickedness, sin, and unrighteousness, and producing the fruit of changed lives and enabling them to receive the gift of the Holy Spirit—it is all a waste and a sham.

Luke has juxtaposed over against the unchanged heart of Simon the responsive and receptive heart of another foreigner, the Ethiopian eunuch, who was in charge of the treasury of Candace, queen of Ethiopia (8:26–40). The eunuch received Philip's ministry gladly and gave every evidence of being genuine, even though he, like Simon, was not Jewish. The Ethiopian eunuch's heart was changed by the Spirit of God.

Conclusion

Alterations in the life of the church that come from outside the church to the inside count for nothing if the heart remains unchanged and resolute. But when God changes the heart, everything takes on a whole new set of priorities. God's rules, not ours, prevail. The quests for power, position, money, recognition, preeminence, and all those lesser goals are suddenly exchanged when the heart is changed.

God's work of revival includes a change of our hearts. And when our hearts are changed, such an impact is made on the cultures in which we live that our hearts are also changed to the glory of God.

For such changes to be worked in us, we must look to our Lord and pray that the work might be his and his alone. Jeremiah 29:13 said it best: "You will seek me and find me when you seek me with all your heart." May our Lord be pleased to send to his church such a hunger to seek him with all our heart.

15 It Is Time to Advance the Missionary Cause of Christ

Revival under the Apostle Peter at Caesarea
Acts 10

---

*S*ince this is the first time in the New Testament that God sent a revival among the Gentiles, it has been called the Gentile Pentecost. It is similar to the previous sending of the Holy Spirit at Samaria in Acts 8 and among the Jews at Pentecost in Acts 2, all of which were further evidences that the apostles and early church heeded the mandate given to them in Acts 1:8—to be Christ's witnesses in all the earth. Even though major prejudices and deeply ingrained patterns had to be overcome, God himself would lead his people as they obeyed, despite all natural hurdles and obstacles. The missionary nature of the gospel, itself one of the deepest concerns of God for the lost among the heathen, could not be overlooked or bypassed if the church was to remain true to her Lord.

Three stages in the advance of the missionary cause of Christ can be seen in Acts 10. Each stage is very similar to the way God has been pleased to work in the Old Testament and the way he continues to work in our day as well. The three stages are

1. The audience and the messenger are both prepared (10:1–23).
2. The words and the works of God are both announced (10:24–43).
3. The evidence of belief and the gift of the Holy Spirit are both received (10:44–48).

Let us see how it was that God led believing Jews to shift from the old emphasis of a separation from the Gentile nations to a new revelation of his purpose that refused to call any person unclean or impure (v. 28).

The Audience and the Messenger Are Both Prepared (10:1–23)

Repeatedly, the Bible emphasizes the fact that God never calls anyone to go witness in his name without simultaneously preparing both the ones to whom the messenger is sent as well as the messenger himself. For example, all the days that Moses was being raised in the house of Pharaoh in Egypt and the lonely time he spent in the desert of Midian, God was just as surely working with the Israelites to ready them for the time when Moses would be prepared to lead them out of Egypt. Neither one was aware of the other; nevertheless, God increased the skills of Moses, while he increased the burdens of Israel. Finally, both met: there was a tremendous outcry from the Israelites, and there was an exasperation in Moses over the way the Israelites were being treated. Eventually, Moses found himself in the desert of Midian, where God finished off his training.

The Preparation of the Audience

Something similar to that happened with Cornelius and the apostle Peter. Cornelius was a Roman captain stationed in Caesarea with the Italian regiment assigned to him. The Scriptures compliment him by describing him and his family as "devout" and "God-fearing" (v. 2a). In addition, "he gave generously to those in need and prayed to God regularly" (v. 2b). Here was a man, though not a believer, who was doing everything he knew how to find God.

One day, when he was engaged in his usual time of prayer, at about three o'clock in the afternoon, an angel appeared to him and informed him that his prayers and almsgiving had come up before God as a memorial (v. 4). Cornelius was certain that this was not a mirage or some type of self-induced apparition, for he said that he had "distinctly" seen "an angel of God" (v. 3). Clearly, it was God's will that Cornelius should know more about God and the way to life everlasting.

This is an important principle, for often the question is asked, "What about those who have never heard about Christ? Will they spend eternity in hell just because no one has ever told them about Jesus?" But in the Cornelius affair, we are given exactly the very same set of circumstances. It is also in this same context that we learn that it is God who now takes the initiative in sending someone to tell Cornelius about the Savior, for Cornelius had done all he could, it would appear, to seek the face of God. But it was necessary that an explicit witness be given to Jesus Christ and that is where God also had to take steps to prepare his messenger, just as he prepares all believers today.

This all came about through the angel who carefully instructed Cornelius to send some men to Joppa. They were specifically told to go to the house by the sea, of one called Simon the tanner, where a man named Peter would be staying. Cornelius acted immediately by selecting two of his servants and one of his soldiers, who like himself was also a "devout" man. Cornelius told these three delegates what had happened to him and where they were to go. It would appear that the time of preparing the audience had come to completion. It was time for a witness to instruct these prepared hearts in the way everlasting.

The Preparation of the Messenger

Now while the three men were on their way to Simon the tanner's house, the next day after Cornelius's vision, Peter had gone up to the roof of Simon's house to pray around noon (v. 9). And as he prayed, he became hungry and wanted something to eat. Now while the meal was being prepared, and no doubt while the aroma was wafting up to the roof by the sea breezes blowing in off the Mediterranean Sea, Peter fell into a trance (v. 10).

In the course of this trance Peter saw the heavens opened and what appeared to be a great sheet being let down from heaven by its four corners with all kinds of four-footed animals, reptiles, and birds of the air (v. 12). With that, he was urged to get up, butcher, and eat these creatures (v. 13)!

But Peter, good Jew that he was, would never even think of doing such a thing. How could he eat those things that were impure and unclean (v. 14)? Had not the book of Leviticus distinctly forbidden him to do so? This did not happen just once—it was repeated three times. Then the sheet was suddenly withdrawn and taken back up to heaven (v. 16).

Peter was still pondering what the meaning of such a bizarre event was when the men whom Cornelius had sent arrived in Joppa and stopped at Simon's place of lodging. They called out, asking if Peter was staying there. But Peter was still trying to get straight in his own mind the meaning of what he had seen in this repeated action of the lowered sheet when he heard someone downstairs calling his name. He was then told by the Spirit to go downstairs off the flat roof. God's explicit word was, "Do not hesitate to go with them, for I have sent them" (v. 20).

When Peter inquired who the men were, they must have momentarily stunned Peter when they announced that they had "come from Cornelius the centurion" (v. 22a). The word *centurion* was enough to conjure up in Peter's mind all sorts of hated associations: Romans, Gentiles, pagans, occupying army, and hinderers of the kingdom of God promised to David. But the Gentile delegation quickly added that Cornelius was "a righteous and God-fearing man, who [was] respected by all the Jewish people" (v. 22b).

The Call of God

But even if that were true, and we know that it was, how did these three men happen to stumble upon Peter's name and current place of residence? The men anticipated that question as well, for they volunteered, "A holy angel told [Cornelius] to have you come to his house so that he could hear what you have to say" (v. 22c).

Peter couldn't argue. Every one of his defenses had been demolished. In all that was happening to him, he had been taught first not to think of any mortal as trash—impure, unclean, or whatever—all mortals were creatures made in the image of God. Second, an angel of God had informed this inquirer where to go and who to find. The fact that they had found Peter was proof enough that this was of God. Third, the obvious sincerity of Cornelius could be seen in the type of life that he lived, which was totally different from what one would expect of the proud, demanding, and brutal occupying forces of Rome.

Even though God used an angel to tell Cornelius where to go, God still used a mortal to preach the gospel to him. Baker makes this same point:

> There is no case on record in which the truth about God and salvation has come to men other than through human agency. In human agency we include the Bible, for that has been penned, translated, printed, and circulated by men. It is a tremendous privilege that God has conferred upon us in making us the channels of the knowledge of His will to our fellow-men. But the privilege is a great responsibility. It means that there are people in the world who will not know the truth if we do not take it or send it to them. Every one of us must take a

share in the work, for it is committed to the whole body.[1]

The Words and Works of God Are Both Announced (10:24-43)

The Ministry of Prayer in a Seeker

The question is often asked, "How does God work in getting his message out to the multitudes on the face of the earth?" The answer is this: first of all God uses prayer, and then he follows that with his word about his Son through human witnesses.

Cornelius was a man of prayer, even though he had not yet known the Savior. Indeed, he had lived up to all the light that he had but on the crucial matter about how he could have eternal life, he, like all who have not yet heard about Christ, was totally in the dark. The more he prayed, the more he sensed his need for something in addition to what he had and to what he presently knew. The directions on how to get that light came from God.

One cannot be satisfied with a little light when what is being sought after is the true light that enlightens everyone who comes into the world (John 1:9). Men and women are judged not only by the light they have but also by the light they could have had. Living by the light that we have must include using that light to obtain more light until our soul's hunger is satisfied, for God will never allow anyone to be satisfied merely with the first beams or flashes of insight. We must press on as Cornelius did. That is why Cornelius prayed to know God more perfectly. And as he prayed, God gave him more light, which opportunity he eagerly seized.

The Ministry of Prayer in One Who Witnesses

We must also consider how God used prayer in the life of Peter. Here was a man of strong prejudices. Not even his three years of following Christ had changed those naturally and deeply ingrained opinions about those who were not Jews. Mentally and theologically he could render a good accounting of himself on the fact that the Holy Spirit must be given to all regardless of gender, age, or race, for he had clearly preached exactly that on the day of Pentecost from Joel 2:28–32, as recorded in Acts 2. God would pour out his Spirit *on all flesh*, including Gentiles. But saying something is true and acting on it are two different things. That fact continues to be most apparent in our own day as new prejudices arise. New sheets will need to be let down from heaven to help us, even where in principle, if not in practice, we continue to affirm the necessary truths of Scripture on these points.

Peter also was a man of prayer, and this is what God used to make his practice conform to his theology. While Peter was praying on the rooftop of Simon the tanner's house, a place that must have smelled to high heaven from the hides of all the animals (talk about clean and unclean!), God perfected his servant in time for the ministry that was to take place shortly. Therefore, what three years of tutoring in the school of discipleship with Jesus could not do, and what our Lord's teaching during the forty days before the ascension was unable to accomplish, prayer was able to effect. Baker made this same point:

> Prayer not only brings more light and corrects prejudices, it prepares us to hear God's call. If Peter had not prayed he would not have recognized a Divine call behind the invitation from Cornelius. The call to Peter was an outward and an inward one, of God and of man. Some people say they have no call to work for God. That is not true. God has given to every [person] his work. But it is true that some people have not heard the call. The call is a still small voice, and it is heard only by the soul that has withdrawn from the world, and is waiting before God. Some of our ears are only open to the world's sounds, to its business, pleasure, excitement, and crimes. The daily newspaper conveys much more to us than God's Word. The voice of God is drowned.[2]

Our Lord has always used prayer about the mission of the church's witness for Christ as the means of preparing each of us to participate in that mission. That is how we get our call.

One day as Jesus was going through the towns and villages, teaching and preaching in the synagogues the good news of the kingdom, he impressed on his disciples how harassed, helpless, and leaderless the masses of people were. With such an enormous harvest to gather in, and with so few who were willing to help, the solution lay in prayer. Jesus urged his disciples, "Ask the Lord of the harvest, therefore, to send out workers into his harvest field" (Matt. 9:38). Prayer was our Lord's solution for getting the job done, massive and formidable as it appeared.

Is it any wonder that prayer plays such a vital and significant role in any revival? God has chosen this method as his means to accomplish his work. It is not altogether clear why God has chosen this method when so much is linked to fallible and disobedient humans, but the fact is that he has and continues to operate in this way.

The Results of the Ministry of Prayer

When Peter arrived at Cornelius's house in Caesarea the following day, the centurion had already assembled his relatives and close friends to hear what Peter had to say (v. 24). As Peter approached the house, Cornelius fell down in reverence and deference to him, but Peter commanded him to "Stand up," since Peter was only a mortal (v. 26). The honor and the glory were to be God's, not man's.

When they had gone inside Cornelius's house, Peter addressed the large group that had gathered. He began with an explanation. As "you are well aware," he began, "it is against our [oral] law for a Jew to associate with a Gentile or [to] visit him. But God has shown me that I should not call any [person] impure or unclean. So when I was sent for, I came without raising any objection. May I ask why you sent for me?" (vv. 28–9).

Cornelius then rehearsed the unusual experience he had had with the angel of God during his prayer time (vv. 30–32). He concluded by urging, "Now we are all here in the presence of God to listen to everything the Lord has commanded you to tell us" (v. 33). One cannot help being struck by the utter simplicity of this man's expectation that God would send more light to the group through Peter. Moreover, he had such a deep consciousness of God's omnipresence that he depicted this hastily arranged meeting as one that was taking place directly in the presence of God (v. 33a). This is an amazing amount of theology for one who, up to this point, probably has not had any formal teaching on the doctrine of God, much less any teaching on how to be saved.

It was Peter's turn to be amazed: "I now realize how true it is that God does not show favoritism, but accepts men from every nation who fear him and do what is right" (vv. 34–35). The fact that God had sent an angel to Cornelius was proof enough for Peter that God had honored the fact that this Gentile had lived up to all the light he had. That is why he now sent someone to tell him about Jesus.

The message, therefore, that God had for these Gentiles was one that he had prepared and sent to them through the people of Israel. They must know the same truth that the Samaritan woman had to acknowledge: "Salvation is . . . [through] the Jews" (John 4:22). That point had been revealed by God ever since 2000 B.C., when God promised Abraham that in his seed all the nations (Gentiles) of the earth would be blessed (Gen. 12:3). The plan of God from the beginning had embraced all the peoples of the world.

Here was the good news: peace was available to all the world through Jesus Christ, who was Lord of all (v. 36). The events that had happened throughout Judea and Galilee, from the days of John the Baptist until then, were widely known. This Jesus of Nazareth was anointed by the Holy Spirit with power to do good, to heal the sick, and to deliver all who were under the power of the devil. Jesus did these works as further evidence that God was with him (v. 38).

But there was more. Jesus was killed and hung on a cross, but God raised him up from the dead on the third day. We and others, Peter interjected, are witnesses of this resurrection. That is why God has called us to preach and testify that it is this same Jesus whom

God has appointed as judge of all who are now alive and of those who have already died (vv. 39–42). Therefore, Peter concluded, I am going to make the same point that the Old Testament prophets have already made about this Jesus, who is the Jewish Messiah: "everyone who believes in him receives forgiveness of sins through his name" (v. 43).

It all may have looked terribly simple, but the power of that divine name exceeded anything one could imagine. Both the powerful words and mighty works of God in Christ demonstrated that he was who he claimed to be: God himself.

The Evidence of Belief and the Gift of the Holy Spirit Are Both Received (10:44–48)

The last stage in the revival experienced here was the mighty outpouring of God's Spirit at this third Pentecost (in addition to the first on Pentecost and at Samaria). Neither the audience nor the Holy Spirit waited until Peter had concluded his talk, but while Peter was still speaking, "the Holy Spirit came on all who heard the message" (v. 44). The Jewish believers who had accompanied Peter on his trip from Joppa were "astonished that the gift of the Holy Spirit had been poured out even on the Gentiles" (v. 45). But there it was—right before their eyes! God had promoted what their theology had said was impossible, because of similar prejudices that Peter had just wrestled with. God was indicating that these non-Jews should also be regarded not only as believers but even as full participants in the gift of the Holy Spirit. There were to be no second-class citizens in this fellowship.

Other signs of the genuineness of the work of the Holy Spirit began to show up: speaking in tongues and praise to God for all he was and had done. That is why Peter asked the rhetorical question: "Can anyone keep these people from being baptized with water? They have received the Holy Spirit just as we have," he reminded them (v. 47). Evidently, if there were any who objected, they held their tongues. The facts were all too evident.

Conclusion

This biblical record of the first Gentile revival makes it plain that, when God renews and revives his church, a new urgency is felt to get the gospel out to every man, woman, and child on the face of the planet. Peter and that small delegation from Joppa must have reflected many a time on what had happened that day in Caesarea.

Just over two centuries of modern missions have passed since the call of William Carey. We have seen an enormous number of people drawn to the Savior through the faithful proclamation of the Word of God. But the most effective moments in the worldwide mission of the church have come on the heels of special times when God has revived his church.

When the lips of the church have been cleansed, just as the prophet Isaiah's were as he caught an overwhelming vision of the greatness of God one day during his worship in the temple, then we too will be able to hear the call of God to be his witnesses around the earth. He waits for a church that has slackened in her response to this missionary mandate to say to her Lord, "Here am I, send me."

After World War II, a veritable army of men and women returned from the former battlefields of the globe to take up the challenge to go as ambassadors for Christ wherever he would have them go. The days have passed and much has been accomplished, but that army of workers has now retired, and some have gone on to glory. As a result, the net number of workers continues to dwindle, to the shame of the present church.

And what shall we say of the rest of Christ's church? Should not all of his people evidence that same indwelling boldness and power of the resident Holy Spirit by carrying a witness into every sphere and walk of life? Instead, we seem to be more intimidated by the world than we are involved in shaking up the world. Those early disciples turned their world upside down for the sake of the gospel (Acts 17:6), even though they were just as ordinary as we are. The difference lay in the fact that they submitted themselves to the work of God's Holy Spirit. Hence it was not by might, nor by power, but by God's Spirit (Zech. 4:6) that they fulfilled the great missionary mandate that our Lord gave to his own.

If it takes another sheet dropped down from heaven to jolt us out of our preconceptions and prejudices about many aspects of sharing the gospel, then let us pray that God will use whatever methods are needed to awaken us to his call in our day.

16 It Is Time to Renew Evangelism in the Church

Revival under Paul and Silas in Europe
1 Thessalonians 1:2–10

*I*t is not possible to include every revival alluded to in the Bible. The path we have chosen is to treat those that form large teaching blocks of text in the Scriptures and those that mark the great turning points and new beginnings in history. Accordingly, along with the revival under John the Baptist, the great works of God at Pentecost in Jerusalem, and later in Samaria and Caesarea, mention must be made of what took place on the first missionary journey of Paul into Europe.

One of the great turning points in history came as Paul and his companions were traveling through what is known today as Turkey. The church there at Antioch sent out Paul and Barnabas to evangelize those in the surrounding areas and beyond as the Spirit saw fit to lead them. It will be recalled that it was in Antioch where the believers were first called Christians, albeit in a derogatory manner (Acts 11:26).

Now when Paul and the team set out from Antioch a second time, they worked their way through what is now called Turkey until they came to its northwestern border, just south of the Black Sea (Acts 16:6–7). As they tried to press on further northeast, on a route that perhaps would have taken the gospel into such modern republics as Russia and on into the Far East, Acts 16:7b records that "the Spirit of Jesus would not allow them to [go there]." Therefore, being prevented in going in a northeasterly direction, they turned south, but especially westward, down to Troas, a city on the seacoast, searching where God would lead them next.

It was while they were at Troas that the apostle Paul had a vision at night of a man in Macedonia, Greece, standing and begging him, "Come over to Macedonia and help us" (Acts 16:9).

Had it not been for that vision, history would have been much different today. No doubt, missionaries would have come from the East to evangelize the West, instead of the reverse pattern that has proven true since the days of Paul. The church would have been strongest in the Far East, not the West. The spiritual leadership of the world would have first come from Russia, China, India, Persia, and Japan. Indeed, America might have been discovered from the other side (i.e., the West Coast area of California, Oregon, and Washington), not the East Coast.

But in the providence of God, the gospel moved westward into the center of the Empire of Rome. The civilizations of Greece and Rome were not all that great spiritually and morally; in fact, they were downright corrupt and filled with moral, ethical, and spiritual decay. Nevertheless, the infusion of the gospel had the effect of arresting or delaying that decay and conserving some of the better parts of the Greco-Roman culture through the preserving salt of the Christian faith.

It was the hand of God that turned the course of events in human history. Paul and his friends had not even thought of a western campaign in Europe: Paul's heart had been set on going into

Asia. But the Spirit of God forbade him; that is the reason why so many in the West have been so fortunate to have been blessed all these years with the light of the gospel and the accompanying benefits that it brought.

It is beyond our human reasoning to assess or explain why the Spirit of God chose to move in a westerly direction rather than an easterly one. This is not to say, of course, that God thereby abandoned the eastern nations, for with the privilege of being the first to receive the gospel came the responsibility of sharing the gospel with those in other parts of the world. This was no different than our Lord's method of calling the Jewish people first and charging them with being a "light for the Gentiles" (Isa. 12:3; Gen. 49:6).

In the same manner, the divine choice of the European nations as the first to have the gospel preached to them was simultaneously a call for those blessed with the gospel in the West to engage in the work of evangelism around the globe. Failure to recognize the purpose God had in mind, when he had so generously gifted the believers in the West, could well result in the same fate that overtook the Jewish people as they too shrunk back from the task of evangelism.

It is interesting to observe the change in strategy by Paul's team of evangelists as they landed in Europe for the first time. Normally, had they been anywhere else, they would have gone to their own nationality first; that is, to a synagogue on the Sabbath day. But there was no synagogue in Philippi, where they had landed after they had sailed from Troas across the Aegean Sea.

The rule of postexilic Judaism was that wherever ten Jewish men lived in a city, they could form a *minyan* (a prayer cell), and thus a synagogue. But this Macedonian center gave no evidence of that many Jews present at Philippi, much less a place of worship. Accordingly, when the Sabbath day came, the evangelistic team was momentarily stumped as to what they were to do.

They decided to go outside the city gate down to the river banks on the Sabbath, hoping that there in the open air they would find a prayer meeting they must have been told about. To the amazement of these Jewish men, they found one—but only women were present! Now that was a cultural shock, for only men, in their previous experience, had gathered to pray.

Undaunted, Paul addressed the small group of women. This was the first gospel sermon in Europe. It was an earnest invitation to these women to come and receive Jesus Christ as their Lord and Savior.

The first convert in Europe was Lydia. Actually, her home was not in Europe, but in Asia Minor at Thyatira (again, modern Turkey). She was in Philippi as a businesswoman, a dealer in purple cloth. When she heard Paul's earnest entreaty down by the riverside, she opened her heart to the Lord. In the process, her whole household came to know the Savior and were baptized (Acts 16:15).

Her prior search for the truth of God may be seen from the fact that, as a Gentile, she had come in contact with the Jewish faith. She had become a Jewish proselyte. Having received all the light that was available to her at that time, she left her paganism and turned to Judaism. But now that these Jewish missionaries had announced the events that had taken place in the life of Jesus the Messiah, she acted in full faith and became the first convert to Christ on European soil that we know about.

The sincerity of her search for God can be seen in the fact that though she became a Jewish proselyte in Thyatira, nevertheless she still sought out a band of those worshiping God while she was in another city away from home—a remarkable challenge even for today's believers! And just as she was resourceful in business, she applied that same resourcefulness in caring for the matters of her soul. Too frequently we wish to blame others for the faults, failures, and weaknesses in today's church. But God will meet each hungry individual just as he met Lydia's spiritual needs. He only asks what steps we have taken with that light and those gifts we have been supplied so far. Not even the demands of Lydia's business would keep her away from tending to what she had made a priority in her life: the needs of her soul. Is it any wonder that God graciously met those needs?

On one of those occasions when Paul and his team were headed to this unusual place of prayer on the city's river banks, they were confronted by a slave girl who had a demonic spirit by which she predicted the future. The girl had followed Paul and Silas for several days shouting, "These men are servants of the Most High God" (Acts 16:17). Paul finally had had enough of this, so he commanded the evil spirit to come out of her.

When the owners of the slave girl realized that their source of income was gone, they had Paul and Silas hauled before the magistrates and imprisoned in an inner cell with their feet secured in stocks. At midnight, however, as Paul and Silas sang, a violent earthquake, of unknown Richter-scale force, shook the prison so severely that the prison doors flew open. When the jailer realized that his prisoners had not fled and escaped, he begged, "What must I do to be saved?" (Acts 16:30). He and all his household were converted, and Paul and Silas were given honorable releases when it was learned that they were both holding Roman citizenship.

After leaving Philippi, Paul and Silas passed through Amphipolis and Apollonia, and then came to Thessalonica. There was a synagogue there, so they attended it on the first Sabbath they were in town.

At the appropriate time in the service, Paul began to reason with the Jewish audience from the Old Testament Scriptures that Jesus must be the promised Messiah. Had he not suffered and been raised from the dead as the Scriptures had predicted? (Acts 17:3). The result was that some of the Jews were persuaded, along with many Greek proselytes and quite a few women.

Now it was to this new group of believers at Thessalonica that Paul wrote his letter to the Thessalonians. There are three evidences, found in 1 Thessalonians 1:2–10, that God had revived this new European group of believers by giving them a wonderful impetus to evangelize those around them.

1. Look at the way the gospel came to them (1:2–5).
2. Look at the way the hearers imitated what they had heard (1:6–8).
3. Look at the way the message brought results (1:9–10).

Look at the Way the Gospel Came to Them (1:2-5)

Paul was joined by Silas and Timothy as he addressed the new church at Thessalonica (v. 1a). This group of believers was identified, not only geographically, but as being located "in God the Father" and also in "the Lord Jesus Christ" (v. 1b). With that kind of address, churches ought to be much more confident about who is their main source of support and stay.

When Paul began to reflect on how the gospel came to these Thessalonians, he could not refrain from giving thanks to God for all that he had done. There were three parts to Paul's thanksgiving: the faith, love, and hope of these believers.

First, the quality of their faith was demonstrated in the way that the believers worked in the cause of Christ. Unfortunately, some are willing to do all sorts of work in the Christian church, but some of it does not spring from faith as its motivating force. God hates and flatly rejects this. But there is a real and genuine faith in Christ that issues forth in a life of dedicated work for God: this is the occasion for great joy to the Savior. The foundation of their new life was faith in Christ. That is what transformed the Thessalonians.

The love of these people exerted itself to the point of weariness. This was no mere sentimental or sensual love but a love that showed that the Savior had loved the Thessalonians first, as exemplified primarily in his death for them. So grateful were these recipients of God's love that they responded by giving themselves in ministries of labor and witness to others. If faith was the root of their new life, then love was the stem. Hope would be its crown.

There was a solid certainty in these new believers that resulted in a hope that produced steadfastness and patience. No matter what the odds were or how severe the persecution, their eyes were fixed on the triumphal return of the one who loved them and gave himself for them. The important thing to note is that hope was not a subjective psychological pep talk that they gave to themselves; it was grounded in a real object: the person of Jesus Christ. Rather than their hope being some kind of ephemeral wishful thinking, Christ himself was the reality that constantly filled their lives and thinking. This was the crowning glory of the work of Christ in their lives.

Believers should never forget all the benefits they enjoy (Ps. 103:2). In fact, we are responsible to rehearse to one another what God has done in the past: in, through, and by us.

What a confidence-builder is the fact that believers are loved and chosen by God (v. 4). What had happened at Thessalonica was no sudden change in God's plans, or even an afterthought. Even before the creation of the world they were chosen (Eph. 1:4)—and so were all believers!

But the heart of the matter can be seen in verse 5. This text is probably the simplest statement of the whole Protestant position. It is almost a formula, which can be put like this:

The Word of God + The Holy Spirit = Dynamite

If someone thinks that what happened at Thessalonica was just words being exchanged, then they had better think again. It was the mighty word of God that Paul and his associates gave out at the synagogue. And it was the Holy Spirit that made the word of God real to all who heard it. That is why it came with such "power"—as the Greek has it, such "dynamite." Thus, when the gospel is declared, whether from a lay witness or from a pulpit, mark it well: God is present there. He is working to effect what mortals are unable to do themselves. Witnessing and preaching are more than bantering about of more words in a world that already is crammed full of words. And it is not that the gospel just describes or talks about power; the gospel itself is power!

The gospel also produces "deep conviction" or "much assurance" (v. 5). It is not necessary to try to produce a guilt trip or to study the ways in which mass crowd psychology works in order to get religious results. There is nothing like that here in the gospel. Why, then, is it that so many attempt to cheapen the mighty working of God's Word and his Holy Spirit by introducing methods that will not carry the day? If we think that the old-fashioned reliance on the Word of God is now passé, we are dead wrong. Lay witnesses, pastors, missionaries, youth workers, and all other servants of Christ should be warned not to bend to contemporary substitutes. These are all weak imitations of the power God has demonstrated in his Word time and time again.

Look at the Way the Hearers Imitated What They Had Heard (1:6-8)

The effects of the gospel did not stop with the first group of believers: these first believers turned around and became mimics of what they had seen the apostle Paul and his friends do. At first they mimicked only the messengers who brought the words of life to them; but then they became mimics of the Lord (v. 6). That is usually the way it happens: so grateful are the recipients of the Word for those who brought the message of life to them that they become imitators of mere mortals; eventually, however, they see it was the Lord who was really responsible for what took place, so they switch their loyalties from mortals over to the Lord (cf. 1 Cor. 4:16; 11:1; Eph. 5:1).

Here, then, is the formula for evangelism, which is so important to the heart, mind, and plan of God for our world. It is this: the imitators themselves were imitated as the next generation of believers were formed (v. 7). The word went far beyond Thessalonica: it spread across Macedonia and Achaia. Here is another test for the truth of the gospel: its universality. Heresy is always local, ethnic, and bound up in a mere human personality. But everyone knew that God had done a work at Thessalonica because of the fruit that resulted from what had happened to those who first heard.

So widespread were the results of those first few converts who responded to the simple arguments of Paul in the synagogue that Paul was confronted with the evidence of their witness everywhere he went (v. 8). It was almost as if Paul had worked himself out of a job. The word of God kept "trumpeting forth" (literal translation of the NIV's "rang out") all over the land (v. 8).

Evangelism is simply sharing the good news of the gospel. The noun *evangel* occurs in the New Testament seventy-six times. It means the "gospel" (i.e., the "God-spell," or the "God-story"). It was the good spiel! It is a narrative about the great acts of God in Christ. The verb *to evangelize* means "to announce" or "proclaim the good news." The verb appears fifty-four times in the New Testament. But way beyond the formal labeling of this event in the New Testament, the act of setting forth the wonderful story of what God did in Jesus is one of the major preoccupations of that testament. Whenever God has revived his people, there has invariably followed a new consciousness of the need for witnessing and evangelizing all who have not heard. So thrilling is the evidence of the work of the Spirit of God in our lives that it is impossible to contain it. It must be shared with those who are in need of God's grace.

Look at the Way the Message Brought Results (1:9–10)

The proof of the pudding is said to be in the eating. Here, it was in the results. The idolatry of the Greek and Roman religions that had infected so much of the culture in that part of the world was immediately forsaken by the believers who came to Christ. Rather than serving a dead god of wood and stone, they now served the "living God"; these people had been transformed.

Should we think that idolatry was limited to the Old or New Testament worlds, we need to reflect seriously on what is the genius of idolatry. It is the act of placing anything, any person or idea, equal with or above God, so as to give ultimate allegiance to that goal, person, or idea. Seen in that light, idolatry is our modern cup of tea. We do tend to put our careers, our schooling, our children, our grades, ourselves, if not a thousand other things, on an equal plane, or even above God. Thus, when the call comes from the Spirit of God for us to witness, to serve, or to minister to the physical, social, or spiritual needs of someone else, we protest and refuse to serve: we have inferred or actually acknowledged higher commitments than our professed allegiance to Jesus Christ. What will we say to the high King of glory in the final day? Are these not further evidences of our need for revival?

And there was hope manifested in these verses as well. It was a hope fixed on the second coming of our Lord Jesus Christ. Then he would raise out of their graves all who had believed on him. Jesus would also rescue us from the wrath that would come on the world (v. 10c).

But look how the newborn converts at Thessalonica now loved the true and living God: they served him in life, witness, and action. They had no other option but to serve him since they had been loved so much by the Savior who died for them. They did not have to be urged to serve: it came as naturally as night follows day. Too frequently this type of love is later replaced with one that appears more refined and cultured. Alas, this latter type of love turns out to be a loss of love, not a more refined love. No longer does it feel the urgency in sharing the good news with others. This can only be another indication that it is time for God to send a revival once again.

Conclusion

The message of our Lord is still just as powerful as it ever was. It is infused with the same words that can bring life to all who will listen. It is still attended by the mighty ministry of the convicting, comforting, and teaching Holy Spirit. Why, then, do we shrink back so naturally from sharing that word in the lives of others?

Will the memory of our labors for Christ bring to the minds and lips of all who recall them thanksgiving to God? Is the type of life and the consistency of our witness such that it is worth imitating and mimicking by those who are now coming to Christ? What kind of advertisement for the effectiveness of the gospel are we? How much work has our faith produced? What kind of labor has our love prompted? What has our hope of personally seeing the Lord Jesus soon done by way of making us more patient and able to bear up under suffering and persecution? All of these are tough questions unless it is the same Lord who called us who is now reviving us by his mighty Spirit to do what we in our own weaknesses cannot do.

Epilogue

Revival on God's Terms
2 Chronicles 7:14

*T*he verb to *revive* in our English Bibles is almost exclusively an Old Testament word. It occurs in the NIV only five times in the Old Testament (Pss. 80:18; 85:6; Isa. 57:15 [*bis*]; and Hos. 6:2). The sole New Testament occurrences were found in the King James Version of Rom. 7:9; 14:9. Thus we are mainly limited to the five passages mentioned in the Old Testament where the Hebrew verb *ḥayah* "to live," "to recover," or "to revive" appears.

The major reference to being revived, of course, is in Psalm 85:6, which we treated in our first chapter of this book.[1] But we must not think that all the references to revival in the Bible will mention this word, for, as we have found out, the Scriptures will refer to the concept of revival without using this word more frequently than it does with it.

In our introduction we have also noted that each of the sixteen revivals in the Bible had very distinctive characteristics. Most of them began as one or two individuals saw the need for a heavenly visitation. All of them were addressed in the first place to the body of believers. In fact, five out of the seven churches addressed in the Book of Revelation were told to repent and return to God. Therefore, revivals are definitely aimed at the believing church and not at the unsaved. The purpose of these revivals is to call the church back to a new hearing of and responding to the Word of God. It must involve a forsaking of sin, a confession of that sin, and a deep desire to reverse the pattern of spiritual declension and apostasy that has begun to typify that ministry, either locally, regionally, or nationally.

Most will agree that the divine response given to Solomon, when he prayed that great dedicatory prayer, after the completion of the temple of God, forms one of the great hallmarks in Scripture for expecting revival in any period of history. Solomon prayed that God would forgive the sins of Israel when they would confess their guilt, after being visited by some future drought, famine, or pestilence as a result of their sin (2 Chron. 6:26–31).

God's reply to Solomon's petition in 2 Chronicles 7:12–16 was put in such formulaic terms that this response would serve forever after as the basis for true revival and renewal to any people in any nation at any time. The heart of this central text, in the gallery of revival texts, was verse 14: "If my people, who are called by my name, will humble themselves and pray and seek my face and turn from their wicked ways, then will I hear from heaven and will forgive their sin and will heal their land." Note that "my people" are identified by the apositional clause "who are called by my name." Since this clause is used in both the Old Testament and the New Testament for all believers, the scope of this promise goes far beyond Israel to include any and all believers in all times.

The Promise of 2 Chronicles 7:14

Philip R. Newell noted three great facts about this remarkable promise, which we will describe here: (1) the promise is intended for us today; (2) the promise is descriptive of current times; and (3) the promise of deliverance is conditional.[2]

This Promise Is Intended for Us Today

We have already described in our introduction the fact that this promise originally was given to the nation Israel. However, the qualifying clause that immediately follows the references to "my people" is one that opens up this promise to more than the Jewish people—it was the clause that read, "who are called by my name." That phraseology is used to describe everyone who had become part of the family of God and over whom God had put his protective name.[3]

We also have the assurance from Romans 15:4 that "everything that was written in the past was written to teach us, so that through endurance and the encouragement of the Scriptures [which, up to this point, was only the Old Testament] we might have hope." Likewise, 1 Corinthians 10:11 exhorts, "These things happened to them [i.e., to the Old Testament saints] as examples and were written down as warnings for us, on whom the fulfillment of the ages has come."

It is incumbent on us to apply these same words of 2 Chronicles 7:14 to our own times, nation, churches, and families, as did the ancient Israelites. The principles by which God operates his kingdom remain the same; we dare not assume less.

The Promise Is Descriptive of Current Times

The conditions of 2 Chronicles 7:13 imply that when national disasters begin to afflict a nation, people, or group of believers, it is time to ask what it is that God is trying to say to them or to us. Naturally, one emergency or disaster cannot automatically be converted into the voice of God, for there are more factors at work in this world than reducing them all to a single factor; there is, however, that which is sinful and wicked. Ask Job about his experiences along this line. But when these tragedies start coming in a series, such as Amos 4:6–12 illustrated, then it is high time for the believers to sit up and take notice. Be sure that God is calling a nation away from unrighteousness and back to himself. In Amos's case, God sent first famine (Amos 4:6), then drought (v. 7–8), then locusts, blight, and mildew (v. 9), then plagues similar to the ones that hit Egypt (v. 10), and finally the defeat of some of their cities (v. 11); but in each case the sad refrain was, "yet you have not returned to me, declares the LORD" (vv. 6b, 8b, 9b, 10b, 11b). Not one of the calamities of that day forced any of the people of God to turn back to him. And because the people had not returned to the Lord, there would not only be no revival; the nation would exist no longer as well: "Therefore this is what I will do to you, Israel, and because I will do this to you, prepare to meet your God, O Israel" (v. 12). Many have taken this verse to be a salvation text, for one used to see it out in the countryside printed on large oval discs as one drove along: "Prepare to Meet Your God!" Unfortunately, that is not what the prophet of God meant here; he meant that since there was no repentance, or heeding to the national signs of disaster that were lovingly sent to those who had ignored the Word of God written and announced by his messengers, God would be obligated to send his wrath and judgment on that nation.

Likewise, God warned Solomon in 2 Chronicles 7:13, "When I shut up the heavens so that there is no rain, or command locusts to devour the land or send a plague among my people," then it was time that Israel met the four conditions of the famous verse 14 in 2 Chronicles 7.

The question needs to be asked by every generation and culture: Have we yet reached the point described in verse 13? Only the Lord knows for sure, but one would hardly need the skills of a prophet to conclude that the current pace of evil in America has accelerated to such a rate that it is almost a foregone conclusion that God must intervene with unusual punishment soon, if an immediate repentance to God and a revival from God is to prevent such judgment from falling on any one of the modern nations of our day.

It is not necessary to spiritualize the drought, famine, or pestilence of verse 13 in order to make the principle of this text applicable to our times, as Newell apparently decided to do. Those spiritual declensions follow the other forms of ethical, moral, and legislative deteriorations already mentioned: both are just as real and of equal importance to our Lord.

The Promise of Deliverance Is Conditional

It is all too easy in these days of stressing the love and grace of our Lord (which is correct and legitimate in and of itself, of course) to ignore the stipulated conditions attached to our participating in the blessings of God. The four conditions mentioned in this text were not of human origin, but divine. This was God's word to Solomon but it is none the less his word to us as well.

Some will object: "But this is yet another form of legalism." However, that would be wrong, for legalism is the attempt to earn our salvation by working for it—a form that is totally antithetical to Scripture. Salvation is God's free gift; it cannot be earned in any shape or form.

But if we are talking about fellowship and communion with our Lord, then let it be noted that God cannot be present or work where sin is present. That is why revival is called for under such circumstances.

The conditionality of "If my people . . . will humble themselves and pray and seek my face and turn from their wicked ways" is no more offensive than John 14:21, "Whoever has my commands and obeys them, he is the one who loves me"; or John 15:7, "If you remain in me and my words remain in you, ask whatever you wish, and it will be given you." The conditions, then, were not for entrance into heaven or possessing eternal life, but for the maintenance of fellowship and communion, and for the enjoyment of life to its fullness in these mortal bodies.

The old hymn writer said it best: "Trust and obey, for there's no other way, to be happy in Jesus, but to trust and obey." And if that is true of an individual, it is also true for a nation and church denominations as well.

The Four Conditions of 2 Chronicles 7:14

1. If My People Humble Themselves

So large is the topic of "humbling ourselves" in the Old Testament that there are more than a dozen Hebrew words translating this single word *humble*, with over eighty references. The one used in 2 Chronicles 7:14 is *kana'*, meaning "to subdue," as Gideon "subdued" Midian (Judg. 8:28). The picture is one of "bending the knee" or bending the neck in deference to another.

God calls for his people to render to him complete and voluntary subjection. The precedent for doing this is to be found in the example of our Lord in Philippians 2:8, where Jesus "humbled himself." Those who follow our Lord must be willing to deny themselves and take up his or her cross and follow Christ (Matt. 16:24).

Humbling ourselves, then, is a voluntary denial of every impulse we have to exalt ourselves instead of following the pattern set by the world. We must go into spiritual bankruptcy ("Blessed are the poor in spirit") if we are to have the mind-set and frame of thinking that was in our Lord Jesus (Phil. 2:5).

The two revivals we have studied in 2 Chronicles indicate what more is intended by this condition of "humbling ourselves." Both Rehoboam and Josiah had to come to the point of saying that if God did not extricate them from the trouble they were in, then no one or nothing else would be able to help them.

That is the point to which the modern church must also come. God dwells with those who are of a contrite and humble spirit, reviving their spirits and reviving the hearts of those who are contrite (Isa. 57:15).

2. If My People Will Pray

There are ten different words for prayer in the Hebrew text, but the one used here focuses on intercession. It is well illustrated by Samuel, who assures God's people, "As for me, far be it from me that I should sin against the LORD by failing to pray for you" (1 Sam. 12:23).

S. D. Gordon, in his *Quiet Talks on Prayer*, combines the various forms of prayer into three groups: petition, communion, and intercession. Most Christians know how to petition God in prayer, for that is what we do best. Like little children, we are always asking—and the Lord does not rebuke us for doing so. Fewer believers have learned about staying in God's presence in order to commune with him and to meditate on the things of God. The joy of worshipful adoration of the Most High God and Lord of lords often goes unclaimed by many who stay in prayer only for a passing minute or two.

But the work of entering into prayer as a ministry of intercession, praying for the world and its problems and needs, is a task that is rarely entered into by believers. In intercession we participate with God in the great conflict between God and our archenemy, the devil. True intercession takes the persons and places in the world where evil is assaulting the kingdom of God and pleads that the strong hand of God might defeat evil. It prays that the lost might see the glorious offer of grace given by our Lord Jesus and that they might come to trust him personally.

Just as Jehoshaphat was taught to stand still and pray for the defeat of the enemy, so too we need to prepare for the work we attempt to do in God's name by means of intercessory prayer. When Moses' hands were held high in prayer by Aaron and Hur, Amalek was vanquished, and his forces fell back in defeat. But when Moses dropped his hands out of exhaustion, thereby relaxing in his prayer for Joshua and the troops engaged in the conflict on the valley floor, the enemy surged forward against the forces of good (Exod. 17:8–15). This is the lesson the church needs to learn in all our current skirmishes with evil. This does not mean that this is all that we must do, for that could be an easy excuse to exempt us from getting our hands dirty in the various services for Christ. But if this is not the very atmosphere in which God's work goes forward, then we must count on being soundly thrashed by the present world system in our families, our churches, our courts, and our nations. Mark it well: where intercession goes thin or ceases altogether, there the saints and the churches drift into spiritual lethargy, and the forces of evil have a field day in the culture.

The weapons our Lord gave for our warfare are only two: (1) "the sword of the Spirit, which is the word of God," and (2) "all kinds of prayer and requests . . . praying for all the saints . . ." (Eph. 6:17–18). No other provisions are needed for us to successfully thwart the devil's attacks.

Newell quoted from both Alexander Whyte and Andrew Murray on this matter of prayer. Cried Whyte,

> My brethren, will nothing teach you to pray? Will all His examples, and all His promises, and all your needs, and cares, and distresses, not teach you to pray? Will you not tell your Saviour what a dislike, even to downright antipathy, you have at secret prayer; how little you attempt it, and how soon you are weary of it? Only pray, O you prayerless people of His, and Heaven will soon open to you also, and you will hear your Father's voice, and the Holy Ghost will descend like a dove upon you."[4]

Andrew Murray, in the introduction to his book *The Ministry of Intercession,* urged us to consider the fact that our Lord attempted, in this connection, to get two main truths across to us:

> [First] that Christ actually meant prayer to be the great power by which His Church should do its work, and that the neglect of prayer is the great reason the Church has not greater power over the masses in Christian and in heathen countries; [and second] that we have far too little conception of the place that intercession, as distinguished from prayer for ourselves, ought to have in the Church and the Christian life.[5]

Murray continued to express amazement that in Israel's day, God

> often had to wonder and complain that there was no intercessor, none to stir himself up to take hold of His strength. And He still waits and wonders in our day, that there are not more intercessors, that all His children do not give themselves to this highest and holiest work . . . Ministers of His gospel complain . . . that their duties do not allow them to

find time for this, which He counts their first, their highest, their most delightful, their alone effective work. . . . His sons and daughters, who have forsaken home and friends for His sake and the gospel's, come . . . so short in what He meant to be their abiding strength—receiving day by day all they needed to impart to the . . . heathen. He wonders to find multitudes of His children who have hardly any conception of what intercession is. He wonders to find multitudes who have learned that it is their duty, and seek to obey it, but confess that they know but little of taking hold upon God or prevailing with Him.[6]

Is it not clear that we ought to pray, and to pray in an intercessory way? What a wonderful discovery it would be if we should suddenly come to the end of all of our attempts to bypass this most inexorable condition, and if we concluded that the condition of praying was what we needed to meet for God to act in our day on our behalf! The world would be changed like it had never been changed in our lifetime.

3. If My People Will Seek My Face

Some things we long for so much that we can almost taste them. But what of our desire to seek God's face?

The "face" of God signifies not his literal face, for, as Scripture often reminds us, no one can see God's face and still live (e.g., Exod. 33:20). What the "face" of God signifies is the joy and the benefits that come from experiencing his presence, his approval, and his communion with the likes of humanity.

So how can we go about seeking his presence, communion, and approval? By drawing near to him, advises James 4:8. That is how God is able to draw near to us.

But how can we draw near to God if we have unclean hands and an impure heart (Ps. 24:3–4)? We must forsake our wicked ways and our unrighteous thought (Isa. 55:7) and ask for the cleansing work of God's forgiveness to take place (2 John 1:9).

Only as we abide in Christ are we able to bear fruit (John 15). So, if we are risen with Christ, we must seek those things that are above, where Christ is seated at the right hand of the Father (Col. 3:1). That is where we will find fullness of joy (Ps. 16:11), for when we seek our Lord with all our heart, then he will be found, promised Jeremiah (29:13).

4. If My People Will Turn from Their Wicked Ways

The fourth and final condition that would allow revival to take place, in the sovereign plan of God, is if God's people would turn from their sin by repenting of the evil they have done. If there is no turning from evil, the genuineness of the confession of sin must be doubted. Newell quotes a bit of quaint verse from another century that admonished us about this very need for being authentic and genuine in our request for forgiveness.

> 'Tis not to cry God mercy, or to sit
> And droop, or to confess that thou hast failed;
> 'Tis to bewail the sins thou didst commit—
> And not commit those sins thou has bewailed.
> He that bewails, and not forsakes them too,
> Confesses rather what he means to do.[7]

Jacob was told that he had to put away the idols that were in his household and to be clean if he wished to experience the blessing of God and his reviving power (Gen. 35:1–4). Likewise, Joshua commanded the nation of Israel that they also had to "throw away the gods your forefathers worshiped beyond the River and in Egypt, and serve the LORD" (Josh. 24:14). No less insistent was the prophet Isaiah when he also rebuked Israel by saying, "Take your evil deeds out of my sight! Stop doing wrong, learn to do right!" (Isa. 1:16b–17a). And in the very same train of thought came John the Baptist declaring, "Repent, for the kingdom of heaven is near. . . . Produce fruit in keeping with repentance" (Matt. 3:2a, 8). The whole case built by all of those we have mentioned can be summarized by the apostle Paul's injunction, "Everyone who confesses the name of the Lord must turn away from wickedness" (2 Tim. 2:19c).

God wants us to be clean persons, channels through which his blessings, witness, and interventions in this sinful world can flow. But if we are to be clean, we must renounce all bitterness, wrath, malice, harshness, unforgiving spirits, filthiness, and immorality; in short, anything that would "give the devil a foothold" (Eph. 4:27) in our lives, in our churches, in our families, and in our nation.

If the constant and key cry of the prophets of the Old Testament was for the people to "turn," and "return to the Lord," can the constant cry of our hearts be any less than that in our day?

Conclusion

Not only have we examined each of the four conditions and requirements that God has made of us if we seek the outpouring of his blessing in revival; we have also examined sixteen revivals in the Bible that have taught us no less about our Lord.

There is only one conclusion that we can draw from all these matters. We all agree that we and our nations are in desperate need of revival. We also agree that if God does not intervene we are headed for a time of divine judgment; probably, such as we have never seen before. So what is this one logical conclusion to which we believers must all come? It is the one found in John 13:17 — "Now that you know these things, you will be blessed if you do them."

Notes

Preface

1. J. Edwin Orr, *Campus Aflame* (Glendale, Calif.: Regal Books, 1971), 101, as cited by Dan Hayes, *Fireseeds of Spiritual Awakening* (San Bernardino, Calif.: Here's Life Publishers, 1983), 36.
2. Walter C. Kaiser, Jr., *Quest for Renewal: Personal Revival in the Old Testament* (Chicago: Moody, 1986).

Introduction

1. Wilbur M. Smith, *The Glorious Revival under King Hezekiah* (Grand Rapids: Zondervan, 1937), vi–vii.
2. For more on these four conditions, see the epilogue to this present volume.
3. H. G. M. Williamson, "1 and 2 Chronicles," *The New Century Bible* (Grand Rapids: Eerdmans, 1982), 225.
4. Stephen Olford, *Heart-Cry for Revival: Expository Sermons on Revival* (Westwood, N.J.: Revell, 1962), 33.
5. Charles G. Finney, *Revival of Religion* (Westwood, N.J.: Revell, n.d.), 7.
6. Ibid., 20.
7. C. E. Autrey, *Revivals of the Old Testament* (Grand Rapids: Zondervan, 1960), 13.
8. Walter C. Kaiser, *Ecclesiastes: Total Life* (Chicago: Moody Press, 1978).
9. Smith (rev. ed., 1954), 7–8.
10. Ibid., 25.
11. I am indebted for this general list of five reasons for studying revivals (though without attributing the substance and general development of the discussion) to Autrey, *Revivals of the Old Testament*, 18–20.

Chapter 1

1. *Hesed* appears 248 times in the Old Testament. The NIV gives 25 different translations for this one word: "love," 129 times; "kindness," 41 times; "unfailing love," 32 times; "great love," 6 times; "mercy," 6 times; "loving," 5 times; "kindnesses," 3 times; "acts of devotion," 2 times; "devotion," 2 times; "favor," 2 times; and one time each for: "approval," "devout," "faith-

ful," "faithfully," "glory," "good favor," "grace," "kind," "kindly," "loving-kindness," "loyal," "merciful," "well," and 4 times it was left untranslated!

Chapter 2

1. George Bush, *Notes on Genesis*, 2 vols. (1860; reprint, Minneapolis: James and Klock, 1976), 2:200.
2. Harold C. Stigers, *A Commentary on Genesis* (Grand Rapids: Zondervan, 1976), 262.
3. Bush, *Notes on Genesis*, 201.
4. H. C. Leupold, *Exposition of Genesis*, 2 vols. (Grand Rapids: Baker, 1953), 2:919.
5. Victor P. Hamilton, "Shaddai," in *Theological Wordbook of the Old Testament*, 2 vols., eds. R. Laird Harris, Gleason L. Archer, Jr., and Bruce K. Waltke (Chicago: Moody, 1980), 2:907.

Chapter 3

1. George Bush, *Notes on Exodus* (1852; reprint, Minneapolis: James and Klock, 1976), 215.
2. Ibid., 224.
3. Ibid., 224.
4. Ibid., 245.

Chapter 4

1. John Shearer, *Old Time Revivals: How the Fire of God Spread in Days Now Past and Gone* (London: Pickering and Inglis, n.d.), 43.
2. C. F. David Erdmann, *The Books of Samuel in Lange's Commentary on Holy Scripture* (New York: Armstrong, 1877), 120.
3. Autrey, *Revivals of the Old Testament*, 53.

Chapter 5

1. A. W. Pink, *The Life of Elijah* (London: Banner of Truth, 1963), 109.
2. Josephus, *Antiquities*, 8.13.2.
3. Pink, *Life of Elijah*, 127.

Chapter 6

1. Ernest Baker, *The Revivals of the Bible* (Capetown, South Africa: Miller, 1906), 37.
2. "Seeking the face of the LORD" appears in 1 Chron. 16:11; Ps. 105:4; Ps. 24:6; 27:8 (twice); Hos. 5:15; 2 Sam. 21:1; and 2 Chron. 7:14. The more

general statements of seeking the Lord are found in Exod. 33:7; Deut. 4:29; 2 Sam. 12:16; Ezra 8:22; Pss. 40:17; 69:6; 70:5; Prov. 28:5; Isa. 51:1; Jer. 29:13; 50:4; Dan. 9:3; Hos. 3:5; 5:6; 7:10; Zeph. 1:6; Zech. 8:21; Mal. 3:1; and the references in 1 Chron. 16:10/Ps. 105:3; and 2 Chron. 11:16; 15:4, 15; 20:4.

3. *Theological Dictionary of the Old Testament*, s.v. "Darash."

Chapter 7

1. Finney, *Revivals on Religion*, 126–27.
2. Ibid., 498.

Chapter 8

1. Baker, *The Revivals of the Bible*, 66.
2. Smith, *King Hezekiah*, 12.

Chapter 9

1. These fourteen references are 2 Chron. 7:14; 12:6, 7 (twice), 12; 30:11; 32:26; 33:12, 19, 23 (twice); 34:27 (twice); 36:12. The root of this word is sometimes associated with "to bend the knee."
2. Franz Delitzsch, *Biblical Commentary on the Proverbs of Solomon* (Grand Rapids: Eerdmans, 1950), 2:85.
3. Baker, *Revivals of the Bible*, 83.
4. Autry, *Revivals of the Old Testament*, 34.

Chapter 10

1. Matthew Henry as cited by Richard Wolff, *The Book of Haggai* (Grand Rapids: Baker, 1967), 27.
2. G. L. Robinson, "Zechariah, Book of," *The International Standard Bible Encyclopedia*, eds. James Orr, et al. (Grand Rapids: Eerdmans, 1952), 5:3137.
3. T. V. Moore, *Haggai, Zechariah, and Malachi* (New York: Carter, 1856), 66.

Chapter 11

1. Baker, *Revivals of the Bible*, 117.
2. Ibid., 114.
3. Ibid., 123.

Chapter 12

1. J. Elder Cumming, *John: The Baptist, Forerunner and Martyr* (London: Marshall Brothers, n.d.), 104–5.
2. There are twenty passages from the prophet Isaiah including: "vipers" from Isa. 59:5; "fleeing from the wrath to come" in 10:3; "fruits fit for repentance" in 3:10; being Abraham's seed in 63:16; "wash you and make you clean" in 1:16; the fan and the threshing floor in 41:16; the axe laid to the tree in 14; the case against exaction, oppression, and false fasting in 58:6–7; the Lamb that takes away the sin of the world in 53:7, 10; the Spirit "remaining" in 11:2; and the "bridegroom" in Isa. 62. Likewise, references and allusions to Jeremiah include the fan in Jer. 15:7; "O generation" in 2:31; "fruit" from a life in 17:10; 6:19; 21:14; 32:19; the axe laid to the root of a tree, the tree being hewn down and cast into the fire in 7:20; 11:16, 19; and God as Husband in 2:32.
3. Cumming, *John*, 34.
4. Flavius Josephus, "Antiquities of the Jews" in *The Works of Flavius Josephus,* tr. William Whiston (Philadelphia: John C. Winston, n.d), xviii, 2, 540.

Chapter 13

1. Baker, *Revivals of the Bible*, 137–38.
2. T. Goodwin, *Works* (Edinburgh: 1861), 6:8, as cited by G. Smeaton, *The Doctrine of the Holy Spirit* (London: 1958), 49.
3. For a more detailed discussion of Joel 2:28–32, see Walter C. Kaiser, Jr. *The Uses of the Old Testament in the New* (Chicago: Moody Press, 1985), 89–100.
4. For a fuller discussion of the work of the Holy Spirit in the Old Testament, see Walter C. Kaiser, Jr., "What Was the Old Testament Believer's Experience of the Holy Spirit?" in *Toward Rediscovering the Old Testament* (Grand Rapids: Zondervan, 1987), 135–141.
5. In 4 of the 23 examples just mentioned, the term "all flesh" is used as a synonym for the "nations" (Deut. 5:26; Isa. 49:26; 66:16; Zech. 2:13 NKJV).

Chapter 14

1. The opposition between the Jews and the Samaritans continued to fester way beyond Sargon's destruction of Samaria in 722 B.C. and his policy of deportation and mixing populations. The Samaritans opposed the rebuilding of the Jerusalem temple when the Jews returned from exile in the fifth century (Neh. 2:10–6:14). The Samaritans, in the meantime, had erected their own schismatic temple on Mount Gerizim around the time of Alexander (cf. Josephus, *Antiquities of the Jews,* XI, 310–11, 322–24; XIII,

255–56). Later, they identified themselves with the Sidonians and joined with the Seleucids against the Jews in the conflict of 167–64 B.C. But the final rupture in relations seemed to come when John Hyrcanus destroyed the Gerizim Temple and the city of Samaria in 127 B.C. (cf. Josephus, *Antiquities*, XIII, 256, 275–77).

2. Luke uses the word *all* (*pantes*) throughout his two volumes in a general sense, leaving each context to limit it. Throughout the New Testament the words *all* (*pantes*) and *many* (*polloi*) are used interchangeably (e.g., Matt. 20:28; Mark 10:45).

3. Baker, *Revivals of the Bible*, 152.

4. See the fuller discussion of this supposition in Richard Longenecker, "The Acts of the Apostles," in *The Expositor's Bible Commentary*, Vol. 9 (Grand Rapids: Zondervan, 1981), 284–85.

5. I am indebted to Richard Longenecker (ibid., 358) for this discussion of Simon Magnes and the references that follow. Justin Martyr, *Apology* 1, 26; *Dialogue* 120.

6. Irenaeus, *Against Heresies*, 1, 23.

Chapter 15

1. Baker, *Revivals of the Bible*, 159–60.

2. Ibid., 162.

Epilogue

1. The title and many of the concepts for this epilogue come from a booklet by the same title mentioned in the introductory chapter. It is the one by Philip R. Newell, *Revival on God's Terms: A Consideration of Scriptural Conditions Which God Waits for His People to Fulfil.* (Chicago: Moody Press, 1959).

2. Ibid., 6–11.

3. See our introduction.

4. Alexander Whyte, *The Walk, Conversation and Character of Our Lord Jesus Christ* as cited by Newell, *Revival on God's Terms*, 30.

5. Andrew Murray as cited by Newell, 31.

6. Ibid.

7. Ibid., 42.

Study Guide

Introduction

1. What are some of the improper definitions for *revival*?

   What is the Bible's definition of *revival*, especially regarding the circumstances when a revival is needed, who are its subjects, what are its conditions, and what are its results?

2. In what way does 2 Chronicles 7:14 supply the outline for the book of 2 Chronicles? What is the pattern for five of the kings of Judah and the four emphases found here?

3. Some may object, "But sin and evil have always been rampant, so why argue so strenuously for revival in our times? Anyway, aren't things supposed to get worse and worse before Christ returns?" What is your answer?

4. Name the nine characteristics of the great revivals of the Bible listed by Wilbur Smith. How applicable is this list for us today?

5. If one is not farming, of what use is it to promise productivity of the fields and prosperity of one's labor on the farm? Does this mean that we should get right with God in order to get rich? Is that a worthy, or even a correct, motive for seeking revival?

6. Name the five reasons, as given by C. E. Autrey, why it is worthwhile to study the revivals of the Bible.

7. Has any revival occurred without being initiated by God? Does this mean that there is nothing we can do to bring revival? When was the last great revival in America and in other parts of the world?

1. It is Time to Ask God to Revive Us Once Again

1. What is so amazing about the fact that God would use the sons of Korah to write Psalm 85? What should this fact teach us about God's treatment of us today?

2. What are the three steps, as signified by the six verbs in Psalm 85:1–3, to our being restored back to God? Does God forgive but not forget? Why are some people so hesitant to ask God for forgiveness?

3. What is the connection between one's joy and the ability of a congregation to sing wholeheartedly to the Lord?

4. Do you think we in the United States of America (or those other countries of the world) need to experience a genuine revival if we are to be spared an almost certain disaster (Ps. 85:4–7)?

5. What three names does God give to believers in Psalm 85: 8–9? Do any of these names make you feel funny about being called that?

6. Name some of the sins the New Testament lists that we need to be delivered from as itemized in our discussion of verse 7. To what extent do these same sins afflict the church today?

7. How can we get a deep passion for the truth together with our need for seeing real harmony among all who believe in Jesus Christ? How successful do you think a real revival would be in bringing all God's people together?

8. How much life and vitality do you think is in the church today? Do we need a heaven-sent revival or not?

2. It Is Time to Get Rid of Our Idols

1. What role do circumstances play in bringing us to the point where we sense our need for revival? Is this the only way God can accomplish this effect? How many years had intervened since Jacob had promised God he would change when he had been in another crisis? Does any of this sound at all familiar to us today? Can we remember vows to change in the past that were never carried out?

2. What three reasons does Genesis 35 give why Jacob, and those like him, should get rid of all idols? What are the modern forms of idolatry that we also must get rid of?

3. The cleansing that God seeks is a holistic holiness. Illustrate this from Moses' experience at the burning bush. How can we apply this to ourselves?

4. Describe the two occasions when God changed Jacob's name to Israel. What was the significance of this name change? Are believers at all changed?

5. There are two hallmarks of this revival: the revelation of God and a place of sacrifice. Of what significance are each of these, and what part do both play in revivals throughout history?

6. With what divine name does God announce the favors he will bring to renamed Jacob? What is the meaning of that name? In what other connections did God announce himself by the same name in the patriarchal age?

7. How can we apply the truth taught in this revival to our day and times? Has God changed his standards in the meantime? What personal idolatries are holding back the reviving work of God in our lives now?

3.   It Is Time to Confess Our Sin

1. Name the sins that Aaron and the Israelites committed in the golden calf incident. To what extent are these same sins symptomatic of sins committed today?

2. Name the four risks that this text warns us about if we refuse to confess our sins to God.

3. Of what significance is the verse in Proverbs 29:18 for the situation Moses faced, and what is its proper translation and meaning? How do we know there is a connection between Moses' day and this verse in Proverbs?

4. Must we view Moses as being more merciful than the Lord in this situation? In what way did Moses offer to serve as an instrument of reconciliation? How is his offer reminiscent of the apostle Paul's? What book is Moses referring to?

5. What is meant by God causing all his "goodness" to pass by in front of Moses? How would that help Moses out of the situation he and Israel were in?

6. What is meant by the "Name" of God? (Name five characteristics.) What was in that name that could have any bearing on what was needed by Israel and by all who are similarly afflicted today?

7. In your estimation, how serious is the issue of unconfessed sin among believers in hampering the effectiveness of the church and for preventing revival in our times?

4. It Is Time to Serve the Lord Only

1. What was the cycle of spiritual life during the days of the judges? What is this so analogous to our own situation today?

2. What relationship is there between the sins of the leaders in Samuel's day (1 Sam. 2:12–17, 22) and the lack of the Word of God being given by them (1 Sam 3:1)? How does this same connection play out in our own day?

3. What contrast does Samuel's regard for the Word of God present with his audience in 1 Samuel 3:19? What does this suggest about the choice of whether we cater to the contemporary tastes of listeners or stick with dependency on the eventual effectiveness of the Word of God?

4. In what sense is serving the Lord a necessary effect and a genuine evidence of a revival? What could serving the Lord include today?

5. What four things took place as Israel confessed their sin and prayed to the Lord? What is the meaning of pouring out water before the Lord? Should believers practice fasting today (other than for purposes of dieting)?

6. If the people of Israel had acted so nobly and spiritually at Mizpah, why were they attacked by the Philistines? One would have thought that their meeting the necessary conditions for revival would have been a guarantee against that sort of thing. Is it a guarantee today?

7. What did the erecting of the stone called Ebenezer signify? How important is it to remember those times when God has met us in the past?

5. It Is Time to Let God Be God

1. Describe the spiritual and moral climate in the fifty-eight years following the death of Solomon and the division of the kingdom in 931 B.C. How does the question of 2 Kings 2:14 function against such a despicable background? Note especially the role played by Baal in the north.

2. What was it that commended Elijah for the role of leading this revival? How is the character of Elijah brought out by 1 Kings 18:1–2?

3. Of what importance are the first small steps of obedience for the larger and more climactic moments later in our lives?

4. In your judgment, was Obadiah apostate in working for the wicked King Ahab and Queen Jezebel? Offer biblical reasons for your conclusion. Should believers hold positions of influence in business and government today?

5. Why was the test for the true God to be fire and not the longed-for water and rain? What is the theology that stands behind this symbol of fire from heaven? What do we learn about the character of God from this episode?

6. Why did Elijah risk being politically incorrect when he chose twelve stones to make the altar and say what he said? What incident flashed through the people's minds when he told them their name?

7. Why does James 5:17–18 think that Elijah serves as a model for prayer to us? Why did Elijah need to pray for what God had already promised in verse 1? What were the characteristics of Elijah's private prayers, and how do these compare with his public prayer?

8. What is our view of God—grand or mediocre?

6. It Is Time to Seek the Lord

1. What differences did Ernest Baker note between Asa's revival and other revivals in the Bible? What is the difference between a revival and a reformation? Some current writers say that what is needed is only a reformation, not a revival. Do you agree? Or disagree? Why?

2. In Asa's case, which came first: revival or reformation? What would you assume is the more typical order and why is it always necessary for God to allow trouble to come before he can send a revival?

3. What is the key phrase repeated so frequently during Asa's revival that it became its hallmark? Judged by its usage in the Old Testament, what does this phrase mean? Mark in your Bibles where this phrase and its parallels appear during this revival.

4. In what ways do the actions of King Asa demonstrate the truth that "righteousness exalts a nation"? Is that teaching of Proverbs 14:34 still true today? Illustrate from your lifetime how the fortunes of your nation have shown a strong tendency to follow the lowest available spiritual quotient of God's people.

5. What happens when a nation decides, for reasons of its own, to forsake God, or to treat him as a lesser reality than the things immediately visible? What are some of the prices we and our nation pay for our godlessness?

6. What are some of the memorable descriptions in this text of the fact that God is incomparably greater than any other reality we can think of, or face? Relate this truth to several of the key problems we currently are facing on a national and international scale.

7. The end of Asa's life is the reverse of the rest of what this revival teaches us. What happened to him? Why? What did Asa use rather than "seeking God's face"? What is the serious warning in this demise of the king?

7.   It Is Time to Pray to the Lord

1. What does it mean to pray? Who or what is the cause of prayer? What should be the aim of our praying? With what sort of attitude and approach should we come to God in prayer? What does God use prayer for in his kingdom?

2. How do you answer the objection that there is no need to pray since God already knows what is wanted and needed? How does the doctrine of divine providence enter into the practice of prayer? Name five suggestions that will help improve our prayer life.

3. What five reasons does 2 Chronicles 20 give for praying? Is it proper to rehearse these reasons to God when we pray? What effect do you think this would have on our petitioning, interceding, and adoration in our prayers?

4. Why base our prayers on the promises of God if they really are promises? Aren't they, as the expression goes, "already in the bag"? Give scriptural support for your position.

5. In what sense is the concept of God as judge an encourage- ment to our prayers? In what sense does God judge the wicked currently as well as in the final day?

6. How do the words of verse 15 about the battle belonging to the Lord remind us of the David and Goliath episode? When we are faced with serious odds against us, what is the repeated command of Scripture (vv. 15, 17) and what is its positive corollary?

7. What happened as a result of King Jehoshaphat's unusual approach to a potential battle with overwhelming odds against him, judged from human standards? Why was he successful? Are these same tactics available to us today?

8. How can having faith in the Word of God rescue a nation? Is Charles G. Finney's strong rebuke of the ministry (and of all forms of Christian ministry) needed today?

8. It Is Time to Turn Back to the Lord

1. In what ways had Hezekiah's father, Ahaz, and his people "cast off all restraint" prior to the revival? What similarities do you observe with the culture of our own day?

2. The key word that symbolized this revival under Hezekiah was *shuv*, "to turn" or "repent." Trace how this word was used in a religious sense from its earliest times down to its fivefold appearance in 2 Chronicles 30:6–9.

3. Can Christians "backslide" away from the Lord? How does this happen? What is the remedy for this spiritual ailment? To what degree is it a current problem in the church?

4. Discuss the positive and negative aspects of the verb *to repent* or *to turn* along with the main prepositions *to* and *from* used with it. What does this tell you about repentance?

5. Name the three commands of verse 8. Based on your observations of prevailing practices of believers, how readily do people "give a hand" to Christian work, cultivate the habit of regular attendance at the house of God, and serve in some regular assignment in God's program of discipling others?

6. What can Daniel 9:4–19 teach us about our roles in intercessory prayer? What other Bible passages are just as instructive in this matter? Is this privilege almost a lost art for most believers today?

7. How do you react to the thesis that the church was rescued from the downward spiral of the 1960s mainly through God's use of the parachurch movement in the 1970s and 80s, but it does not appear at this point that this will be the main avenue of deliverance again, for the ball has been bounced back into the lap of the church?

9. It Is Time to Humble Ourselves before the Lord

1. In what sense(s) are revivals the sole work of God, and in what sense(s) do they employ secondary causes or human means? In what class does the revival in Josiah's time belong?

2. Discuss the appearance of the phrase "humble yourselves" in the eras of Rehoboam and Josiah. How does the writer of Chronicles arrange his emphases on this concept of "humbling oneself"? What does this suggest about the importance the writer attached to this concept?

3. Is the idea of humbling oneself equivalent to becoming a doormat for everyone to trample on? What are some of the key concepts included in

this command to humble oneself? Give some positive examples of persons who humbled themselves in the Bible, including our Lord.

4. Recite the family heritage of Josiah. How did he avoid being influenced for evil or escape the adage that the sins of the fathers visit their children to the third and fourth generation? What does this say to persons who blame the devil, their parents, their bad luck, or others for what they have become morally? (Victim mentality!)

5. Once again we see a reform movement taking place without a revival happening as Josiah cleaned out the temple and rid the land of debauchery. What key factors had to be introduced in order to made a difference here for a revival?

6. How did Josiah unwittingly fulfill the strange prophecy of 1 Kings 13:1–31? Name some of the lessons we can learn from the incident in 1 Kings 13.

7. How central must the role of the Word of God be for a genuine revival to take place? How central is the role of that Word in our churches and ministries today? What can be done about it?

10. It Is Time to Renew the Work of the Lord

1. How many years elapsed between Hezekiah's revival and Josiah's? How many years between Josiah's revival and the one under Haggai and Zechariah? How long has it been since there was a worldwide revival in our times?

2. What can we learn from the dateline of Haggai 1:1 about the times and the seasons of the work of God? The shift in cultural eras? The date on our Julian calendars? And the shift in the royal line of David?

3. How does the word *time* function in verse 2? What does such an accusation tell us about ourselves and our unwillingness to face up to our responsibilities? What are some contemporary excuses for putting off the work of God and hiding our failures?

4. What areas are affected when we seriously set out to designate priorities for the work of God? Why are claims of lordship proven false when verbal allegiances to God are not matched with deeds? What is the remedy? What is the connection between the moral/spiritual condition of a people and their economic and material status? How far back does this connection go in the Bible?

5. What is the real purpose of obedience to God? What are the alternatives to obedience both then and now? How will God use the things around us to speak to us?

6. What has God provided for us to do his work? Is that same provision still available today for those who complain they just can't do what is expected of them?

7. How did Zechariah's message supplement Haggai's summons to the people? What was permanent? What was temporary? What was the condition of all of God's blessings?

11. It Is Time to Rejoice in the Lord

1. How many groups returned from the exile? In what year did Ezra lead his return? How many years was this after the one led by Zerubbabel with Haggai and Zechariah? When did Nehemiah's return take place? How was Nehemiah called into the service of God?

2. How does Ezra 7:10 provide the key to Ezra's life? Of what significance is this fact for revivals?

3. What activity was central in the revival in Nehemiah 8? How did the thirteen Levites function at this time? How did this extended exercise contribute to the formula for success? What would that suggest about what we should do in our day? What do we tend to substitute for this proven method that God has used time and again in the past?

4. Why did Nehemiah tell the people not to weep over their sins? What did he mean by the fact that "the joy of the LORD is your strength"? How would that joy function today? What should the joy and communion with God naturally lead to?

5. Once we get a real taste of what the Word of God is like, how is our appetite whetted and shaped for the future?

6. How should we define what godly fellowship and unity of the brethren is like? Will a revival restore this to us? Or are there other complicating factors?

7. What is the significance of the Feast of Tabernacles and the Day of Atonement? What do these days of feasting and fasting tell us about what is needed in revivals?

12. It Is Time to Prepare for the Lord

1. To what extent did John the Baptist rely on the Old Test- ment for his teaching and doctrine? What does this suggest about the seriousness with which we should take the Old Testament?

2. How can we measure the success or usefulness of our lives? Think about this in connection with the fact that John only had a six-month ministry. What do you hope to accomplish in your life for the Lord?

3. What six prophecies about John the Baptist were fulfilled by his birth? What does this suggest about the dependability of the Bible?

4. How was John affected by the conditions of his day, and in what way did they set the conditions for revival? What are some of the conditions in our day that seem to indicate that we too are in need of revival?

5. What three preparations should we make for the coming of the Lord? Is it necessary for believers to repent?

6. What are some of the evidences of repentance that we can produce today?

7. How did the baptism of John differ from that of Jesus' baptism? How do we participate in Jesus' baptism today?

8. What are some of the ways that we can be offended because of Christ? How should we react to these things?

13. It Is Time to Embrace the Gift of the Holy Spirit

1. According to Ernest Baker, what was so startling and unusual about the revival that took place on the day of Pentecost? What day in Israel's religious calendar did it celebrate?

2. Was Pentecost the first time the Holy Spirit had been revealed in the Bible or history? What was new about his coming at Pentecost?

3. Name the four features of Pentecost that will encourage believers today to be prepared for a similar outpouring of the Holy Spirit? Which feature strikes you as being the most impressive, given our modern situation?

4. Which Old Testament prophet had predicted such a downpour of the Holy Spirit? What three basic items did he predict? Did Pentecost exhaust the fulfillments that the prophet had anticipated? How does this prophecy affect some of our modern concerns, such as the legitimate roles of women, the extent of the missionary movement, and the average person's ability to be effective?

5. What comfort can we give to those who have a dread of dying? How much power does God reserve for those who will serve him? What limits are placed on this power?

6. How can we "save [ourselves] from this corrupt generation" (Acts 2:40)? Suggest some specific actions.

7. What preceded Pentecost? What does this tell us about the preparation we must make if we wish to see something similar in our day?

8. What is your own view of the person and work of the Holy Spirit? Why are contemporary Christians so nervous about the doctrine of the Holy Spirit, and how can we overcome that?

14. It Is Time to Ask for a Change of Heart

1. What verse in Acts 8 did the author of this book argue was the focal point for the revival in Samaria? In what way did Simon the sorcerer violate this central concern? What are some modern analogies of these same kinds of dual loyalties and empty professions that are attempted in our day?

2. Sometimes our Lord must use many different circumstances to motivate his church to get into action. What did he use in Jerusalem? Does that mean that God automatically approves of all the means he allows if he still is willing to use them? Give some biblical examples.

3. Explain the relationship of the Samaritans to the Jews. What kinds of social, class, ethnic, mental, and emotional blocks do we experience today when it comes to witnessing to others? What about the large number of "hidden people" groups that still have not heard the gospel?

4. How much of the Bible did the Samaritans accept as norm- ative? What prophecy did they link with the coming Messiah?

5. Some think that "if the price is right," you can buy almost anything. What is the danger of applying this type of thinking to spiritual things? What are some modern examples of attempting to do the same thing?

6. Why do you think Luke placed the conversion of the Ethiopian treasurer of Queen Candace in Acts 8:26–40 right alongside Simon the sorcerer? What does this say about race, attitude, and the extent of the gospel?

7. What changes need to take place in our hearts about some facets of our walk and ministry for our Lord? For example, about lay evangelism, the ministry of prayer for revival, about praying for the restraint of evil in our day, etc.?

15. It Is Time to Advance the Missionary Cause of Christ

1. What evidences are there in Scripture that God never calls someone without simultaneously preparing the audience or person to whom we are being sent? What assurance should this give us when we feel prompted by the Holy Spirit to talk to someone about Christ?

2. Will there be some persons in heaven who never knew about Jesus, but who, like Cornelius, lived up to the light that they had? Why, then, does Scripture give us this story about Cornelius, the angel, and Peter, if the answer to the first part of this question is yes? How important are human agents in the spreading of the gospel message?

3. How does God work to overcome the cultural and theological "hang-ups" that his messengers sometimes have? Did Peter believe that the gospel was for all races (cf. Acts 2)? Then why did he need to have a sheet let down from heaven? Is it true that our beliefs sometimes outstrip our actions? Name some areas. Where in the New Testament did the distinction between clean and unclean cease?

4. Does God hear the prayers of someone who doesn't know him as yet, but is only seeking him? What is the role of prayer in this situation?

5. Given the fast pace of our culture, is it any wonder that we are experiencing more difficulty than former days did in knowing the will of the Lord for our lives? Put this statement together with the role that prayer plays in receiving the call of God.

6. Why is it correct to affirm that "salvation is from the Jews" (John 4:22)? Give the Old Testament evidence for this truth.

7. What was it about this third "Pentecost" that startled the small delegation that went up the coast from Joppa to Caesarea with Peter? What area will this fact impact the most, when we think about the results that revival should have in our day?

16. It Is Time to Renew Evangelism in the Church

1. Explain how the Macedonian call to Paul was one of the "turning points in history." What could some of the results have been had Paul been allowed to go where he wanted to go? Can you think of other pivotal points in history that have likewise affected us today?

2. How did Paul have to revise his strategy when he first entered Europe with the gospel? What does this tell us about the relationship of the gospel itself to the methods we use in spreading that gospel?

3. Who was the first convert to come to Christ in Europe? What facts about her life indicate that she was: (1) devout, (2) sincere, and (3) exhibited a similar situation to that of Cornelius?

4. What are the three evidences found in 1 Thessalonians 1:2–10 that God had revived this new European group of believers? In what ways could these same three evidences characterize our churches?

5. What were the three qualities of the faith of the Thessalonians (vv. 2–5)? How do these motivating forces differ from those we normally associate with God's work?

6. Verse 5 gives us the simplest formula of the reformation. What is it? What does this formula suggest about the way the church and persons ought to engage in evangelism today?

7. Give some examples of how individuals tend to imitate and mimic those they admire. Relate this to the theory of reproducing Christians in verses 6–8.

8. What modern strategies and pivotal points do you think should be pursued to evangelize this generation?

Epilogue

1. What is the main purpose of a revival? Is a revival aimed primarily at the believing community or the unbelieving?

2. Philip R. Newell names three great facts about the promise of 2 Chronicles 7:14. What are they?

3. How can we be sure that the promise of 2 Chronicles 7:14 is for our day and our kind of people? What in the text of 2 Chronicles 7:14 argues that way? And what other New Testament texts support the same conclusion?

4. If we do not have the gift of prophecy, in what way are we responsible for understanding that it is God who is speaking to us in our day and generation? What part does a text like Amos 4:6–12 play in alerting us to the fact that God is warning us of an impending national disaster if we do not repent and turn back to him?

5. Name the four conditions listed in 2 Chronicles 7:14 for revival and the reversal of impending national disaster.

6. Doesn't the condition of "humbling ourselves" run counter to the modern emphasis on self-esteem and finding one's own self-identity? What is the balance between these two?

7. S. D. Gordon combined all forms of prayer into what three groups? Which did he think was the most difficult and most neglected of the three? Do you

agree? Would a change of our habits in prayer on this matter really make a difference and be instrumental for a national revival? Give some biblical examples of this type of prayer.

8. What is involved in "seeking the face of God"? Give some biblical examples. How can we do this in our day?

Subject Index

Scripture Index

Reformation & Revival Ministries

Reformation & Revival Ministries, in partnership with Christian Focus Publications, has an imprint line of books for the purpose of providing resources for the reformation of the Christian church through the life and work of Christian leaders. Our goal is to publish and distribute new works of pastoral and theological substance aimed at reforming the leadership, life and vision of the church around the world.

Reformation & Revival Ministries was incorporated in 1991, through the labors of John H. Armstrong, a pastor for the previous twenty-one years, to serve the church as an educational and evangelistic resource. The desire from the beginning has been to encourage doctrinal and ethical reformation joined with informed prayer for spiritual awakening. The foundational convictions of the ministry can be summarized in the great truths of the sixteenth century Protestant Reformation and evangelical revivals of the 18th & 19th centuries.

To accomplish this vision the ministry publishes a quarterly journal, *Reformation & Revival Journal*, designed for pastors and serious readers of theology and church renewal. A more popular magazine, *Viewpoint*, is published six times a year. The ministry also has an extensive array of books and tapes.

Dr. Armstrong speaks in conferences, local churches and various ministerial groups across the United States and abroad. The ministry has a no debt policy and is financed only by the gifts of interested people. The policy from the beginning has been to never ask for funds through solicitation, believing that God provides as he will, where he will, and when he will. An office and support staff operate the ministry in suburban Chicago.

Further information on the ministry and resources can be found at -

Reformation & Revival Ministries
P. O. Box 88216
Carol Stream, Illinois 60188
Tel: (630) 980-1810 Fax: (630) 980-1820

E-mail: RRMinistry@aol.com

Web: www.randr.org